ALSO BY THIS AUTHOR

ALIX & MINNIE: *Queen Alexandra of England & Empress Marie of Russia*
Book Two: Adventure, Wealth and Scandal

ALIX & MINNIE: *Queen Alexandra of England & Empress Marie of Russia*
Book Three: Widowhood, War, Revolution and Legacy

A CHURCH OF TRADITION: *What Every Catholic Should Know*

THE CHURCH VISIBLE: *The Ceremonial Life and Protocol*
of the Catholic Church—Revised Expanded Edition (Sterling Press, 2012)

THE CHURCH VISIBLE: *The Ceremonial Life and Protocol*
of the Catholic Church, Papal Commission, (Viking, 1996)

BOOK

ROYAL SISTERS PREPARING FOR GREATNESS

ALIX & MINNIE

BOOK

ROYAL SISTERS PREPARING FOR GREATNESS

ALIX & MINNIE

JAMES-CHARLES NOONAN

ISBN: 978-0-578-24990-2 (Paperback)

Interior Design by FormattedBooks.com

This book is dedicated to
Michael F. Burke
The finest person I know

TABLE OF CONTENTS

ACKNOWLEDGEMENTS

No study of this size and scope, taking more than eight years to complete, would be possible without the profound support of dear friends and academic colleagues. Foremost amongst these I wish to thank Michael, Nancy and Judy Burke for their steadfast support and love. Likewise, I thank Rev. Monsignor William A. Hodge for his always enthusiastic and continual support and unwavering friendship, as well as, his special aid in this project . Without each of them this work would not have seen the light of day.

I offer thanks also to my numerous research agents and their assistants who spent untold hours in archives worldwide, particularly those working on my behalf in the great archives at Windsor and elsewhere in The United Kingdom, in Copenhagen, Saint Petersburg and Moscow, in Vatican City, and in Greece, and in numerous German royal house archives as well. To each and to all I thank you for your research on my behalf, without which this study would never have materialized. In a particular way, I thank Alexander N. Bokhanon who directed my research assistants to the proper repositories in the early stages of this work as the Romanov research fully began, opening to us new avenues of study and research.

I thank also the numerous translating services engaged and their professional staffs. I likewise offer thanks to Devin Burke for his tech support, guidance and expertise and to Linda P. Nicholson who always offers the finest advice and guidance with the most artful eye. Thanks for cover design by Michaelstar. And to you, the reader, I thank you for taking interest in these two beautiful royal sisters who changed Europe, most certainly for the better, during the second half of the nineteenth and the first decades of the twentieth centuries. I am pleased to introduce the fascinating story of their brilliant, complicated lives and those of so many others intertwined in their story.

PREFACE

This is the story of two women, sisters born in Denmark, who never expected to lead extraordinary lives. Their father was an impoverished minor northern German prince with no prospects for greatness. But events in neighboring Denmark in the early 1850s changed the prince's life and that of his wife and children forever. The prince and princess' mutual blood links to a Danish king at the time moved them both closer in the line of succession to the throne in Copenhagen. In just a decade, this young couple would become the king and queen of Denmark and their children would suddenly gain the interest of people across Europe. The two eldest daughters of this young family became the first royals to ever experience ardent international attention. Free press with newspapers founded in every capital of Europe routinely copied their images and promoted their life story.

Nature had been very good to both sisters. Each in her own way was very beautiful and each possessed a distinct charm which drew everyone closer to them wherever they went. In time the eldest daughter married the Prince of Wales and would become the Queen of England after the death of her mother-in-law Queen Victoria. Her name was Alexandra but she was known within the Danish and British royal families as *Alix*.

Alix was very much the Princess Diana of her day. Everything she did, all the clothes she wore, the way she wore her hair, and the causes she took up were watched and copied by women everywhere, not only inside the British Empire, but across Europe and into America as well. Alix's younger sister Dagmar (known as *Minnie* within the family) would soon marry the heir the Russian throne, heir to the richest and mightiest empire the world had ever known. After this prestigious marriage, Minnie's world became filled with wonder and fascination as well as with profound wealth. She never again wanted for anything. No one on earth since her time in Russia has lived in a whirl-wind of wealth, extravagance, privilege and largesse as enjoyed by Minnie, the Dowager Empress Marie Feodorovna of Russia before the Russian Revolution. Minnie had become empress and then dowager empress long before Alix even became queen after Queen Victoria's death in 1901. But Minnie's career had not waned in widowhood. She became empress at thirty-four and was widowed at forty-eight. The Romanovs lost the throne in 1917. For the twenty-three years she lived as dowager empress in Russia, Minnie's influence remained substantial although her hold on her son, Tsar Nicholas II, lessened as his wife's influence over him grew. In exile, as horrible as it was for her, Minnie never ceased to view herself as a consecrated empress, the richest woman in the world, and the doyenne of surviving European royalty.

Alix was fifty-seven when she became queen. She had been the Princess of Wales for thirty-seven years; she would be queen consort for nine years between the years 1901 and 1910, the year of Bertie's death. For the remaining years of her life, ending with her death in 1925, she would be dowager queen. Alix, of course, perpetually young at heart and always in appearance never saw herself as a widow or a dowager, nor did she wish to have the public think of her as an old woman.

As both Princess of Wales and queen, Alix personified the epitome of Queenship. In daylight hours she typically appeared in a designer creation, simple but elegant at all times, even when alone at Sandringham. At her neck she wore a sautoir, a long thin chain of diamonds reaching to her waste at which point hung a diamond cluster in the shape of a small tassel. At her neck, either upon a velvet ribbon or a chiffon scarf to conceal the scar which she hid all of her life was pinned one of several possible diamond brooches, bows, or lockets. In evening, whether at home at Sandringham with only family and intimate friends present or on state occasions with the cream of society present, Alix glittered like no other. Leslie Field, one of the great authorities on the British royal jewelry collection wrote of Alix as queen on these occasions: She wore a tiara, a high pearl dog-collar, and rows of sparkling diamond chains, while pinned to her low-cut bodice were brooches—stars, crescents, butterflies and flowers. To this she typically added a diamond stomacher (a highly decorative ornament of diamonds and other gemstones reaching from the bodice to the waist or stomach). To this array, Alix also always wore the most spectacular diamond earrings and a half-dozen diamond bracelets on each arm; placed over her pure white kid gloves. On every state occasion, especially on the day of her coronation at Bertie's side, Alix always made certain that she appeared ablaze with light.

Alix did not own a jewelry collection of the quality and scope possessed by Minnie in Russia, but in England her jewel collection was one of the finest in private hands. After her eldest son, Prince Eddy's death, Alix preferred to wear only diamonds and amethysts. This stone's purple hue matched her favorite choice of dress color. In addition, in Victorian and Edwardian times, after the loss of a close loved one, women wore black for a specific period of time. Thereafter they did not return to normal clothing. Instead their wardrobes went from black to the light purples and grays—known as half-mourning. Alix loved lavender and lilac so this change to half-mourning was no trial for her as it was for other women. She wore these colors routinely. After Eddy's death, she preferred these hues to all except white and creams. Her amethyst collection, including two diamond and amethyst tiaras, worked best with this change in style and women the world over took note and copied their favorite fashion icon.

The two sisters remained extremely close throughout their lives despite more than the thousand miles which separated them in their new homelands (in an age where written letters and telegrams were the only way to communicate). The sisters faithfully wrote to each other and to other family members as well, nearly every day of their married lives. They often gathered for reunions in London, in Denmark, in Greece and in Russia. These frequent reunions were marked by exuberance and practical jokes, the hallmark of the Danish Royal House. And yet, despite their very charmed lives, tragedy, sorrow, and scandal befell them both just as it did their subjects.

This is the story of the brilliant lives of these two glamorous women, Queen Alexandra of England and the Empress Marie of Russia, who were the epitome of dignity, class, and grace in the late 19th and early 20th centuries. It is additionally the story of their immediate and extended families. Both

Alix and Minnie were the staunchest defenders of the family bond and neither lost their love for, and support of, each other and their extended families as it spread across Europe.

Alix and Minnie possessed determined, powerful personalities. By the sheer, steely strength of their characters each sister influenced their immediate family's political opinions at home as much as they did their adopted nation's foreign policy. They likewise set the manner in which each royal house experienced its own rhythm of life, due entirely to each sister bringing a Danish informality and relaxed charm into the rigid Court protocol in their two adoptive lands.

Alix is the great-grandmother of the present queen, Elizabeth II. She was the most beautiful woman to ever marry into the British royal family and many of her Danish customs remain a part of the lifestyle of the current British royal family today. Minnie was the mother of the fated Tsar Nicholas II who perished in the Russian Revolution, as did another of Minnie's sons, her five grandchildren by the tsar, a sister-in-law, and a host of other relatives and close friends. She was once the richest and most influential woman in the world, people fawning over her at every turn, but at the fall of the Russian Empire she suffered abject poverty, exile and loneliness.

Alix & Minnie, the story of these two Danish princesses, covers events in Russia, Great Britain, Denmark and Greece as well as places throughout Europe during the eighty years of their lives beginning with obscurity in Denmark in the 1840s and ending with each sister's death in the late 1920s.

This dual biography covers the military drama in Denmark early in the girls' lives resulting from the aggression and territorial ambitions of the Kingdom of Prussia to the south. The first chapter in this three volume series introduces the early lives of the enchanting Alix and Minnie in light of the difficulties these territorial wars imposed on Denmark and the Glucksburg family to which they belonged. It is included in this study not because war history is the most interesting story to tell but because the outcome of the war with Prussia affected the Danish royal family (as well as subsequent generations of this royal house who married royalty across Europe) leading to a hatred for Germans for generations, culminating in a continental-wide hatred for Germany leading into the First World War. All subsequent chapters detail the glamor, wealth, and pageantry of both royal courts—Saint Petersburg and London—as well as the scandals and hardships which each sister endured as well.

Like all biographies and histories, the original backstory is sometimes laborious to work through, but once the reader works through it, one will find the brilliance which marked Alix and Minnie their entire lives long both fascinating and charming. My hope is that each reader will come away from this biography with a great appreciation of these two royal women heretofore unsung in European royal history.

Before the story begins…it will help to know a few things about the people and the protocol surrounding the lives of Alix and Minnie…

NOTE ABOUT PERSONAL NAMES

The subjects of this study are Alexandra and Dagmar of Schleswig-Holstein-Sonderburg-Glucksburg, who became in time princesses of Denmark. Before we begin to explore their life stories we must take a moment to explain the names and titles by which these two women would be known for the remainder of their lives.

The first of the two sisters was Alexandra. She was known within her family as Alix and would continue to be so-called in the British royal family after her marriage to the Prince of Wales in 1863.

The younger of the two sisters was born Dagmar. Her situation is more complicated. She was known throughout her life in both Denmark and later in Russia as Minnie by those closest to her. Once she married the heir to the throne of Russia she converted to the Orthodox religion, there upon she took the formal name of Marie Feodorovna in accordance with Russian custom. All three of the names attributed to her during her lifetime will be seen in this study: Dagmar as we begin and progress to her marriage, alternating with Minnie when appropriate, and after her marriage as Marie or as Marie Feodorovna.

Hopefully this brief explanation will alleviate any confusion which may otherwise arise as we progress through the story of the lives of two of the most amazing women of the nineteenth and early twentieth centuries.

As to other familiar names, it should also be noted that in the case of the sisters' younger brother, Prince Wilhelm of Denmark, he will be referred to as Willy throughout these pages since this is how he was known within his family even after he had become the king of Greece as George I. In cases where more formality will be required, references to this younger brother will not be in a more formal style: George I, King of the Hellenes.

All other names appearing in this text, both formal and familiar, shall be introduced, and thus made clear, as the study progresses. As to the Russian names which appear throughout this study, an English language version shall prevail, both in spelling and for ease of pronunciation.

Russian names and titles appearing throughout this study typically appear in standard English language translation. They have been rendered into the simplest format as in English there is no single way to cite the Romanov names and titles. For instance, one could properly write the monarch's title as *tsar*, *csar* or *czar*. The wife of the monarch could be entitled empress, tsarina or czarina and as to proper names within the imperial family, two or more alternative spellings exist for each—the most understandable form of each has been chosen for this work. For instance, the name Grand Duke Constantine Constantinovitch could also be written as Konstantine Konstantinovitch (and in some instances both versions will appear) and Grand Duke Alexander Nichaelovitch could just as easily be rendered as Aleksandr Nikolevitch. For the sake of simplicity and uniformity, therefore the names and titles which appear in this study are presented in the simplest format. Different spellings may be seen occasionally, however. In particular, when quotations appear within the text, spelling used by the original author is followed for accuracy sake even when it is contrary to the style selected for this work.

In regards to Russian names, in the Orthodox Church the Romanovs and all other Russians bore both a baptismal first name and a patronymic second name. The baptismal name always had to be taken from the Russian Orthodox litany of saints. The patronymic, or second name, was determined by the baptismal name of an individual's father. Male children take on a patronymic name with the added ending of 'ovitch' or 'evitch' which roughly translates to 'son of' while female children take on a patronymic name with the ending 'ovna' or 'aevena' which similarly translates to 'daughter of.' An example therefore would be: Grand Duke Nicholas of Russia (later Tsar Nicholas II) who in this system of naming children was known within his family as Nicholas Alexandrovitch. Similarly, his sister Olga was entitled the Grand Duchess Olga

Alexandrovna as their father was Tsar Alexander III. Although this may seem cumbersome to non-Russians, it made for an easy way of identifying family members who so often shared a baptismal name. So within the Romanov family one would not just refer to 'cousin Serge'. One would properly say Serge Alexandrovitch or Serge Michaelovitch and in this way each member of the family automatically knew which person was being discussed.

When a foreign princess married into the house of Romanov, she generally assumed a new first name from the established calendar of saints of the Orthodox Church since many of the Protestant names common to German princesses at that time were not found on the Russian Orthodox calendar. These women also had to take on a Russian patronymic which reflected either her father's baptismal name (if his name was an approved Orthodox name) or one which honored someone within the history of the imperial house. This patronymic name was either of the brides' choosing or was one chosen for her. Sometimes the choice made was to honor the reigning emperor such as "Alexandrovna" for Tsar Alexander. More commonly, however, the patronymic "Feodorovna" was granted a foreign-born bride in honor of the *Feodorovskaya Icon of the Mother of God*, also known as the icon of *Our Lady of Saint Theodore—the Black Virgin Mary of Russia*. This image of the Mother of God is the patronal icon of the Romanov family and one of the most venerated icons in all of Orthodoxy. The name Theodore translates in Russian to Feodor and thus the patronymic for Saint Theodore in the feminine form in Russian would be *Feodorovna*. Like all Russian names transliterated into English, this name can be rendered in many ways.

At her marriage to the future Tsar Alexander III, Princess Dagmar of Denmark legally and ecclesiastically ceased to exist. Upon her sincere conversion to Orthodoxy she was instantly transformed into *Her Imperial Highness the True Believing Grand Duchess Marie Feodorovna*; her first name was adopted from one already included in the long list of names given her at baptism as an infant in Copenhagen (Marie Sophie Frederikke Dagmar—Marie being the only one of her given names approved by the Orthodox Church) and Feodorovna her patronymic was chosen for her in honor of the holy icon of the Romanov family.

The imperial family also had additional customs governing the various branches of the ruling house in the same manner that Japan's imperial family continues to do today. There were several of these branches within the imperial family, each branch taking a distinct title to distinguish members of one branch from the other. During the period of time of this study, each branch of the imperial family was named after either a son of Tsar Nicholas I or of Tsar Alexander II as these grand dukes headed their particular branch of the family at this time.

In order of seniority was extremely important in imperial Russia. The branches of the Romanov family being:

> The *Alexandrovitchi,* were the senior line of the Imperial House, from which descended the line of the last two tsars of Russia. They took their branch name from Alexander III who headed it.
>
> The *Vladimirovitchi* headed by the second living son of Tsar Alexander II, the Grand Duke Vladimir Alexandrovitch, from which descends the current, most senior, members of the imperial house.
>
> The *Pavlovichi* were headed by the youngest son of Tsar Alexander II, the Grand Duke Paul Alexandrovitch.
>
> The *Konstantinovitchi* were headed by the Grand Duke Konstantine Nicholevitch, descendent from Tsar Nicholas I.
>
> The *Nicholivitchi* were headed by the Grand Duke Nicholas Nicholevitch, descendent of Nicholas I; and
>
> The *Michaelovitchi* headed by the Grand Duke Michael Nicholevitch, descendent of Nicholas I.

Although all the grand dukes were equal in birth, their precedence at Court and their place within the line of succession to the imperial throne was determined by the place which they held within their individual branch of the Imperial House; this standing was determined entirely by order of birth.

PERSONS YOU SHALL MEET
British, Russian, Danish & Greek Relatives

ALEXANDRA was born *Alexandra Caroline Marie Charlotte Louise Julia* of the princely house of Schleswig-Holstein-Sonderburg-Glucksburg on 1 December 1844. She was the daughter of Prince Christian of Schleswig-Holstein-Sonderburg-Glucksburg and Princess Louise of Hesse-Cassel. In time her parents would become the king and queen of Denmark. As a princess of this house, *Alix* held the rank of *Serene Highness*. When her father was designated heir presumptive of the Danish throne in 1853, Alix and her siblings were raised to the rank of *Highness*. Finally in 1858 they were designated as princes and princesses of Denmark with the rank of *Royal Highness*. Alix was Christian and Louise's eldest daughter, and their most beautiful child. She married the Prince of Wales, eldest son of Queen Victoria and Prince Albert, in 1863, forever-after winning the hearts of the British nation. From 1863 until 1901 she was styled Princess of Wales but as a princess by birth she was also generally known as Princess Alexandra. In 1901, at the death of Queen Victoria, her husband *Bertie* became King Edward VII. As his consort, Alix became Her Majesty Queen Alexandra, the title by which she was known until her death at age eighty on 20 November 1925. Her speech and memory became impaired in the last two years of her life but she continued to appear in public until her frail health made this impossible. Her death came rapidly after a heart attack at Sandringham. Alix's siblings were Frederick VIII of Denmark, Marie Feodorovna of Russia (Minnie), George I of Greece (Willy), Thyra and Waldemar of Denmark.

MARIE FEODOROVNA was born *Marie Sophie Frederikke Dagmar* of the princely house of Schleswig-Holstein-Sonderburg-Glucksburg on 26 November 1847. She was the second daughter of Christian and Louise, and was known officially in Denmark as *Princess Dagmar.* Within the family Dagmar was always known as *Minnie.* It would be this familiar name that she would bear until her death. At her marriage to Grand Duke-Tsarevitch Alexander Alexandrovitch (known in the Romanov family as *Sasha*), the second son of Tsar Alexander II, her thoroughly Danish name "Dagmar" disappeared forever. At conversion to Russian Orthodoxy, Minnie became Her Imperial Highness the Grand Duchess-Tsarevna Marie Feodorovna. The Romanovs continued to call her Minnie which helped the princess ease into an entirely new identity in Saint Petersburg. Minnie's prestigious marriage to Sasha came after first being engaged to his elder brother Nicholas who died suddenly at age twenty-one before the two could marry. Tsar Alexander II was assassinated in 1881. Sasha and Minnie mounted the Russian throne in the aftermath. Sasha died in 1894. At that time Minnie transitioned from Empress-Consort to Dowager Empress and in this final role she found her balance and her true power. Like all the Romanovs, Minnie suffered the terror of the Russian Revolution which began in 1917. No surviving member of the Romanov family suffered as much as Minnie. She died in exile, having lost two sons, five grandchildren along with the children's mother, a sister-in-law and many other close relations. She also lost the empire, wealth and the position she loved. Minnie went from being the richest woman on earth to absolute penury thereafter depending entirely on the kindness of royal relatives until her own death in 1928. Like her beloved older sister, Alix, Minnie was eighty years old at the time of her death.

EDWARD VII was born Albert Edward, Prince of Wales. He was known in the family as *Bertie,* the husband of Alexandra of Denmark *(Alix)* and the eldest son and heir of Queen Victoria. He became King-Emperor in 1901 reigning until his death in 1910, dying after suffering several weeks from severe bronchitis resulting from years of smoking numerous cigars and cigarettes each day. On the last day of his life, Bertie endured several consecutive heart attacks but he refused to take to his bed as his physicians had requested. Bertie married Alix in 1863 and together they had six children, five surviving to adulthood: Albert Victor (Eddy), George, Louise, Victoria, and Maud. Prince Alexander John did not survive infancy. Although both Alix and Bertie admired one another, it was only Alix who bought true love into their marriage. Bertie was a serial philanderer, many times bringing shame to himself, and embarrassment to Alix as a result of numerous, very public sexual liaisons.

ALEXANDER III was born in 1845. In accordance with Russian custom he was given the name of Alexander Alexandrovitch. He was the second son of Tsar Alexander II and Marie of Hesse-Darmstadt. Within the Romanov family, and later throughout wider royal circles, Alexander was known as *Sasha*. The first-born son of Tsar Alexander II and Marie of Darmstadt was named, Nicholas Alexandrovitch. He died at age twenty and so at his passing, the next oldest son, Sasha, became heir to the Russian throne. Sasha married Minnie in 1886at his parent's urging in 1866 after a proper period of mourning for his late brother. Sasha would eventually be known as *the Peacemaker* as under his rule Russia avoided foreign wars. In reality Sasha ruled Russia with an iron fist. His rule was marked by fear and intense police control. Sasha died at age forty-nine in 1894. His marriage to Minnie had been an arranged one. Sasha was in love with a princess of noble, but not of royal, birth and thus she was unacceptable as a bride for the future tsar. Minnie was still mourning Nicholas whom she genuinely loved, but in time this new arrangement with Sasha developed into friendship and friendship developed into love. By the time their children were born, both loved, admired and respected one another and their union could best be described as a love match. Sasha and Minnie's family included Nicholas (the future Nicholas II who was named for Sasha's late older brother), Alexander (who lived just short of eleven months), George, Xenia, Michael and Olga.

THE BRITISH FAMILY

QUEEN VICTORIA was arguably the most impressive monarch Britain had until then known. She was a granddaughter of George III and Queen Charlotte through her father Prince Edward, Duke of Kent. Victoria's mother, also named Victoria, was born a princess of Saxe-Coburg-Saalfeld, a minor German ducal house then relatively unknown. She married firstly Emich-Carl, 2nd Prince of Leiningen, but this much older prince died soon-after and Victoria found herself in need of another husband. She and Emich had two children together. Their son stayed behind at Leiningen when Victoria married Edward of Kent, the fourth son of George III. She and her daughter Feodora followed Victoria's new husband to London where the couple's only child was born. It was intended the infant be named for her mother but the Prince Regent (the future George IV) insisted that his niece be named for the Russian tsar. She was therefore given the names Alexandrina Victoria, known as *Drina* in the family until her teenage years when she ordered her first name to be consigned to history. Victoria reigned from 1837 until her death in 1901. She was the mother of Edward VII (Bertie) and the mother-in-law of Alexandra (Alix).

PRINCE ALBERT was born Prince Albert of Saxe-Coburg-Gotha in 1819, son of Duke Ernst I and Princess Louise of Saxe-Altenburg. He married Queen Victoria in 1840. Together they had nine children—four sons, including King Edward VII (Bertie), and five daughters, including the first born child, Victoria Princess Royal (later crown princess of Prussia and German empress). Albert died in 1861 at age forty-two leaving Queen Victoria to retreat into perpetual mourning until her own death in 1901.

ALBERT VICTOR was the eldest son of the Prince and Princess of Wales (Bertie and Alix), and was heir after his father to the throne of Great Britain. Known in the family as *Eddy* the prince was born slow and backward and had great difficulty adapting in social settings. He was the source of great worry for his parents and the subject of great scandal as an adult, so much so had his lifestyle been known to the public at-large it could have bought down the British crown. He died of pneumonia following a bout of influenza in 1892.

GEORGE OF WALES was known in royal circles as both *English Georgie* and as *Georgie Wales*. He was the second son of Bertie and Alix and would in time become King George V. He was born in 1865 with no prospect of becoming monarch. His older brother Eddy should have been king in time but when he died from influenza in 1892 George was propelled to second in the line of succession. George married May of Teck in 1893. She would go on to become known as Queen Mary. Together George and Mary had four sons, including two kings (Edward VIII and George VI) and a daughter who would become Princess Royal in 1932. George died at Sandringham in 1936.

VICTORIA MARY OF TECK was known in the family as *May*. She was the only daughter of Princess Mary Adelaide of Cambridge (Fat Mary) and Francis, Duke of Teck who was a morganatic son within the Royal House of Wurttemberg. May Teck was originally selected as the ideal bride for Prince Albert Victor (Eddy) but after his untimely death it was decided that what had been good for Eddy would now be good for George and so she was betrothed to the new heir after a suitable period of mourning had passed. Queen Mary lived until 1953. She was the grandmother of the current queen.

MARY ADELAIDE OF CAMBRIDGE was known within royal circles simply as Mary but affectionately by the British public as *Fat Mary* because of her immense girth. She was a princess of Great Britain as a male-line granddaughter of George III with the corresponding rank of *Royal Highness*. Her father was the Duke of Cambridge (and through him she was a cousin to Queen Victoria and to Bertie). Her mother was Princess Augusta of Hesse-Cassel. As such she was entitled by birth to be included in the frequent Rumppenheim reunions of this fun-loving German family. She was a maternal cousin of both Louise of Denmark (born a Princess of Hesse-Cassel) and her daughters Minnie and Alix. Despite her inability to manage money, always being in terrible debt, Fat Mary was universally loved. Her enormous emeralds were won by her mother in a lottery in Germany. These passed to her great-granddaughter the current queen. Mary Adelaide died in 1897.

AUGUSTA OF CAMBRIDGE was the elder sister of 'Fat Mary' and the daughter of Adolphus, Duke of Cambridge and Augusta of Hesse-Cassel. As such, she was Queen Mary's aunt. In fact the two women were very close and Augusta was clearly the expert at that time of all things concerning British royal protocol and family history. Augusta was married in 1843 to her first cousin Frederick William Duke of Mecklenburg-Strelitz. Although she would be a German Grand Duchess for more than seventy years she identified as a thoroughly English princess to the end. Just before her death, as she was dying in Germany during the First World War, she sent word to her niece Queen Mary and her husband George V through neutral Sweden saying—*Tell them that it is a strong old English heart that ceases to beat.*

GEORGE OF CAMBRIDGE was the only son of Adolphus Duke of Cambridge and Augusta of Hesse-Cassel. He would succeed his father in the title in due course and was the only brother of Fat Mary and the Duchess of Mecklenburg-Strelitz. He was also a first cousin of Queen Victoria and was considered a formidable member of the 'old royal family.' Throughout his lifetime George refused to marry a woman of equal rank. Instead he married his mistress Sarah Fairbrother who later became known as Mrs. Fitz-George. Their offspring also took this surname. George rose to high rank in the army where he had made a stellar career.

LOUISE, DUCHESS OF FIFE was the eldest daughter of Alix and Bertie. She was born in 1867. From 1905 until her death she was entitled *Princess Royal*. Extremely shy by nature, Louise preferred to keep out of the royal spotlight. When it came time to marry, Louise chose to avoid a dynastic royal match with a foreign prince. Instead she married a friend of her father, Alexander Duff, the Earl of Fife, who was eighteen years Louise's senior. Upon their marriage Queen Victoria elevated Duff in rank. He became the first Duke of Fife.

Louise and Fife had two daughters, Alexandra and Maud. He died in Egypt in 1912. Louise died in 1931.

MAUD was the third daughter of Bertie and Alix. She was born in 1869 and in 1896 she married her cousin Carl of Denmark. She never found joy outside of England, always longing for her home at Sandringham, and so in 1905 when her husband was elected first king of independent Norway (as Haakon VII) Maud found herself heading for a very public life in a new nation. She and King Haakon had only one child, a son named Alexander, but when they assumed the Norwegian throne his name was changed to Olav. Maud died in England in 1938. Haakon died in 1957 and their son Olav died as king of Norway in 1991.

VICTORIA OF WALES was the fourth child of Bertie and Alix. She was born in 1868 and was known within royal circles as *Toria*. She never married, staying by the side of her mother as companion and gloried maid. She died in 1935.

EMPRESS FREDERICK was born Princess Victoria of Great Britain in 1840 and was the oldest child of Queen Victoria and Prince Albert, the Prince Consort. Known as *Vicky* within the family she was the most intelligent of the queen's nine children and the most ambitious. At eighteen she married Prince Frederick William of Prussia. In short order they would become crown prince and crown princess of Prussia and in 1888 they became the emperor and empress of Germany, and king and queen of Prussia. Frederick III would reign for three short months, dying of throat cancer before he had the opportunity to bring their liberal ideals to fruition in Germany. After her husband *Fritz*'s death, Victoria chose to be entitled *Empress Frederick* in her husband's honor, and as a means to keep alive the title of his brief reign. Fritz and Vicky had eight children. Their oldest son was the infamous Kaiser Wilhelm II and their third daughter Sophie married Minnie and Alix's nephew Crown Prince Constantine of Greece.

CROWN PRINCE FREDERICK was known in the family as *Fritz*, he became crown prince of Prussia in 1861, the German crown prince when the empire was proclaimed in 1871, and emperor at the death of his father Kaiser Wilhelm I in 1888. He would live for only three months as emperor, already suffering from the end stages of throat cancer. He married Queen Victoria's oldest daughter, the Princess Royal, in 1858. His death came at the *Neues Palais* in Potsdam on 15 June 1888.

ALFRED was the second son of Victoria and Albert. He was known in the family as *Affie*. He entered the British navy as a teenager and during his naval career he developed a true seaman's personality. He was a heavy drinker, loved to tell off-color jokes, and spoke in a very salty manner. As he aged his once pleasant personality soured and he became greatly embittered and difficult to be around. Alfred married Grand Duchess Maria Alexandrovna, the only daughter of Tsar Alexander II. Marie was the first Romanov to enter the British royal family. This union was not favored by Queen Victoria but Alfred's determination to marry one of the richest princesses in Europe forced the queen to acquiesce. Alexander II was likewise not pleased by the proposed match, wishing his beloved daughter to remain in Russia, but in the end both monarchs granted their permission. This youthful union seemed to be a true love-match and the couple soon settled into happy bliss in London. Queen Victoria granted them lifetime use of Clarence House, the Georgian extension of Saint James's Palace now the home of the Prince of Wales and the Duchess of Cornwall (and once the residence of the late Queen Mother). Clarence House at this time (1874) was not the first-class town mansion it is today. Alfred filled it with trophies of his hunting adventures and prizes won by his many journeys abroad. An Orthodox chapel was furnished on the top floor and an Orthodox priest was installed to attend to Maria Alexandrovna's spiritual needs. Alfred became the heir to the dual duchies of Saxe-Coburg and Gotha when his father, Prince Albert, died. Victoria's oldest son Bertie could not ascend to both the British throne and the German duchies and so he resigned his rights in favor of Alfred who looked forward to becoming a sovereign in his own right, albeit of a small domain. He looked to the legendary wealth of the Coburgs which would come, he thought, to him in time. By the time Duke Ernst II died, however, most of the family's holdings had been wasted on dozens of mistresses and illegitimate children. As a result, Alfred inherited nothing but great debts. He was named Duke of Edinburgh by his mother in 1866 and he succeeded to the German duchies in 1893. He died before his mother, Queen Victoria, in July 1900.

MARIA ALEXANDROVNA Duchess of Edinburgh, Duchess of Saxe-Coburg and Gotha, was born the only daughter of Tsar Alexander II and the Empress Marie (of Hesse-Darmstadt) in 1853. One of the richest, if not *the* richest, princess in Europe at that time, Maria wanted for nothing, and nothing was ever denied her. Whereas her father was cold and stern with her brothers, the tsar was loving and devoted to Maria. Tsar Alexander II did not support Maria's desire to marry Alfred of Edinburgh, however, and he did all he could to stall the marriage, short of refusing his permission. The marriage was celebrated at the Winter Palace in 1874. The tsar endowed his daughter with a huge dowry, including one of the finest jewelry collections in Europe. As Duchess of Edinburgh, Maria found herself lower in precedence in England as the wife of the second son, than she had enjoyed in Russia as the only daughter of the tsar. Her resentment festered for years as a consequence. Maria longed for Alfred's succession to Coburg so that she could be the premier lady of a realm, albeit a small one. She lived through the revolutions in Russia and Germany, losing many members of her family, all of her wealth, and her position simultaneously. She and Alfred had drifted apart long before his death in 1900, both growing more difficult and aloof with each passing year. Their eldest son, Alfred, died from a self-inflicted gunshot wound leaving his parents without an heir for Coburg and Gotha. Their four daughters made successful marriages: Marie married Ferdinand of Romania (although both she and George of England had strong feelings for one another), Victoria Melita had a failed first marriage thanks to Queen Victoria who pushed the union of two of her favorite grandchildren when she should not have (Ernie of Hesse-Darmstadt was homosexual) but her second marriage to another cousin, Kyril Vladimirovich, despite the scandal that this new union initially caused, was happy and successful. Alexandra married the Prince of Hohenlohe and Beatrice married the Infante Alfonso, Duke of Galliera, cousin to King Alfonso XIII of Spain. Maria Alexandrovna, Duchess of Edinburgh, dowager duchess of Saxe-Coburg and Gotha died a broken woman in exile in Switzerland in 1920.

WILHELM II was the first-born grandson of Queen Victoria, son of Frederick III and Victoria, the Princess Royal. He was born in 1859 after a difficult birth that left him partially deformed. He succeeded his father on the Prussian and German thrones in 1888 and set out to rival Great Britain on the seas and in Europe which led to a rift between him and his Uncle Bertie which was never healed. Wilhelm lost his throne along with the other German monarchs in 1918 following Germany's defeat in World War I. He fled to Holland with his wealth intact and there lived a very comfortable exile until his death in 1941.

ALICE was the second and most rebellious daughter of Queen Victoria and Prince Albert. She was born in 1843. Alice married Ludwig IV, Grand Duke of Hesse-Darmstadt in the year following her father's death (1862)and began a new life in Germany where she introduced the most modern methods in nursing, religious teaching, and female education. She was a heroine to her people who grieved her sudden death from diphtheria at age thirty-five in 1878. Alice had contracted this deadly disease from her children when their nursery fell to the disease. Alice was the mother of Alicky, the future Empress of Russia—wife of Nicholas II and Minnie's daughter-in-law. Her surviving son Ernie became the Grand Duke after his father's death, her daughter Victoria married Prince Louis of Battenberg. This younger Victoria would in time become the grandmother of Prince Philip, Duke of Edinburgh. Alice's daughter Elizabeth married Grand Duke Serge and became known in Russia as Grand Duchess Elizabeth Feodorovna (Ella).

HELENA was the third daughter of Queen Victoria and Prince Albert. She was born in 1846. She was the least favorite sister of Bertie, Prince of Wales. She did not make a brilliant marriage as so many of Victoria's offspring tended to do. Helena, known in the family as *Lenchen,* instead married Alix's distant cousin, Prince Christian of Schleswig-Holstein-Sonderburg-Augustenburg which caused much strife within the British royal family. Christian's branch of the family claimed the dual duchies of Schleswig-Holstein for themselves and during the war with Prussia they sided against Denmark. As such Christian IX and Louise and all their extended family turned against them. They never forgot or forgave their cousins' treachery. Victoria sided with Helena and her new husband. She tired of the anger that constantly simmered in the Danish family after that war. The issue had already caused a rift between Bertie and his sister Vicky since she was married to the crown prince of Prussia who was the main aggressor in this war. It was Vicky who suggested the much older Christian of Schleswig-Holstein-Sonderburg-Augustenburg as a bride for her headstrong sister and this interference Bertie and Alix also resented. Helena married Christian in 1866 with the proviso that he settle in England and live with the queen as Helena was to continue to serve her mother as private secretary. Their marriage was unusually happy, producing five children, three sons (Christian Victor, Albert and Harald who died in early childhood, and two daughters—Helena Victoria and Marie Louise. Helena lived on until 1923. Only her two daughters lived into old age.

LOUISE was Queen Victoria's fourth daughter and the one with the most difficult personality. She refused to marry a foreign prince, rich or poor, and so a British nobleman had to be found to suit her, something that had not been seen in Britain since the Tudor period. Louise married Scottish Lord Lorne who was the heir to the Duke of Argyll. Their union was friendly but not a love match as John Campbell (Lord Lorne) was homosexual. In fact, Louise had a large window opening onto her garden at Kensington Palace bricked over to keep Lorne from using it as a means to sneak away late at night to have sexual assignations with soldiers in nearby Hyde Park. In 1878 Prime Minister Disraeli posted Lord Lorne to Canada as Governor General. He remained there for five years. The famous *Princess Hotel* in Bermuda was named after Louise after she made a prolonged visit to the island in 1883. The cold Canadian winters had taken a toll on her health and she was induced to visit Bermuda which at this time was being promoted as a health resort. Lorne died in 1914 having been the 9th Duke of Argyll for fourteen years. Louise died in 1939 at age ninety-one.

LEOPOLD was Queen Victoria's youngest son. He was born in 1853. Sadly he had inherited the hemophilia gene and was one of the worst sufferers of the disease within the British royal family at that time. Because of the disease, the queen sheltered Leopold and strictly limited the activities permitted him. He was one of the queen's more sensitive children but also had a very determined personality. He insisted on going off to university, where he excelled, and as an adult became Queen Victoria's confidential secretary. This appointment resulted in a rift between Leopold and Bertie who was forbidden access to confidential government papers despite being heir to the throne. Leopold was Alix's favorite brother-in-law and the two enjoyed many hours together sharing ideas and common interests. Alix, who always hated Prussian-Germans, was nevertheless very pleased when Leopold chose Princess Helena of Waldeck and Pyrmont as his wife. Queen Victoria thought sexual activity might very well kill Leopold and therefore wanted him to remain celibate. Leopold and Helena's marriage was a brief but loving union producing a son, Charles-Edward, and a daughter, Alice, who would go on to marry Queen Mary's brother. Charles-Edward was given the duchies of Saxe-Coburg and Gotha after both the deaths of Alfred of Edinburgh-Saxe-Coburg and his son. Queen Victoria created Leopold Duke of Albany upon his marriage. He died at age thirty from the effects of hemophilia after having fallen down a staircase at a vacation villa in the South of France.

ERNST LUDWIG OF HESSE was a grandson of Queen Victoria through her second daughter Alice who had married Ludwig IV of Hesse-Darmstadt. Known in the family as *Ernie*, he was born in 1868 and became the grand duke of Hesse und bye Rhine in 1892 at the death of his father. Ernie was homosexual but accepted pressure from his grandmother Queen Victoria to marry his maternal first cousin, Victoria Melita of Edinburgh, in 1894. The marriage was naturally unhappy although a daughter, Elizabeth, was born to the couple.

The little girl died in 1893 at age eight. After their divorce, shortly after Queen Victoria's death, Victoria Melita (known in the family as *Ducky*) went on to marry Grand Duke Kyril Vladimirovitch. Ernie would later marry again, to Princess Eleonore of Solms-Hohensolms-Lich, with whom he had two sons—Georg Donatus and Louis. His siblings included Alexandra Feodorovna, wife of Nicholas II (Minnie's daughter-in-law), Elizabeth Feodorovna, wife of Grand Duke Serge Alexandrovitch, Victoria, who married Prince Louis of Battenberg (grandparents of Prince Philip, Duke of Edinburgh), Irene who married her first cousin Prince Henry of Prussia (another grandson of Queen Victoria) and two other children, Marie and Frederick, who died in childhood. It was long rumored that Ernie entered Russia secretly during World War I to attempt to secure separate peace negotiations with his brother-in-law Tsar Nicholas but the House of Hesse has always steadfastly denied such allegations. Ernst Ludwig died in 1937.

THE RUSSIAN FAMILY

ALEXANDER II was known in the family as *Sasha* just as would his son Alexander III after him. He was born in 1818, the son of Tsar Nicholas I of Russia and Empress Alexandra, born Charlotte of Prussia. He married Marie of Hesse-Darmstadt in 1841. Together they had seven children—Alexandra Alexandrovna who died at age six, the Tsarevitch Nicholas Alexandrovitch who was Minnie's first love and her fiancé until his death in 1865, Alexander Alexandrovitch, who was also known as *Sasha*, (Minnie's husband who became Tsar Alexander III), Vladimir Alexandrovitch, Alexis Alexandrovitch, Maria Alexandrovna who married Prince Alfred Duke of Edinburgh, Serge Alexandrovitch and Paul Alexandrovitch. When the Empress Marie died in 1880, Alexander II quickly married his long-time mistress, Princess Catherine Dolgoruky with whom he already had four illegitimate children. Known in history as the *Tsar-Liberator* for freeing the serfs, Alexander II was assassinated on 13 March 1881.

NICHOLAS II was the son of Alexander III and Marie Feodorovna. He was born on 18 May 1868 at the Alexander Palace at Tsarskoye Selo but his early childhood was spent at the Anitchkov Palace in Saint Petersburg. After the assassination of Tsar Alexander II in 1881 Sasha and Minnie moved their family to relative safety at Gatchina. Minnie's children grew to adulthood in near total isolation being kept from the sycophantic influences of Court life and away from possible terrorists. *Nicky* to the Romanov family, the tsarevitch enjoyed a healthy lifestyle within the Russian military. He met the ballerina Mathilde Kschessinska as a young officer with whom he had his first love affair. He remained with her until he married Alexandra of Hesse whom he first met when she was a girl who had come to Russia to visit her elder sister, Elizabeth, the Grand Duchess Serge. Like her sister and Marie Pavlovna before her, Alicky did not wish to convert to Orthodoxy and so any engagement between her and Nicholas was stalled. Unlike the other two grand duchesses, Alicky was to one day become empress and a Russian empress had to embrace Orthodoxy. Nicky and Alicky did eventually marry on 26 November 1894 after the sudden death of his father Alexander III. It was said that Alicky came to the Russians *behind a coffin* which to the highly superstitious peasants harkened darkness and sorrow. Nicholas called Alexandra '*Sunny*' while she called the tsar '*Sunshine*.' Together they had four daughters and a son: Olga, Tatiana, Marie and Anastasia and Alexis. Nicholas was forced to abdicate on 15 March 1917. Afterwards, he was escorted to Tsarskoye Selo where he joined his wife and children under house arrest. The entire family was later moved to Siberia where they were murdered by the Bolsheviks on the night of 17 July 1918.

ALEXANDRA FEODOROVNA was born a princess of Hesse-Darmstadt, a granddaughter of Queen Victoria and a distant relation of the first wife of Tsar Alexander II. She was known as *Alicky* to her family but to her husband she was called *Sunny*. Alexandra was the last empress-consort of Russia. She possessed a shy and difficult personality. After she embraced Orthodoxy in order to become the wife of the tsarevitch, Alexandra Feodorovna also became a religious zealot and a social bigot. She removed her husband and their children from Court because she thought that the Romanovs and the highest levels of the Russian nobility were generally immoral. Alicky fell under the influence of Rasputin whose wishes for government appointments for his friends and his thirst for graft for himself she readily facilitated. Much of the hatred which came to the Romanovs during the failed war fell at her feet. Nicholas and Alexandra's relationship was a true love match, their ardor for one another never died. She and Nicholas had five children, four daughters and a long awaited son: Olga, Tatiana, Marie, Anastasia and Alexis. Nicholas, Alexandra and their children were assassinated by the Bolsheviks in July 1918.

MARIA ALEXANDROVNA (Empress) was the mother of Alexander III (Sasha) and Minnie's mother-in-law. She was born a princess of Hesse-Darmstadt in 1824. She married Tsar Alexander II in 1841. Her time in Russia was not happy. Marie could not adapt to its bitter winters and so spent many months each year in her native Germany or in France. Due to widely different personalities and Marie's long periods outside of Russia, the marriage between Alexander II and Marie was never happy. They did, however, produce Alexandra Alexandrovna who died at age six, the Tsarevitch Nicholas Alexandrovitch who was Minnie's first love and her fiancé until his death in 1865, Alexander Alexandrovitch, (Minnie's husband), Vladimir Alexandrovitch, Alexis Alexandrovitch, Maria Alexandrovna (who married Prince Alfred Duke of Edinburgh), Serge Alexandrovitch and Paul Alexandrovitch. Marie suffered many indignities at the hands of her husband, including his long-time affair with her former lady-in-waiting, Princess Dolgoruky. During the last months of her life, Marie had to endure one final insult from the tsar when he installed his mistress and their children in apartments in the Winter Palace very near to her own. She died a lonely tragic figure at age fifty-five in 1880 after suffering a long battle with cancer. Her indifferent husband remained unconcerned for his wife to the end.

MARIE PAVLOVNA was born Duchess Marie, the daughter of Grand Duke Frederick Francis II of Mecklenburg-Schwerin and Princess Augusta of Reuss-Köstritz. She also possessed Romanov blood. She was a great-great granddaughter of Tsar Paul I. Marie met Grand Duke Vladimir, son of Alexander

II, in 1873 but the two would not marry for another year because of Marie's refusal to accept Romanov law that all imperial brides must first convert to Orthodoxy. Their marriage took place in 1874. She took the name Marie Pavlovna at marriage, identifying herself at the Imperial Court as a direct descendent of Paul I. Because of her refusal to abjure Lutheranism, her household included a Lutheran minister to service her spiritual needs. Known within the family as *Miechen,* Marie Pavlovna became the second most powerful woman in Russia after Minnie. The two women were friendly but never friends. Miechen set up rival courts to those of Empress Marie Feodorovna and later Empress Alexandra Feodorovna. Marie Pavlovna miraculously escaped Russia during the Revolution, as did all of her children. She settled in France where she died in 1920 at age sixty-six. Her husband Vladimir predeceased her, dying in 1909 before the fall of the dynasty.

MARIE PAVLOVNA (The Younger) was the daughter of Grand Duke Paul Alexandrovitch, youngest brother to Alexander III, and his first wife, Alexandra of Greece. When Alexandra died after a fall in a boat which led to the early birth of Grand Duke Demitri, Alexandra's children were placed with Grand Duchess Elizabeth Feodorovna (Ella) and her husband Serge. Serge and Ella were childless and readily agreed to raise Paul's children. This move was legalized in 1902 when Paul married a second time to Olga Pistohlkors, a commoner and divorcée with four existing children. Having married morganatically and without the tsar's expressed permission, Marie and Dimitri officially became Serge and Ella's wards. Paul was subsequently exiled from Russia. Ella had no real love for the children but Serge was devoted to them. He was assassinated in Moscow in 1906. Ella went on to found a religious order of nuns after Serge's murder. Thereafter the children became the wards of Nicholas and Alexandra. Marie married William of Sweden but this union was unhappy and ended in divorce. She subsequently married a Russian nobleman, Prince Sergei Mikhailovich Putyatin, and escaped the Revolution with him. She died in 1958.

ELIZABETH FEODOROVNA was born a princess of Hesse-Darmstadt. She was a granddaughter of Queen Victoria through the queen's daughter Alice. Known inside royal circles as *Ella* (and by her husband as *Titinka*), she was prized for her beauty, being referred to as the prettiest of Victoria's Hessian granddaughters. Ella married Grand Duke Serge whom she had come to know in childhood when his mother Empress Maria Alexandrovna came home to Darmstadt for annual family visits. Ella and Serge were deeply fond of one another but Serge was homosexual with a trail of scandalous whispers surrounding him even as a youth. Ella married Serge but used Miechen's earlier permission as a precedent to retain her Lutheran faith. The two would have no children of their own. Ella would never speak to rumors that her husband was homosexual or that their marriage had never been consummated. After Grand Duke Paul's first wife, Alexandra of Greece, died in childbirth, Serge and Ella took on the role of foster parents to Paul and Alexandra's two children. This continued until Serge's assassination in 1906 and Ella's subsequent conversion to Orthodoxy. Eventually Ella founded a new order of nuns. To independently accomplish this, she sold all of her possessions. Not wanting to lose control of the vast sums realized from this sale, she personally retained the funds achieved. In fact, Ella never turned these funds over to her new foundation which she named the Serving Order of Saints Martha and Mary. What jewels she did not sell, Ella gave to family members. Her Appanages payments continued and although garbed in a nun's habit (which was made for her by a couturier in Paris), she was still a very rich woman despite her new quasi-religious lifestyle. After years of good works for the poor of Moscow, Ella was arrested by the Bolsheviks along with other Romanovs. She was murdered in Siberia in 1918.

OLGA CONSTANTINOVNA: *See Greek Family*

VLADIMIR ALEXANDROVITCH was born the third son of Tsar Alexander II and his first wife, Maria Alexandrovna. After Alexander III, Vladimir possessed the strongest personality in his generation of the Romanov family. He was born in 1847 and was interested in both the military and the arts. He married Marie of Mecklenburg-Schwerin in 1874 and although it was rumored that Vladimir had several mistresses during their long marriage he and Marie Pavlovna were immensely happy together and very well suited to each other's personalities. Marie, known as Miechen in the family, was as ambitious for herself as she was for her husband just as she would become for her children once they were adults. Together they had five children—the eldest, a son by the name of Alexander Vladimirovich, died in infancy. Surviving to adulthood were Kyril, Boris, André and Elena. Vladimir was fiercely protective of his children's imperial rights and often argued with his brother and nephew about them. Vladimir died suddenly in 1909. He never fully accepted or respected his nephew Nicholas II whom he found weak and unable to rule Russia as he felt Russia needed to be governed. He likewise never liked Nicky's choice of wife.

ALEXIS ALEXANDROVITCH the fourth son of the Tsar Liberator, he was born in 1850. He died of a heart attack 1908 at the age of fifty-eight, before the Revolution and war. Alexis never married although rumors circled suggesting that he had married a former lady-in-waiting to his late mother by the name of Alexandra Zhukovskaya. She gave birth to a son which Alexis claimed to be his own. Alexis sought a Russian noble title for the boy as well as for his mother but none was forthcoming which suggests that real doubt existed within the imperial family as to the validity of the supposed marriage and to the reality of the boy's paternity. Alexis Alexandrovitch was both an admiral and a general, excelling particularly in his naval service. He modernized Russia's naval infrastructure and was responsible for the building of new, modern ports for new classes of war ships which were being built for the Russian Navy under Alexis' watch. When it became known that many of these new ships, built under Alexis' direction, were defective, he was forced to resign in disgrace. This did not affect his high standing within the imperial family. He was named godfather and namesake to Tsar Nicholas' only son, Alexis Nicholevitch. Grand Duke Alexis was likewise interested in the arts, particularly in writing and through his efforts the Imperial Library was founded and fully funded making it the finest repository of Russian literature in the empire.

Alexis lived the high life. He was one of the famous Russian grand dukes who frequented the *Casino de Monte Carlo* where he won and lost great fortunes. His high living and rich diet eventually led to his early death by heart attack in 1908 at age fifty-eight.

PAUL ALEXANDROVITCH was the youngest son of the Tsar Liberator. He was born in 1860. He was married firstly to Alexandra of Greece, daughter of George I and Queen Olga. Thus he was both a nephew by marriage to Alix and Minnie and he was also Minnie's brother-in-law. After Alexandra died in childbirth (she had two children—Marie Pavlovna 'the younger' and Grand Duke Dimitri) Paul married Olga Pistohlkors morganatically. With her he had three more children, Vladimir, Irina, and Natalia. Later each of these morganatic Romanovs was granted the title of prince or princess Paley. By this marriage Paul also became the stepfather of three other children. Because he married against the tsar's strict prohibition, Paul was forced into exile. He was stripped of his paternal rights over his Romanov children and he was removed from the annual Appanages payment. His banishment from Russia was long-lasting, continuing from 1902 through 1914 when he was finally permitted to return from Paris. It was then that the tsar gave Olga and her children the Paley title. Upon his return Paul became commandant of the Imperial Guards in 1915. As Russia moved towards Revolution, Paul and several others in imperial circles drafted a new constitution that intended to convert Russia from an autocracy into a constitutional monarchy like that found in Great Britain. His efforts were thwarted by of Tsarina Alexandra. Like all Romanov grand dukes, by this time Paul's days were already numbered. The Danish ambassador in Saint Petersburg offered to smuggle Paul out of Russia in the uniform of an Austrian officer, as he had arranged for an exchange of prisoners of war and could get Paul safely to Vienna in that disguise but he refused. To don the uniform of an Austrian soldier would be tantamount to treason. Paul Alexandrovitch died at the hands of his executioners on 20 January 1919. His son Vladimir Paley was executed before him on 18 July 1918.

SERGE ALEXANDROVITCH was the most difficult personality in the Romanov family during the end of the nineteenth century and the early years of the twentieth century. He was arguably the most hated man in Russia before Rasputin. Serge was the fifth son of Alexander II and Maria Alexandrovna. He was born on 11 May 1857. Serge was a brutal, ruthless officer and an extreme anti-Semite. He ruled the Moscow Province for his nephew Nicholas II with a cruel, iron fist. His hatred for the Jews knew no bounds. Serge was very handsome as a youth but as he aged his internal torment and his many prejudices showed on his face. He always appeared severe and angry, even when sitting for photographs. Serge only smiled in private family circles. He made a practice of always surrounding himself with handsome young men and he was known for his avid homosexual lifestyle. Serge was also a sado-masochist. He married his distant cousin, Elizabeth of Hesse-Darmstadt, in 1884, but he was greatly disturbed by her refusal to convert to Orthodoxy. This did not stall the marriage. Serge went through with it all the same but he harassed and belittled his young wife about it for years to come. There has always been talk that their marriage was never consummated. Serge was murdered outside the Kremlin on 17 February 1905.

ALEXANDER MICHAELOVITCH was known as *Sandro* within the Romanov family. He was the husband of Xenia Alexandrovna, the eldest daughter of Minnie and Sasha. He was thus the brother-in-law of Tsar Nicholas II, as well as Nicky's cousin and best friend. Sandro was born in 1866 and was the fourth son of Grand Duke Michael Nikolaevich and Cäcilie Auguste of Baden who took the name of Olga Feodorovna at her marriage and subsequent conversion. Sandro was raised on the family estate in the Caucasus where his father served as viceroy. This estate was larger than the nation of Belgium and the Michaelovitchi branch of the House of Romanov enjoyed tremendous wealth. Sandro's marriage to Xenia was therefore considered to be a great match. He was not only extremely rich, he was also very handsome and by marrying within the family, Minnie could assure that Xenia would remain close-by, which is what she desired most of all. Sandro and Xenia had seven children together, all with princely rank as they were not male-line grandchildren of a reigning tsar and could not then be entitled to grand ducal status: Princess Irina Alexandrovna, Prince Andrei Alexandrovitch, Prince Feodor Alexandrovitch, Prince Nikita Alexandrovitch, Prince Dmitri Alexandrovitch, Prince Rostislav Alexandrovitch, and Prince Vasili Alexandrovitch. Sandro survived the Revolution, as did Xenia and all their children. He died on 26 February 1933.

MICHAEL MICHAELOVITCH was born in 1861 and was the second son of Grand Duke Michael Nikolaevich and Cäcilie Auguste of Baden. Known in the Romanov family as *Miche-Miche,* like his brother Sandro he was raised on the family estate in the Caucasus. Michael refused a royal marriage. Instead he fell in love with a commoner, Countess Sophie of Merenberg, who was the morganatic daughter of Prince William of Nassau and Natalya Pushkin. Natalya was the granddaughter of Russian poet Alexander Pushkin. Although she had illustrious ancestors on both sides, Sophie was not of royal birth and so Miche-Miche was forbidden to marry her. He did not fear Alexander III but after the couple married Miche-Miche was banished from Russia. Together the couple had three children: Anastasia, Nadejda and Michael. Miche-Miche and Sophie settled in England, living at Hampstead Heath for much of each year. Eventually the Luxembourg title of Countess de Torby was granted to Sophie. This title also passed to their children. Michael and his family were outside of Russia when Revolution broke out. He died in Great Britain on 26 April 1929.

MICHAEL ALEXANDROVICH was Minnie and Sasha's youngest son. He was known in the family as *Misha* and was born on 4 December 1878. Misha was the favorite child of Alexander III and despite his many antics, his father never got seriously angry with him. Michael was a practical joker as a boy, a trait that he inherited from his Danish relations. After the death of his brother George, and until the birth of the Tsarevitch Alexis, Michael served as the heir to the Russian throne, a position he did not want. When Alexis was finally born to Alexandra Feodorovna, Michael openly celebrated his nephew's birth as much as he did his loss of his role as heir to the throne. Michael had numerous infatuations, always surrendering his heart to those women who caught his fancy. Eventually he fell in love with a most unsuitable woman—a twice divorced Russian commoner with children. She was also not someone generally admired for her morals. Her name was Natasha Wulfert. Michael did not care about the consequences he would face if he married Wulfert against his brother's orders. He knew, first-hand, from the aftermath of other Romanov mésalliances what he would face but he married Wulfert all the same. Wulfert was pregnant with Michael's child while still married to her second husband. George Michaelovitch was the couple's son and it would be he who was the last male-line descendent of Tsar Alexander III. Michael and Natasha lived the life of exiles in England for some time, returning to Tsarskoye Selo at the outbreak of the war in 1914. Like other Romanov grand dukes, Michael was arrested when the Bolsheviks seized power. He was technically Russia's last tsar as the throne had automatically passed to him when Nicholas II abdicated for himself and for his son Alexis. Michael would not accept the throne, however, until it came by popular acclaim. He was the first Romanov to be murdered in the purge of 1918-1919. Natasha was later created Princess Romanovska-Brassova with the rank of *Serene Highness*.

GEORGE ALEXANDROVITCH was Minnie and Sasha's third son, born in 1871. He had weak lungs and later developed tuberculosis which greatly restricted his activity. He and his brother Nicholas were extremely close. They lived together in the various nurseries of the imperial palaces where their parents frequently stayed and they were educated side-by-side until George's health decline caused them to be separated. From the time of their father's death in 1884 until his own death in 1899, George was the official tsarevitch of Russia. He was named for Minnie and Alix's brother George I of Greece but inside family circles he was known as *Russian Georgie* (to distinguish him from *Greek Georgie* and *English Georgie* who was also known as *Georgie Wales*). George Alexandrovitch was eventually forced to take up internal exile because of his declining health. A royal lodge was built for him at Abbas Touman in the Caucuses where he led a lonely life many days' journey from his family in

Saint Petersburg. He never married and left no known survivors. Grand Duke George Alexandrovitch died on 9 August 1899.

XENIA ALEXANDROVNA was the eldest daughter of Alexander III and Marie Feodorovna. It was said that she was manlier than her brother Nicholas, never afraid to speak her mind or to defend the actions of her fellow Romanovs. She was born in 1875. Xenia married her cousin Grand Duke Alexander Michaelovitch who was known in the family as *Sandro*. Together they had seven children—Princess Irina Alexandrovna, Prince Andrei Alexandrovitch, Prince Feodor Alexandrovitch, Prince Nikita Alexandrovitch, Prince Dmitri Alexandrovitch, Prince Rostislav Alexandrovitch, and Prince Vasili Alexandrovitch. This branch of the imperial family survived the Revolution. All of them made their way to safety outside off Russia. Xenia died in exile in London on 20 April 1960.

OLGA ALEXANDROVNA was the youngest child of Minnie and Sasha. She was also the least pretentious of her generation of Romanovs, being quite at ease with ordinary Russians. She was born in 1882 and chose to marry early so as to escape her mother's demanding control. Sadly, the husband chosen for her was homosexual and thus the marriage was both unconsummated and unhappy. Olga, like most of the Romanovs, had a very healthy libido and soon took a lover to satisfy her physical needs. She fell in love with this man, Colonel Nicholas Kulikovsky, and since her husband, Duke Peter of Oldenburg, would not continence a divorce, the three set up house together. The duke lived his life, and Olga and Kulikovsky led theirs, all under the same roof independent of the other. In 1916, Nicholas II formally annulled his sister's first marriage freeing her to remarry which she did in the presence of her mother, the dowager empress in Kiev later that same year. Olga and Kulikovsky had two sons together, Tikhon and Guri—neither of whom held royal titles as sons of a commoner. All four escaped Russia and initially settled in Denmark with Minnie. After her mother's death, Olga and Kulikovsky purchased a farm in Denmark but they worried they may be extradited to the

Soviet Union and so they sold the farm and immigrated to Canada where they ended their days. Olga died in 1960; Kulikovsky died before her in 1958.

OLGA NICHOLEVNA was the oldest child of Tsar Nicholas II and the Empress Alexandra Feodorovna. She was born in 1895 and was murdered by the Bolsheviks with her family on July 17, 1918. She was twenty-two.

TATIANA NICHOLEVENA was the second child of Tsar Nicholas II and the Empress Alexandra Feodorovna. She was born in 1897 and was murdered by the Bolsheviks with her family on 17 July, 1918. She was Twenty-one.

MARIE NICHOLEVNA was the third child of Tsar Nicholas II and the Empress Alexandra Feodorovna. She was born in 1899 and was murdered by the Bolsheviks with her family on 17 July, 1918. She was the subject of many false claims by imposters after her murder. Marie was nineteen.

ANASTASIA NICHOLEVNA was the fourth child of Tsar Nicholas II and the Empress Alexandra Feodorovna. She was born in 1901 and was murdered by the Bolsheviks with her family on 17 July 1918. She was the subject of several false claims by imposters, the most famous of these being the Polish woman commonly known as Anna Anderson. She was seventeen.

ALEXIS NICHOLOVITCH was the fifth child and only son of Tsar Nicholas II and Alexandra Feodorovna. He was thirteen at the time of his death at the hands of the Bolsheviks when the entire family was murdered on 17 July 1918. He was the last tsarevitch of Russia.

KYRIL VLADIMIROVITCH was the oldest son of Grand Duke Vladimir and Grand Duchess Marie Pavlovna. As such, he was a first cousin of Tsar Nicholas II and one of the most powerful men in Russia in his generation. He was born in 1876. Kyril fell in love with his maternal first cousin, Victoria Melita of Edinburgh, but any thought of a marriage had to be abandoned because Orthodoxy did not permit marriages between first cousins. Victoria, known in the family as *Ducky*, went on to marry her paternal first cousin Ernst Ludwig of Hesse-Darmstadt. Protestantism had no prohibition against cousins marrying, but this marriage ended badly. After her divorce, Kyril proposed to Ducky and eventually their marriage took place at the Duchess of Edinburgh's home in Germany despite Orthodox prohibitions. As Ernst Ludwig was the young empress' brother, Alexandra Feodorovna never forgave her former sister-in-law for the disgrace which followed her brother's divorce even though his sexuality was mainly to blame. Nicholas banished the couple. Further he stripped Kyril of all his military ranks, his titles, his Appanages income, and all his honorary positions. Victoria Melita was also denied the rank of grand duchess. The couple eventually had three children together: Maria Kirillovna, Kira Kirillovna, and Vladimir Kirillovich. Nicholas II eventually restored them to their rank and income and permitted their return to Russia. Kyril was the first Romanov to swear allegiance to the Provisional Government which overthrew Nicholas. As such, many in the Romanov family thereafter turned their backs on both Kyril and Victoria.

DIMITRI PAVOLVITCH was the only son from the marriage of Alexandra of Greece and Grand Duke Paul. Alexandra died in childbirth giving birth to Demitri in 1891. He was raised mainly by Serge and Ella but several years were spent at Tsarskoye Selo with the tsar and empress. He was one of three murderers of Rasputin. He survived the Revolution, dying in Switzerland in 1942.

FELIX YUSOPOV was the scion of the second richest family in Russia, after the imperial family. Prince Felix was flamboyant and outrageous in both his dress and his behavior. He married Minnie's granddaughter, Irina, and was with Minnie in the Crimea for their last days in Russia. They escaped the Soviets with the dowager empress on-board the HMS *Marlborough*, settling in Paris where he died in 1967. Irina died in 1983.

IRINA ALEXANDROVNA was the granddaughter of Minnie and Sasha and the daughter of Xenia and Sandro. She was born in 1895 and married Prince Felix Yusopov in February 1914. Xenia and Sandro opposed the marriage because of Felix's scandalous bisexual past and a history of cross-dressing but once he won over Minnie, marriage plans preceded with haste. They both escaped Russia with Minnie and eventually settled in Paris. Irina and Felix had one child—Irina who was born in 1915. Felix died in 1967, Irina in 1970 and their daughter Irina in 1983.

THE DANISH FAMILY

CHRISTIAN IX, also known as *Apapa*, was the first king of Denmark from the House of Glucksburg. He was married to Louise of Hesse-Cassel (also spelled Kassel) and he was also the father of Queen Alexandra (Alix), Empress Marie Feodorovna (Minnie), King Frederick VIII of Denmark (Freddy, also spelled Freddie), King George I of Greece (Willy or Willie) and Prince Waldemar of Denmark and Thyra, Duchess of Cumberland. He was known as the *father-in-law of Europe* and as the *grandfather of kings*. His descendants ruled in Denmark, Greece, Russia, Great Britain, Norway, Belgium, Luxembourg, and Spain. He lived from 1818-1906.

QUEEN LOUISE, known within the family as *Amama,* was born Princess Louise of Hesse-Cassel in 1817. She was closely related to the kings of Denmark and was an heiress presumptive to the Danish throne in her own right. She married Christian of Glucksburg in 1842. He also was a presumed heir to the Danish throne but one less closely linked to it than Louise. Together they had six children—Frederick, Alexandra, Wilhelm, Dagmar, Waldemar and Thyra. Louise became the queen-consort of Denmark after the throne was offered to her husband Christian. She and others in the family abdicated their own rights to the crown so as to smooth the way for Christian's ascendancy. She was a master match-maker and placed her children and grandchildren in advantages positions which resulted in prestigious marriages and offers for foreign thrones. Louise was known for her kindness and her intellect. She was expert in the fine arts and was the catalyst for the founding of the Danish Royal Collection. This collection owes its origins to her efforts to form a fine collection of art and artifacts owned by the Danish crown. She died in 1898 at age eighty-one.

FREDERIK VIII was known as *Freddy* within the family. He was the eldest son of Christian IX and Queen Louise. As a child he was known as *Freddy with the pretty face* because, it was said, he was the most beautiful baby ever born in Denmark. Frederik served as crown prince for more than forty years. He did not share his father's conservative views and often times the two men openly disagreed. He married Princess Louisa of Sweden and together they had eight children, two of these becoming kings in their own right—Christian X of Denmark and Haakon VII of Norway. Frederik was born in born in 1843 and died in 1912.

LOUISA OF SWEDEN was known somewhat sarcastically within the wider family as *Aunt Swann* because of her high neck and the imposing way which she carried her head. She was born a princess of Sweden in 1851. She married Frederik of Denmark in 1869 and became queen in 1906. She died in 1926. She was the mother of two kings, having given birth to eight children in all. Although born Louise, she chose to be known as Louisa to distinguish herself from her mother-in-law Queen Louise. With each passing year, she grew deeper in Protestant piety to the annoyance of her husband and children, and to her extended family, especially Alix and Minnie.

PRINCE WALDEMAR was born in 1858. He was the third son and fifth child of Christian IX and Queen Louise. He was also the favorite uncle in the wider royal family. Waldemar had an interesting life. His relationships were unique. He had been offered (and refused) the throne of Bulgaria but he made a fine career for himself in the Danish navy in which he rose to the rank of admiral on his own merits. He married Catholic Marie d'Orleans, a princess of the royal house of France. They had five children together. Waldemar died in 1939.

PRINCESS MARIE D'ORLEANS was a princess of France, the daughter of Jean, Duke of Guise, head of the royal house of France. She was known as *Mimi* in her family. She remained Catholic after her marriage to Prince Waldemar of Denmark in 1885. Their marriage contract called for all sons to be raised as Protestants and all daughters in the Catholic faith of their mother. Marie and Waldemar had five children: four sons raised as Lutherans and one daughter raised a Catholic. Marie was known for her peculiarities and fierce loyalty to France but this uniqueness of character endeared her to both the Danish royal family and the Danish people.

CHRISTIAN X was the eldest son of Frederick VIII and Queen Louisa. He was born in 1870 and died in 1947 having lived long enough to have to endure the forced occupation of his nation by the Nazi regime. During the last three years of his life, he road out in Copenhagen every day on his horse just to show his people he shared their plight and to encourage them to resist foreign occupation by whatever small ways they could. He married Duchess Alexandrine of Mecklenburg-Schwerin whose maternal ancestor had been a Romanov. They had two sons—Frederik IX of Denmark and Prince Knud. King Christian X offered sanctuary to Minnie after the Russian Revolution but he and his aunt disliked one another and the two found building a rapport difficult at best.

ALEXANDRINE was the wife of Christian X and the queen consort of Denmark from 1912 until 1947. At the death of her husband she became the dowager queen but she refused to be known as such, preferring instead to be entitled simply as Queen Alexandrine in the same manner that her husband's Aunt Alix had done at the death of Edward VII. She was born in 1879 in Mecklenburg-Schwerin to Grand Duke Frederick-Franz III and Grand Duchess Anastasia Michaelevna of Russia. She died in 1952.

CARL (HAAKON VII) was born the second son of Frederik VIII and Queen Louisa. He entered the Danish navy in emulation of his Uncle Waldemar. In 1896 he married his maternal first cousin, Princess Maud of Wales, who was Bertie and Alix's youngest daughter. In 1905, after the dissolution of the union between Sweden and Norway, the Norwegian parliament formally elected Carl (known as Charles within the British royal family) as their king. With the permission of his grandfather Christian IX, (who was also his monarch), Carl accepted the Norwegian invitation becoming King Haakon VII of Norway. Maud, who never expected to be queen, was astounded at how the fates had turned in her favor. She and Haakon and their young son Alexander, who was rechristened with the Norwegian name Olav, set sail for their new home. Carl reigned in Norway as King Haakon VII from 1905 until his death in 1957. He was succeeded by his only son, Olav V.

THYRA, princess of Denmark and Duchess of Cumberland, was the third daughter and last child born to Queen Louise and King Christian IX. She was not as beautiful as her oldest sister Alix or as clever as her sister Minnie but she had an endearing charm that enchanted everyone. After a rocky start entering into adulthood, Thyra married the heir to the defunct throne of Hanover in 1878. Her husband called her *Tyrie*. She and Ernst August, the third duke of Cumberland, had six children. The family lived at Cumberland Castle in Gmunden in Austria where they held court as if they still occupied a grand throne. Even though she was far younger than her two older sisters, her hair had turned snow white before age thirty-five. What no one realized was that for years both Alix and Minnie had also lost their natural hair color and began expansive wig collections, as had their mother Queen Louise, to hide this fact. Alix had lost her luxurious auburn hair and Minnie had already lost her deep chocolate brown color at similar ages but few knew it. Thyra and Erni did not care for such ostentation and looked much older than their actual ages as a result. Thyra's more glamorous sisters remained the envy of women across Europe for decades.

ERNST AUGUST, known as *Erni*, was the third Duke of Cumberland and Teviotdale and heir to the throne of Hanover. His father was the last Hanoverian king, dethroned by Bismarck in the aftermath of the Austro-Prussian War which Prussia had won. Hanover had sided with the Habsburgs over the Hohenzollerns and as a result at the war's end Bismarck absorbed

Hanover into Prussia. Ernst never ceased working to restore his nation's independence and to reclaim the huge family fortune which Bismarck had stolen from them during the war. Erni was tyrannical, unsociable, and unpleasant. He was also quirky and strange-looking. He wore Hanoverian national dress every day even wearing the lederhosen when visiting Denmark and Russia. Even though he was quite possessive of Thyra, Ernst August offered her a good life, one that she found most comfortable, and the two genuinely loved one another. They enjoyed a very happy, comfortable married life for forty-five years. Ernst-August died in 1923.

FREDERIK VII was the last king of the Oldenburg line. He preceded Christian IX on the Danish throne. Christian was the father of Alix, Minnie, Freddie, Willy, Thyra and Waldemar. King Frederik was childless and had divorced two royal wives before taking his mistress, Countess Danner, as his third wife. The Danes forgave Frederik all of his many foibles as it was this king who transformed the Danish crown from autocracy to constitutional monarchy. Frederik reigned from 1848 to 1863.

THE GREEK FAMILY

GEORGE I was born Prince Wilhelm of Glucksburg in 1845. He was the second son of Christian IX and his wife Louise. He was known in the family as *Willy,* the name he carried proudly for the rest of his life. He was later lovingly referred to as *Uncle Willy* by his Hanoverian, British, Danish and Russian nieces and nephews. Willy was elected king of Greece in 1863 while still a teenager. He took the Greek name of George and reigned as George I, King of the Hellenes, from 1863 until his assassination at the hands of a madman in 1913. He had ruled Greece for fifty years. Willy married the teen Grand Duchess Olga Constantinovna of Russia in 1867. They enjoyed a very happy marriage until the king's death. Eight children were born to this union. He was succeeded by his eldest son Constantine I.

OLGA CONSTANTINOVNA was the daughter of Grand Duke Constantine Nikolaevich of Russia and Alexandra of Saxe-Altenburg who upon her marriage became the Grand Duchess Alexandra Iosifovna. Constantine was the head of the Constantinovitchi branch of the imperial family and thus a very important man. Alexandra Iosifovna was a beloved and wise doyenne in Saint Petersburg. Olga was the oldest of five children born to this union. She was only sixteen when she married Willy and was still very innocent. She won over the people of Athens when she first arrived dressed in the Greek national colors—blue and white. Olga came to Greece with two large, oversized trunks. The first was filled with her jewelry and expensive wardrobe. The second was filled with her dolls. Although in time she would love Greece, and she used her dowry and annual Appanage income to generously support her charity work there, she returned to Russia every year for prolonged visits with her Romanov relations. She made certain to be present at every historic event and as a result was caught up in the terror of the Revolution. In fact, she had great difficulty escaping the fate of her kinsmen. Greece abolished the monarchy several times and Olga had to go into her first exile when her son Constantine I was dethroned in 1919. She died in 1926 and was initially interred in the Greek Church at Florence. In 1936 her remains were returned to Greece for reburial at Tatoi after the Greek throne was once again restored.

CONSTANTINE I was known as *Tino* within the family. He was the son of King George I *(Willy)* and Olga Constantinovna, the first Glucksburg king and queen of the Hellenes. He was born in 1868, succeeding his father King George in 1913. Constantine first ruled Greece between 1913 and 1917. Greek political vicissitudes drove him to quit his country. He lived in exile in Switzerland, his second son Alexander, replacing Constantine on the throne. Constantine returned to Greece after his son's death, ruling for a second time between December 1920 and September 1922. Again due to heated politics Constantine was forced from his throne once more. He abdicated on 27 September 1922, dying in exile in Sicily on 11 January 1923. He was only fifty-three years old. Constantine married Princess Sophia of Prussia, daughter of Frederick III and Victoria, Princess Royal.

SOPHIE OF PRUSSIA was the daughter of Kaiser Frederick III and his English wife, Princess Victoria, the eldest daughter of Queen Victoria and Prince Albert. Sophie married Crown Prince Constantine of Greece, Minnie and Alix's nephew, on 27 October 1889. Soon after, Sophie decided to convert from the Evangelical Church of Prussia to the Greek Orthodox faith which sent her brother, Kaiser Wilhelm II, into fits of rage. As head of the German church he told his sister he would forbid her entry into Germany if she took such a step. Wilhelm's wife Augusta Viktoria informed Sophie that were she to proceed with her plans she would find herself in hell one day. Unlike her other siblings, Sophie was not afraid of her tyrannical brother and ignored the tantrums her conversion generated. Constantine and Sophie had six children—three of their sons would sit in turn on the Greek throne while one of their three daughters would become queen mother of Romania. Sophie died in exile on 13 January 1932.

NICHOLAS OF GREECE was the third son of King George I and Queen Olga. He was known in royal circles as *Greek Nicky* to distinguish him from his cousins, Tsar Nicholas II and King George V. Through his mother Nicholas was half Russian. He married his mother's cousin, Grand Duchess Elena Vladimirovna, the only daughter of Miechen and Grand Duke Vladimir. They married in 1902 but Elena's mother saw the marriage as a *mésalliance*—Nicholas being neither a king nor a reigning grand duke, nor wealthy. Elena, now a princess of Greece, never ceased in her own thoughts or actions to present herself as an imperial grand duchess and lived as if she were still frequenting the Winter Palace in Russia. Despite her imperious ways, Nicholas and Elena's marriage was quite happy, producing three daughters—the youngest of these being Princess Marina who would go on to marry Prince George, the Duke of Kent, the fourth son of King George V and Queen Mary.

ALEXANDRA OF GREECE was the daughter of King George of Greece and Olga Constantinovna but she is better known as the Grand Duchess Alexandra Georgevna, a title that she assumed when she married her mother's cousin, Grand Duke Paul Alexandrovitch, son of Tsar Alexander II. Alexandra thus became Minnie's sister-in-law as Grand Duke Paul was Sasha's younger brother. Alexandra Georgevna died at age twenty-one after a fall in a boat while seven months pregnant. The fall had been serious but no one realized just how bad it was until the following night when while dancing at a ball she collapsed in the pain of early child birth. Her second child, Demitri Pavlovich, was born healthy, and survived, but Alexandra died. Paul was so struck by grief he had to be restrained from jumping into his wife's grave. He later married morganatically forcing a crisis for the Imperial Household.

GEORGE OF GREECE was known within the family as *Greek Georgie* to differentiate him from his British and Russian cousins. He was the son of George I and Olga Constantinovna. Prince George was born in 1869 and at age fourteen he was sent to Denmark where he lived with his Uncle Waldemar and his family while preparing to enter the Danish Navy. George and Waldemar developed a highly unusual attraction to one another which even their respective wives later on had to accustom themselves to accepting. The two remained close until Waldemar's death in 1939. Eventually both men married as convention demanded of them. George took as his wife Princess Marie Bonaparte, a non-dynastic member of the House of Bonaparte, and Waldemar took as his wife Marie d'Orleans of the rival royal house of France. George was loved by his Greek, Danish, and Russian relatives. He died in 1957.

MARIE BONAPARTE was the daughter of Prince Roland Bonaparte and Marie Blanc, the daughter of the immensely rich casino owner, François Blanc. She married Prince George of Greece and Denmark in 1907, coming to the marriage with half of her late mother's estate and nearly all of her grandfather's wealth—nearly sixty million French francs in all. The couple would have two children together but their married life was best described as independent. Marie would have affairs of the heart, including a long-term relationship with French politician Aristide Briand. She was a devotée of Sigmund Freud becoming an expert, herself, in human sexuality and the female climax. She died of a blood disease in France in 1962.

ALEXANDER I was the second son of King Constantine I of Greece and Queen Sophie. When Constantine was first driven out of Greece in 1917 Alexander was the sole prince acceptable to both the great powers and Greek politicians. He assumed the throne reluctantly, being cut off from every other member of his family who continuously reminded him that he only sat upon his throne in trust for his father's eventual return. Alexander was only twenty-three when he became king and was forced to live under a dictatorship despite his exalted rank and regal title. Lonely and alone, Alexander met and fell in love with a Greek girl, Aspasia Manos. They married despite the union being an unacceptable morganatic one. Anger and scandal resulted in Greece but from this union was delivered a daughter, Princess Alexandra. The young king was visiting Tatoi, the family estate above Athens, when his German shepherd and another dog began to fight. The king stepped in to separate them when his over-excited pet monkey bit him. It was not long after that the twenty-seven year old king died from blood poisoning. His father Constantine I eventually was permitted to return to the throne of Greece.

MARIE OF GREECE was the daughter of King George I and Queen Olga. She married her mother's cousin, Grand Duke George Mikhailovich, and took the title Grand Duchess Marie Georgevna. Her marriage was not altogether happy although she and the grand duke produced two daughters. They were separated during the war, Marie and her daughters being in London with their Aunt Alix when war erupted. This provided Marie with a respite from her estranged husband who died in the Revolution in 1919. Marie married for a second time in 1922. Returning to Greece in 1920 she fell in love with the ship's captain, Admiral Perikles Ioannidis. The two remained married, albeit morganatically, until Marie's death in 1940.

And so now begins the story of Alix and Minnie,
A queen for England and an Empress for Russia...

CHAPTER ONE

THE DANES' DESIRABLE DAUGHTERS

Copenhagen: 1840-1858

ALTHOUGH BORN INTO A TITLED family of solid royal stock, Alix and Minnie's family origins were quite humble. As Glucksburgs they possessed genuine titles and had wealthy relations, but their own family finances were modest. Although their mother's father was quite well off, their own father, Christian of Glucksburg, was impoverished by royal standards.

The sisters did not live the type of grand lives during their childhood in Denmark which would later mark them both as queens. Their mother Louise, although a princess of royal blood, was forced by the circumstances of her marriage to sew her daughters' clothes, and these same daughters cleaned the home given them gratis by the king of Denmark as a large staff was impossible for the family to engage. The king's gift of a new home was a blessing for the Glucksburgs. Christian did not have the means to establish himself and his future family in grand style. Louise's dowry at the time of her marriage came in the form of an annuity and there was no large infusion of cash early-on to purchase a proper family home.

Neither Alix nor Minnie entertained hopes for prestigious marriages. The best possibility for either girl seemed to be a marriage with Danish officers who possessed prestigious family names. At the time, no marriageable royals from abroad turned their eyes towards Denmark and few even knew of the existence of the Glucksburg children. Of course, no one could imagine that Alix and Minnie would one day win the two greatest thrones in Europe. Despite their beauty, it was not until political changes in Denmark moved their father close to the throne that anyone actually took note of these two young girls. There were far more prestigious reigning houses in Europe than the Oldenburgs who ruled Denmark at this time, or the Glucksburgs who soon were to reign after them. There were also princesses by the score waiting for their opportunity to seize a crown through marriage. Once Alix and Minnie's father became heir to the Danish throne, however, every European monarch quickly viewed the two prettiest princesses on the continent as potential wives for their sons.

Denmark in the mid-nineteenth century could best be described as bucolic. It certainly was peaceful—at least on the surface—but it suffered from political malaise brought on by national poverty from a heavy war indemnity imposed upon the country by the victorious powers after the Napoleonic Wars. Two decades had passed since those wars. Denmark was still crippled by the debt, and its agricultural economy had been totally stalled. At the same time, a new political crisis was at-hand. The Oldenburg family, which had ruled Denmark since the middle of the fifteenth century, was dying off. The ruling king, Christian VIII, had only one son and no prospects in his advanced age of producing any others. His only child, Crown Prince Frederik, had always been a problem child. In adulthood, he had married and divorced twice without producing an heir. He favored the delights of Parisian dancers and prostitutes and kept several as mistresses throughout the years. It is believed that he also suffered from syphilis and few thought he was even capable of fathering a child. To make matters worse, he fell in love with an unsuitable woman and would not consider a third royal match. Europe was watching, particularly Germany, as the German states (especially Prussia) had designs on two border duchies which Denmark controlled. Technically these two duchies, Schleswig and Holstein, were fully independent states. If Frederik lived to succeed his father and if Frederik did not produce a royal heir, there would be no Oldenburg to become the next king. If this were to happen, a succession crisis would ensue which might lead to a European war. Prussia would probably use the pretext of an empty throne to seize the two duchies outright.

This looming crisis, and how it was eventually resolved, brought Alix and Minnie to the world stage. Both girls were born in Copenhagen, but technically they were not Danes. They spoke Danish, they called themselves Danish, the Danes were extremely proud of them, and Denmark was the only home they ever knew. But like so many of Europe's royal houses their family was actually German. Their father was born Prince Christian of Schleswig-Holstein-Sonderburg-Glucksburg. In royal circles he was known simply as Glucksburg. He was the best man his clan had produced and he knew it. As a minor princeling, he was penniless and totally without prospects, but his family had origins in the two coveted duchies as well as distant claims to the Danish throne. His future wife Louise was a princess of Hesse-Cassel. Both Louise and Christian were Danish in their sympathies just as much as they were in their devotion to Denmark. Since both were related to Christian VIII and because the king despised his profligate son, Frederik, the king directed his misplaced affections to the young couple who in time he had come to regard as the saviors of his dynasty. But these sentiments were still in the future, as Glucksburg's marriage to Louise was yet to come.

Why Christian VIII took an early liking too young Glucksburg is not known. In every way the two men could not have been more different. Both generation and interests separated them. The king's interests lie in the arts and sciences. He was a man of the Enlightenment. Glucksburg was grounded in common sense and conservative Lutheran principles. He had few outside interests before he married beyond his horses and a career in the military. In this he was a typical parochial German prince. He also experienced real poverty as a youth living in the simplest manner, which came to mark his character in adulthood. Glucksburg was also somewhat prudish as a young man. The old king, in contrast, was a libertine. He fathered ten children with his many mistresses in addition to his only royal heir, Crown Prince Frederik. Despite these differences, King Christian admired both the manliness of young Christian of Glucksburg and his steadfast support of Denmark in the face of growing German hegemony in the region. The king arranged a commission in the Danish Royal Guard for Glucksburg, which carried enough of a salary for the prince to support himself. The king next offered the prince a residence rent free, near his own palace. The mansion long before had been painted a bright yellow and since that time became known as the Yellow Palace. The house was anything but a palace. Its front door opened directly onto the street and only three windows stood on either side of the central portal marking the house's humble width. In the early decades of the nineteenth century the Yellow Palace resembled more a cheap hotel or pensione than it did the residence of a prince. The palace was not furnished and it was also very dingy, but this did not matter to Glucksburg. He had been brought up in a castle with no furniture. His widowed mother had to sell it off to make ends meet. What was not sold was eventually burned as fuel to keep her family warm. Glucksburg was used to hardship and so an empty house did not present a problem for him. And since he could not afford the number of servants necessary to run the house, little effort was initially put into making the Yellow Palace shine.

In time, Christian VIII came to think of the younger prince as his own son. The king certainly liked Glucksburg more than he did Frederik. In addition to providing the young prince with a proper home, and also a posting in the Royal Guard, there were always satisfactory gifts provided at birthdays, name days, and Christmas. The king even filled Glucksburg's stables with good horses which became young Christian's pride and joy.[1]

Glucksburg owed all he enjoyed to the Danish king. In addition to his commission and its accompanying salary and his homes (he had also been given Bernstorff, a castle outside of Copenhagen for holidays and summers), the king also arranged Glucksburg's marriage to one of his nieces.

Christian VIII's sister Charlotte had married the margrave of Hesse-Cassel some decades before and when she came on a visit to Copenhagen in 1840 accompanied by her two daughters, young Glucksburg quickly sought the king's permission to marry Louise, the prettier of the two. The princess readily accepted him and for a nineteenth century royal marriage, theirs was actually a rare love match. Once the two married, Louise's dowry in the form of an annuity granted by her father, along with train cars filled with furniture, paintings and *object d'art* made both the empty Yellow Palace and Bernstorff much more presentable, cozy and comfortable.

The Glucksburg marriage was happy from the start. Christian and Louise's first child appeared in 1843. He was named Frederik and one day he, too, would become king of Denmark. In the family he was called Freddie. Alexandra Marie Charlotte Louise Julie followed on December 1, 1844. She instantly became the heart of the family, a position which she would never surrender. At home, they called the new baby Alix, the name by which she would affectionately be known throughout her lifetime. As child followed child, King Christian VIII began to take a closer interest in this young family. His own son was still childless while the Glucksburgs were quickly producing children—two heirs had already been born and a third was now on the way. Wilhelm was born the following year. Marie Sophie Frederikke Dagmar, called Minnie by the family and known amongst the Danes as Princess Dagmar, followed next. She was born on 26 November 1847 and quickly became the great instigator of family fun.

The king showered all the Glucksburg children with gifts. Louise would not become pregnant again for some time after Minnie's very difficult birth. Thyra did not follow until 1853 and six years after that the sixth child arrived. He was called Waldemar. With so many robust children now in the Glucksburg household, King Christian believed the Glucksburg clan offered the best solution to the looming Danish succession problem.

The Danes did not really love their king. He had steadfastly refused to grant them a modern constitution because he felt they were not yet ready for modern government. Subsequently he ruled over them with a firm hand, but he did so more as an enlightened despot than a belligerent dictator. With each passing day the Danes clamored for a constitution. King Christian viewed Denmark as a powder keg which he feared would soon explode. He knew if a war caused by political unrest broke out in Denmark, it might bring the entire continent into conflict. Were the Danish throne to become vacant, many outside powers would clamor for control of the country and its two dependent southern duchies, Schleswig and Holstein. King Christian could not count on his errant son Frederik, always so unlike his father, to provide an heir. The king was tall and stately with a gentle temperament in most things, but Frederik in appearance was squat, plump in his middle age with a flabby belly, full cheeks, and a tight mouth which always seemed to suggest anger or disapproval. He was also quick-tempered and did not share his father's political views. Nevertheless, Frederik was the last in the direct male line of the Oldenburg dynasty. King Christian worried day in and day out about Denmark if Frederik ascended to the throne.

Many Danes hoped Frederik would die before his father—mostly because of his many debaucheries. They did not really dislike Frederik, in fact many admired him for his infamous peccadilloes, but he was not respected either and most Danes did not wish to see him as king. Christian steadfastly pressured his son to abandon his mistresses for a wife of royal blood so he might produce a legitimate heir before it was too late. If Frederik were to die without an undisputed heir waiting in the wings, a fierce dynastic struggle would tear the nation apart.

It was almost impossible to please both the Danes and the Schleswig-Holsteiners at the same time. The two duchies wanted total independence and Holstein in particular was determined to achieve it. Denmark had no intention of permitting these smaller states to secede. Schleswig was mainly Danish in ethnicity and in its customs, but Holstein's population was thoroughly German. Since 1448, the Oldenburgs who also reigned in Copenhagen had governed Schleswig and Holstein. The Danish king ruled all three of these lands simultaneously, but he ruled each as a separate realm. Each duchy reluctantly recognized the king of Denmark as their sovereign duke but neither was a vassal of Copenhagen. Although the Danes considered the two duchies to be an integral part of the kingdom, both duchies, especially Holstein, sought their independence.

The people of Schleswig nevertheless saw themselves as subjects of the Oldenburgs, but not of the greatly resented Danes. In Schleswigers' minds, their ducal family was quite a separate issue from Danish nationality. Until the Holy Roman Empire collapsed at the fall of Napoleon, Holstein had been under the protection of the German emperors and thus they were thoroughly German in political as well as ethnic sensibilities. It was only recently that they had come under Copenhagen's thumb. The Holsteiners enjoyed tremendous independence in the governing of their small duchy. By the middle of the nineteenth century they began to look across the frontier to Germany for encouragement in their move towards total independence. When Bismarck rose to prominence in Prussia, the Holsteiners finally achieved it. Meanwhile, to further aid their cause against Denmark, the Holsteiners attempted to poison the feelings of their neighbors in Schleswig. The leader of this critical subversive movement was a cousin of the Danish king—Duke Christian of Schleswig-Holstein-Sonderburg-Augustenburg. He was also a distant cousin of Christian of Glucksburg.

The Augustenburgs were an older branch of the Oldenburg family and Christian of Augustenburg was actually the nearest male claimant to the throne after the childless Frederik. If Frederik were to die without issue, almost certainly now the case, Christian of Augustenburg would succeed him unless he could be legally blocked from doing so. Augustenburg was anathema to the Danes because of his fervent support for Germany against Danish interests. The Danes resisted his candidacy vigorously. After it became clear that he was behind the Schleswig-Holstein independence movement, which once achieved would enable him to seize both duchies for himself, the Danes promised revolt if Augustenburg set foot in Copenhagen. The Danish king used Augustenburg's unequal marriage to disqualify him from the Danish throne, but this did not preclude him from inheriting the two duchies. Being blocked from the royal crown in Copenhagen only intensified Augustenburg's determination to win the two ducal crowns for himself. It was imperative for King Christian VIII to find a valid claimant other than Augustenburg for the three thrones. The problem was the only legitimate claimant was a woman, the king's sister, Charlotte of Hesse-Cassel, Princess Louise's mother. The old king began to ponder how best to move Glucksburg to the forefront in order to eventually name him heir after Frederik.

Women could inherit the throne of Denmark, there was no prohibition against it, but women could not inherit the two ducal thrones and so either a viable male candidate had to be found for all three thrones or Denmark would certainly lose the two duchies to Augustenburg. The Danes did not really care for Charlotte of Hesse-Cassel either. She had lived outside of Denmark for decades as the wife of a German monarch who, unhappily, had supported German interests over those of Denmark. After much angst, King Christian came upon a solution. His throne would rightfully pass to his son Frederik. If he died without a legitimate heir, the throne would then pass to Charlotte who would abdicate her rights to the throne in favor of her daughter Louise. Louise, in turn, would also abdicate her rights to the Danish throne in advance to her husband Prince Christian, who was Danish in every way except the origins of his birth. Glucksburg could then legally mount the three thrones without any claimant interfering with the smooth transfer of power.

After years of concern for the future of his country, Christian VIII had cleverly averted a succession crisis, which had become a major political concern from London to Saint Petersburg. The king ordered the creation of all necessary legal documents and Glucksburg was finally proclaimed legal heir to the throne with formal approval by the major European powers to follow in time.[2] Peace, however, did not come with Christian VIII's solution. Prussia refused to recognize the change in the succession and war erupted in 1848. It was at this moment the Glucksburg family developed a deep-seated hatred for all things Prussian and for the ruling House of Hohenzollern in particular which would remain steadfast in them all well into the second decade of the twentieth century. Two years after war with Prussia began, Russia, Britain, France, and Austria imposed peace. A congress met in London in 1852 at which the Danish succession was finally assured by treaty.

King Christian died before this took place. Frederik followed his father as expected, reigning as Frederik VII. The new king was filled with pride and also with disdain. Fredrick showed bland distaste for his new role as he walked into the Amalienborg Palace on his first day as king.[3] He was publicly rude; he certainly did not exhibit any sense of common politeness. At his side was his mistress, Louise Rasmussen, a former Parisian dancer and suspected prostitute whom hours before was created Countess Danner. Frederik married her two days into his reign.[4] King Frederik readily accepted his father's plan for the succession and deferred to the Great Powers: Great Britain, France and Russia's decision to confirm Glucksburg as crown prince. King Frederik would have entered Danish history as a generally unimpressive monarch had he not had the foresight to grant his countrymen its first modern constitution. The year was 1848, the year of political upheaval across Europe and one of the most revolutionary periods in European history. Every sovereign was either dealing with open revolution or with losing his throne.[5] Frederik VII was wise enough, or clever enough, to thwart Danish revolutionaries by advancing the nation a more liberal form of government. Once the new laws were in place, Frederik absented himself much of the time from Court. For granting a new constitution to his people, Frederik earned the deep respect of the Danes, a sentiment which endures to this day. Frederik was a surprise to his people for reasons beyond his granting the desired constitution. He led his people to war to secure the dual duchies for Denmark once and for all; he expelled Christian of Augustenburg, granting him a generous annual annuity so long as he remained in Germany and did not incite further insurrections; he welcomed the Glucksburgs with more generosity than they had shown him; and eventually the Glucksburg allowance from the Crown was increased. Frederik was folksy and relaxed. Most of all, the humble Danes especially appreciated their new king's homespun ways.

As king, Frederik appeared at Court functions when required, but otherwise did not interfere in the governing of his nation. The Glucksburgs, now the newly minted crown prince and crown princess, wanted nothing to do with their new king and his scandalous wife although the countess had won over many Danes by her graciousness. The Glucksburgs absented themselves from the Amalienborg Palace whenever possible—Christian devoting his time to his regiment and to his horses while Louise spent her time educating their growing family.

Christian and Louise led the Court's quiet opposition to the king and his lowborn wife. Countess Danner withstood many humiliations as a result. On one occasion early in the new reign, the king and his countess presided over a gala dinner welcoming foreign diplomats accredited to his Court. Christian and Louise had to be present at the dinner, but had no intention of honoring the countess with a toast. Frederik had to marry morganatically; that is to say the countess could be his wife, but never share his rank, title or wealth, nor could any of their offspring. The countess also fell far below the Glucksburgs in rank and her rumored notorious past in no way inspired them to honor her. Christian and Louise were determined not to accord Danner any respect in public. Diplomats and the nobility present took their cue from Christian and Louise. No one rose after dinner to offer a toast to the king's wife, which had been the custom at the Danish Court for centuries. Frederik and Danner patiently awaited the toast, and whatever goodwill it would offer, but nothing happened. The Glucksburgs dared to look at the king, knowing that Frederik's anger would be centered entirely on them. Rightfully so! Breaking the uncomfortable silence, Frederik spoke to his guests:

"As no one here will propose a toast to my wife, I will do so myself." [6]

All present stood politely but silently, raising their glasses in the countess' general direction without any fawning over their king's wife. No one present would repeat the words of the toast as was the Danish custom nor would anyone present offer the countess the customary Danish salute—*skål.*[7] Silence overtook the room, but Frederik was determined this would be the last time he and his wife would suffer at the hands of own his Court.

Soon after this episode, the king and his countess chose to live a life as quiet country squire's life far away from the capital. As such, the king ignored his duties to the state whenever legally possible. Life was now far away from Court and certainly the government preferred it this way. During this time, in 1851, the countess gave birth to a daughter. The Danes were not informed of the birth, which was kept as secret as possible, but the royal family knew of it, of course, and soon word of the infant's birth spread across Europe by way of a host of trusted spies and special messengers. When Prussia's King Frederik William III initially heard the news, his public response was to ask who might be the father of the child. Without saying so officially, he was only repeating the long-held belief in Europe that the Danish king suffered from both syphilis-induced infertility and impotency. Other monarchs likewise openly doubted that Frederik of Denmark could possibly be the child's father, including Queen Victoria.

On his wife's birthday, 21 April 1854, Frederik acquired Jægerspris Castle from the government. He gave his wife the large red brick manor and estate west of Copenhagen outright. The castle, built in 1722 as the Oldenburg hunting seat, had fallen into disuse since the government took it over in 1849. The government sold it back to Frederik more than happy to see Countess Danner living a comfortable distance from Copenhagen. Jægerspris remained their home until Frederik's death in 1863. When the countess died in Genoa at the age of fifty-eight on 6 March 1874, the Danes were surprised to learn that she had left the estate to the foundation she had earlier created to help women in distress.

By the absolute terms of the London Protocol of 1852, the Danish throne would pass to Christian and after him to his children by the natural process of primogeniture. With the elevation of their father's position came new attention directed towards the two beautiful daughters of the house—Alix and Minnie. Each Glucksburg child was raised to the rank of royal highness and were now worthy of marriage into every prestigious palace in Europe.

Meanwhile, when Louise's paternal grandfather died in 1837 he left one of his many residences, Rumppenheim Castle, to all of his heirs in common. He formed a trust to run the castle after his death. Rumppenheim sat on the edge of the Main River near Frankfurt. It was built in the mid-eighteenth century and was quite modern for its time. Louise's grandfather's testament directed his family to meet there in reunion during the summer of every second year and for this purpose he left a sizable burse to meet everyone's expenses, also covering all the upkeep and the staffing of the castle. And, every two years thereafter Rumppenheim was congested with excited travelers from Russia, Denmark, Nassau, Baden, the Mecklenburg states, and even London. Louise particularly loved these gatherings of her huge family. In fact, these reunions were the only thing German Louise ever admitted to loving.

Rumppenheim was built in a quadrangle form with a large inner courtyard. It stood four stories high and could accommodate hundreds of individuals at one time. But it was in no way luxurious. It stood empty again after each family reunion gathering dust for another two years until the return of the family. In the interim, the castle served as a comfortable home to resident rodents and bats. A block of rooms euphemistically referred to as 'apartments' were assigned to each family group depending on its size and the size of their retinue. Each family was responsible for cleaning their own set of rooms upon arrival despite the presence of a permanent skeleton staff. The Hesse-Cassel family considered these reunions the highlight of their lives. For the adults, Rumppenheim represented whimsical chatter and international intrigue. The children saw the place as a rambling, haunted refuge, a world of magic and hidden surprises. To the Hessians, Rumppenheim can best be described as a rustic gathering of a deeply affectionate, rambunctious clan who thoroughly enjoyed international gossip, childish pranks, flirtations, matrimonial intrigues, new friendships, and most of all, each other's company; all within the beauty and serenity of a remote German countryside.

Those who were excluded from these exuberant summer holidays were keen to dismiss them as overly raucous. This jealousy eventually led to an antipathy for the Rumppenheim summers, especially in Queen Victoria who had no links herself to this German family herself and thus was not welcome despite her exalted status on the European stage. Victoria's cousin, Fat Mary, and her Cambridge siblings were always certain to attend. Their mother was a Hesse-Cassel princess. It was from Rumppenheim that Alix was first mentioned in England. The year was 1847. Mary Adelaide of Cambridge, Fat Mary, and her family had returned to Hesse for the family reunion. Here she met Alix for the first time. Fat Mary wrote to Victoria that this little girl, although only three-years old at the time, already showed promise of a fairy-like beauty. A few years later Mary Adelaide again told Victoria that she had *completely lost her heart to the four eldest* [Glucksburg] *children.*[8] At this time the Glucksburgs would have been the shabbiest of their extended family. Perhaps Fat Mary showed Alix and her siblings more interest simply because of their poverty at that time.

Victoria's antipathy for all things Hessian was long lasting. It would later cause her son Bertie's romance with Alix to stall. Victoria was quick to pronounce the Hessians 'wicked' and 'frivolous,' almost entirely because of how the family reportedly carried on with one another at Rumppenheim. Regardless of what outsiders may have thought of them, the Hessians reveled in the time spent in one another's company. Louise cherished the Rumppenheim reunions. She developed a strong attachment to family, to nostalgia, and to fun making, and soon enough Christian of Glucksburg also fell under the spell of his wife's family and their scenic castle on the Main River. In fact, they would later recreate these exuberant days at Fredensborg Castle each year once they inherited the Danish throne.

Louise had developed early on into a beautiful young woman with sparkling blue eyes and a lovely figure. It was at Rumppenheim where Christian proposed to her long ago, a gesture, which won for him the admiration of Louise's extended family, with the exception of her father who did not want his daughter to marry a penniless prince. The Danish succession rights had not yet been confirmed when the two became engaged and so Christian was still without any prospects of wealth or position. In the end, Louise had her way and married Christian in a very simple ceremony with only King Christian VIII and Queen Caroline Amelie and their chamberlains as witnesses.

Within a few years of marriage the sound of little children's voices could be heard inside the Yellow Palace and at Bernstorff. The birth of their first child promised a secure future for Denmark. According to long-standing tradition, the first male-child was named Frederik if his father's baptismal name was Christian. This assured that Danish kings would reign alternately by each name. Each of the first five Glucksburg children were born at the Yellow Palace, but the last child, Waldemar, was born at the Bernstorff estate. Neither the Yellow Palace nor Bernstorff were palatial by royal standards but the family loved their lives, well lived, in both homes.

Despite their new exalted position, no great income accompanied the post of crown prince and crown princess. An additional sum, however, came from the widowed queen and something more substantial was promised from the Hesse-Cassel family. There was also the meager stipend which Christian already received from the army. Prince and Princess Christian were now secure. In fact, they were now quite comfortable especially since they had two homes at their disposal rent-free. Despite the added income, the family preferred a minimal of staff to assist them—six people in all. The family of eight lived quite modestly and they had great difficulty keeping up with other army officers, the only social set to which they really belonged. Many of these officers and their wives came from Denmark's more prestigious families and they had access to far more financial security than Christian could hope for himself, at least until he was king. There was rarely any excess money available for luxuries such as exotic foods or fine clothes and they seldom entertained. Although Bernstorff provided a country setting, they did not have the means to travel anywhere for vacations or family visits other than Rumppenheim reunions, which were paid for by the trust established by Louise's late grandfather. Nor were various governesses and tutors engaged for each child as was customary at that time. They simply did not have the money to pay for them. The Glucksburgs were also unable to commission portraits of each child when they were still toddlers, which was also the custom amongst royalty then. Therefore, sadly, images of Alix and Minnie in early age do not exist. Neither are there lesson books, childhood letters, children's diaries or any journals of their parents, since none survive to help reconstruct the early lives of the Glucksburg children. We only know of these early years from Alix and Minnie's later public reminiscences. The first mention of Alix by an English stranger came in 1854. Alix was ten at the time. Minnie was seven. Bessie Crew had arrived in Copenhagen from London and by chance came upon the sisters with Anne Larsen, a young Dane engaged to look after the girls from time to time when Louise was busy elsewhere. The three were spending a summer afternoon in the gardens of Rosenborg Palace:

> "We saw a go-cart drawn by a goat that was led by a very smart looking footman [from the palace] in green and gold livery, with another one behind. Someone who looked like a lady's maid or nurse walked beside the cart. Seated in the cart was the most beautiful little girl about eight years old [she

was in fact nearly ten] *wearing a little fur bonnet. That is the little Princess Alexandra. She waved as she drove past. Beside her was a younger girl, perhaps five or six years of age* [Minnie was actually seven] *who seemed preoccupied with her doll. Both girls were enchanting to witness."*[9]

Both Christian and Louise had to assume responsibility for educating their own children. Louise was expert in languages, these coming to her with ease. She spoke five modern languages perfectly and passed her linguistic successes on to each of her children. She also read Latin and could understand a bit of classical Greek, something at the time only men of means had been exposed to. She also had a genuine talent for painting and drawing and possessed a wide grasp of art history. Louise was also expert in music, particularly the piano. The Glucksburg children mastered all these accomplishments. Christian took charge of physical exercise, particularly fencing, equitation, shooting, fishing, gymnastics and boating. He also loved to stand on his head and taught each of his children how to do headstands as well as cartwheels. Both Alix and Minnie continued to perform these indelicate stunts well into advanced age. The Glucksburgs were healthy, robust, and active. In winter, when Denmark was buried deep under heavy wet snow, the family enjoyed ice skating parties at Bernstorff. Alix preferred skating to all other sports. Minnie at this time preferred summer sport—especially riding horses with her father, and by age ten she could rival him in their daily afternoon rides. For their skating parties, the girls would bake doughnuts in the morning, keeping them warm in the coals of the fires burning near the lake until the party was finally ready to eat. Then they would dunk their doughnuts into hot beer punch, soaking them all the way through, before eating them.

In winter and summer the sisters enjoyed extended walks through the forests or along the seashore. Sports and outdoor recreation came easy to all of the children and none were particularly bookish. Only Minnie enjoyed reading and only then the literature and poetry of the day, the racier the better. The Glucksburgs were great animal lovers. The children loved to feed the swans at Fredensborg Castle and in Copenhagen parks. They always seemed to be surrounded by a herd of dogs—large, small and miniature. They loved all breeds and no stray was ever turned away. They even befriended a herd of domesticated deer near Bernstorff, which they fed by-hand nearly every day while living in the country.[10]

As the boys passed out of childhood, their education at home was replaced by attendance at the local public school. The girls remained in the day nursery under their mother's watchful tutelage. Young Freddie, the eldest son of the family, was eventually removed from the public school and educated by special tutors at home to prepare him more fully to one day become king. At eighteen, Freddie was enrolled in the military academy, where like his father he was commissioned as a second lieutenant in the Danish Army. Before he left home for camp training, he and Alix were confirmed together at the Lutheran church at Kongens Lyngby where the family often worshiped.

Through it all, the tone at home was one of absolute frugality. If they even entertained the thought of their father becoming king one day it was a sense of duty and devotion to Denmark which came to mind. None of the children considered their father's destiny to be a pathway to glory for him or for them. Such thoughts would have been offensive to their sincere patriotism. Until that day arrived, simplicity and hard work continued to reign in the Glucksburg home. Louise personally kept the household accounts and she paid all invoices. It was she who met with merchants and the purveyors of supplies not the customary majordomo, as there was none employed at either home. The girls sewed their own clothing and waited upon the table when the maids had their day off. They also did the laundry for the family when the staff was busy elsewhere. Throughout their childhood, Alix and Minnie shared a room on the third floor of the Yellow Palace and another in the attics at Bernstorff, but such economies did not worry or disturb Alix. Minnie meanwhile continually dreamed of better, more glamorous days ahead. Closet space was minimal at both homes but so were the girl's wardrobes. By the time they moved full-time to Bernstorff, Frederik was nine, Alix was eight, Willie was seven, and Minnie was five. They each had impressive winter and summer clothes for Sundays and for when they may be called to Court. Other than these, each child had two additional sets of clothes for daywear, but nothing more. Clothes were passed down from one child to the next as in ordinary families. Boots, in particular, were highly valued and well-cared for because of their cost and, as the children grew out of each pair, they were packed away until a younger sibling would grow into them. They created their own dresses based on outdated Parisian patterns found in magazines which family members sent them occasionally. The two girls mended the underclothes of the entire family as these were rarely replaced. Patches were typically applied in any color available. The move to Bernstorff brought new horizons for the family, but austerity still endured.

The girls even helped with the cooking, creating new concoctions to please their father. They quickly mastered the Danish breakfast favorite Øllebrød—a mixture of day-old black bread boiled in dark beer and poured out over brown sugar with heavy cream added for good measure. All the Glucksburgs loved it and once Alix and Minnie learned to prepare it, they offered it nearly every morning to their parents and siblings. Later, when in far off London and Saint Petersburg, the two girls would crave this old family favorite and make it themselves in the cavernous kitchens of their palatial homes, since no one on their staffs knew how to prepare it. In summers, when the fruit from the orchards and berry patches ripened, Louise taught her oldest daughters to make Rødgrød with red berries and other red fruits. Boiling renders down the fruits, and then flour, sugar and cream are added and it is served warm. The Danes love it. So, especially, did the Glucksburg children.

Tall for a woman of her time, stately with bolt upright posture, and a bit Germanic in her demeanor, which is to say quite domineering at home, Crown Princess Louise was determined to secure a prosperous future for each of her children. With an eventual increase in their income, Louise slowly began to return to a lifestyle similar to the one she once enjoyed as a youth. As life began to improve, Christian was able to build up his stables behind the Yellow Palace, and the couple soon was able to purchase a custom phaeton, the first carriage they would personally own. They had it emblazoned with their new coat of arms proudly confirming their new status as members of the Danish Royal House. Crown Prince and Princess Christian as the Glucksburg couple were now known were full-fledged Danish royalty, which meant they belonged to that magical club whose members were addressed as "your royal highness." With it came entrée across Europe.

Prince Christian was a heavy smoker, a habit begun with his brothers when all were young boys. His endless cigars, one after another from breakfast to bedtime, created plumes of blue smoke everywhere in both homes, providing an odorous environment strangely appreciated as fragrant by his children. Louise was quite content to keep her children close at home. She created a cozy environment of simplicity and wanted her children near her and to remain intellectually and socially unpracticed, innocent and far more youthful, than their actual years.

Louise herself was very unassuming by nature while Christian cared nothing at all for ceremony or social life. Theirs was very much a bourgeois spirit. Several months before King Frederik's death, Louise was diagnosed in the early stages of marked deafness, which increased rather rapidly until she would eventually become entirely deaf by age forty. She suffered from an inherited disease of the ear canal known as otosclerosis, a condition she passed on to her eldest daughter Alexandra and for which there was no cure in the nineteenth century.

As the children became teenagers, the Danes realized just how beautiful the oldest Glucksburg daughter was. In many ways Alix was most like her mother. She certainly had Louise's beauty, in fact she surpassed it, and she also possessed her mother's calming mannerisms. In temperament Alix was quite balanced. She had few airs or ambitions. She embodied a natural simplicity. She had childlike tastes and qualities and a delightful ease of interacting with everyone regardless of class or rank, but at times she did possess a stubborn streak. The wife of a British diplomat posted in Copenhagen at this time later wrote of Princess Alexandra:

> *"Alix was secretly bourgeoise all of her life, in spite of her brilliant and apparently effortless success as Princess of Wales and later as Queen of England."*[11]

Certainly, in her late teen years Alix exuded a happy spirit and tranquil personality. Minnie, three years younger, on the other hand, was already the epitome of high-spirited fun and full of mischief. She would sew the pockets of her brothers' trousers closed so when they would reach to put a small treasure inside, they could not. Minnie would also spend time making special dishes for them, knowing that she had heavily laced her concoctions with salt. She once found a mouse in her bedroom just before going to bed and quickly placed it inside Alix's pillow, waiting in the dark for her sister to scream when the rodent began to move. Minnie was also a talented mimic. She could imitate almost anyone. Once, on the day before Alix's wedding at Windsor, Queen Victoria received her and Minnie for an interview. After they returned to their rooms, the sisters discussed what had just transpired. Victoria could be intimidating when she wanted to be. Suddenly Alix began to imitate her future mother-in-law.

"No, no, no! That is not how it was"[12] Minnie responded. *"It's not like that at all!"*[13] To present her own impression of the audience, Minnie gathered her dignity, walked across the room, and began to speak. Her impression of the queen was exactly as Victoria had spoken to them moments before. Alix tried hard to restrain her laughter. Minnie noticed it:

> *"Of course you can laugh Alix...but I think the queen is magnificent, tremendous, and terrible. No sovereign in Europe could ever stand up to her, I am sure."*[14]

The sisters enjoyed a good laugh at Victoria's expense. *"You might make a good queen yourself,"*[15] Alix told her sister. *"Not as good as her,"*[16] Minnie was quick to reply, *"Because I would want to laugh if I were a queen—or an empress!"*[17] And there it was, Minnie already had her young eyes set on Russia.

With this same thought in mind, Queen Victoria wrote to her daughter Vicky in Berlin about the encounter:

> *"Alix is calm, sweet and gentle and lovely...Minnie was cleverer and I am sure would be very fit for the position in Russia; she is a very nice girl."*[18]

Of the two sisters, Minnie was the more adventurous. Alix was always timid outside the home. It was Minnie who proposed the two should dress alike—at least in the same colors and patterns. Alix always aimed to please and readily agreed to Minnie's impulsive ideas. Alix secretly admired Minnie for her sense of fun and her willingness to try new things. This was an age when unmarried teenage girls were never seen in the forefront of any occasion, and so the sisters' adventurousness was quite refreshing and something altogether new for both their family and for the public. This sense of fun, always inspired by Minnie, would continue during various times of their adult lives. The sisters were mischievous and full of tricks and practical jokes. When Alix was fourteen, she told Minnie that the king was coming to call on their mother. This meant that the children would have to quickly bathe and change into their finest clothes. Taking a bath in those days was not an easy process. Water had to be heated and carried to the bathroom three floors above the kitchens. The girls did this routinely when the servants were occupied elsewhere so Minnie did not notice anything amiss. In her excitement, she certainly had not taken note that Alix had not bothered to change into her best dress. Of course, King Frederik never came. Alix sat with her needlepoint near the window patiently waiting for Minnie to return. At first Minnie thought the king had been delayed until she realized their mother was not at home and none of the servants were scurrying about in preparation, as they should. Alix said nothing; she merely enjoyed putting Minnie through her paces.

More than any other branch of the Hessian clan, the Glucksburgs embodied the Rumppenheim spirit year round. They were also a very handsome family. Most of all they loved each other dearly, emotions which no other generation of Danish royalty had ever displayed before. Fiercely loyal to each other, they were always the first to spring to the defense of any family member wronged by others. Often when the entire family gathered at Rumppenheim, older male cousins would pounce on Freddie and Willie who were substantially smaller in stature and viewed as weak. Alix and Minnie beat their cousins to a pulp in retaliation. Later when Willie was king in Athens she and Minnie would rush to his aid, imposing their determination to have money sent out to help him or to influence policies at home which would benefit Greece.

Few who knew the family when the children were very young would have guessed that one daughter of the house would become a queen of England and an empress of India while another would become the empress of mighty Russia; and the oldest son would wear the crown of Denmark and the next that of Greece.[19] Alix was now seventeen and all of the Protestant royal courts, and Orthodox imperial Russia as well, were very interested in her. Foreign diplomatic missions in Copenhagen were ordered to send regular reports home about her. All of a sudden everybody was discovering that the eldest daughter of Christian and Louise of Denmark was the most enchanting young princess in Europe. Alix accepted this new attention off-handedly, almost ignoring it, but Minnie noted it well and dreamed of the time this attention would also come her way. Minnie, at fourteen, resented the three years she would have to wait for such adulation to also be hers. There were rules about royal life and all she could do for the next three years was dream. And dream she did. All too often Princess Louise punished Minnie for acting too grand for her own good. Louise particularly wanted to squash a rising coquettishness Minnie was beginning to exhibit. She began wearing her hair in the manner of an older woman, and she flirted with officers posted at Bernstorff, always going just a bit too far for Louise's taste. Mother and daughter did not always see eye to eye, but Minnie always deferred, in the end, to her parents' will. Minnie was emerging from childhood. She did everything in her power to further the process along more quickly. In those days, childhood ended when puberty was completed. Adolescence as we know it today was unknown then.

Children grew up quickly, not because they were precocious, but rather because life was shorter and the young, especially royal youth, were promised in marriage by sixteen and married by eighteen or nineteen at the latest. In Protestant nations, adulthood officially came when one was confirmed, which generally took place at sixteen or seventeen. In the Catholic world, where the sacrament of confirmation was imposed at a younger age, adulthood officially arrived at age sixteen for females and seventeen for males. So as Alexandra now turned seventeen, and her beauty and poise caused seasoned diplomats to take every opportunity to report on her activities, Minnie at fifteen was actively clamoring for adulthood to erupt in her too. Diplomats posted in

Copenhagen were eventually ordered to send photographs of both girls (or at the very least to rapidly commission charcoal studies of each), which only increased general interest in the two young women.

Unlike Alix's beautiful piercing blue eyes inherited from her mother, Minnie possessed dark violet eyes. They were soft and welcoming. As her figure developed, and as she grew in size and bearing, Minnie equaled her older sister in grace of movement, and appealing appearance, but she never did match Alix in height or beauty. It was evident to the Danes that the younger sister was far more charming than the more beautiful and reserved elder sister. Alix and Minnie, when seen side-by-side on the streets of Copenhagen or in the capital's parks and gardens, or strolling together on the grounds of the Bernstorff property, appeared so much alike that many thought them to be twins. At close observation their faces were very much different. Alix's facial structure mimicked her mother's while Minnie's was rounder, more like her father. Alix's classic perfection always held the steady gaze of those people intent on admiring her physique and her sparkling face.[20] All of Christian and Louise's offspring showed great promise, but the historic destinies of the two eldest daughters of the family would prove the greater surprise.

Christian and Louise decided to abandon Copenhagen altogether because of the increased interest in the family. The Yellow Palace sat alongside the street and pedestrians could actually stop and peer in the windows while the family was eating dinner or when they were formally entertaining. For privacy, the Glucksburgs settled in the country and would only use the Yellow Palace when their presence at Court functions required an overnight stay in Copenhagen. They all loved the green park setting that Bernstorff offered. It reminded them of their summers at Rumppenheim. The very modest style of living at Bernstorff was far more comfortable for them than the grander, claustrophobic city life in Copenhagen.

While their brothers were being properly educated, Alix and Minnie continued to be occupied with deportment, dancing, fine arts, languages, music and decorum—all the disciplines young princesses were required to master. Most of all, all the Glucksburg children were drilled in punctuality. Louise and Christian had peppered their English cousins—Mary Adelaide

(Fat Mary), Augusta, and George of Cambridge—with questions about how the English Royal family was educating their young. Punctuality was the topic of most concern in palaces throughout Europe at that time, especially in the homes of the British queen. Royals were always punctual down to the very second they were due to appear at a function. Tardiness was not tolerated. And so, punctuality and good manners became a matter of habit for the Glucksburg children. By nature they were an unruly family, but Christian was determined to create a firm sense of punctuality in each child. To achieve this, he imposed a series of penalties for tardiness.[21] He could put the fear of God in his children when he wanted to and arriving late was cause enough to bring forth his wrath. Typically he would stand bolt upright at his place at the head of the table, demanding in a deep voice to know the nature of his children's lateness.

Fifty years after Christian's regimen was put into place in Denmark, the sound of the dinner gong at Buckingham Palace, at Sandringham House or at Balmoral still caused Alix to shudder at the thought of arriving late to the table. As a child at Bernstorff, it was not unusual to find Alix eating her meals each evening in solitary disgrace with no second helping permitted and certainly no offer of dessert. Denying food was Christian's initial way of teaching his children the lesson he wanted to drive home. It seemed something always occurred to delay Alix's arrival, just as it would decades later when she became Princess of Wales, and later still queen-consort. Initially Christian set the penalty as standing in place at table while the rest of the family ate the first course. The stern imposition of this method worked for Christian's always hungry sons, but it seldom worked for Minnie and almost not at all for Alix. And so in time Christian changed the penalty to a more severe measure. He now permitted any offender to sit down when they eventually arrived at the dining room, but he directed the staff to cut the portions of every course by half. There would also, of course, be no dessert served to anyone arriving late. Princess Louise sometimes was forced to endure her husband's rule, as well, since she tended towards tardiness from time to time, especially after she grew deafer and could not hear the gong. Even as a grown woman, during the weeks leading up to her marriage, Alix was forced to endure her father's strict penalty as if she were still a child.

Although quite curious for a princess of her time, Alix did not initially excel as a pupil except in subjects that came to her naturally, particularly languages. She spoke perfect Danish, German, English, French and 'Scandinavian' (a sort of slang mixture of all the Scandinavian languages). After Christian and Louise became crown prince and princess, the staff began to grow. French was taught by Mlle. Sidonie L'Escaille, a Belgian called in to replace the Swiss girl who left the Glucksburgs to marry. English was inculcated in the children very early. By the time the sisters were in their teen years, the family's resources permitted the addition of Matilde Knudson, who taught English grammar and English history. The children continued with the study of German, and Louise and Christian served as the tutors. The Glucksburgs always spoke Danish at home. Despite her grasp of these tongues, Alix never lost the guttural accent common among Germanic people speaking foreign languages. Both girls excelled in exercise, equitation, music, gymnastics, and the art of dressmaking. With their still finite income it was necessary for the girls to learn how to make the clothes they wore. Even Louise mostly wore clothes she had created for herself, even for Court functions. Dressmaking was quite a complicated art because of the numerous layers of undergarments which had to be worn, but Alix's growing expertise would serve her well for the remainder of her life. It would also give her the reputation of a woman with a sense of her own esthetic authority among designers and tailors in the great couturier houses of Paris and London.

Later, as Princess of Wales and queen, Alix preferred silk and cashmere. These were always her favorites for daytime. She could spot the finest quality from a distance. Satins and bejeweled netting were preferred for evenings as were *mousselines de soie* and rich velvet. Suedes were her preference in shoes, which were custom-made for her in London. She wore evening slippers in kid leather and satin and seldom wore a pair of these formal slippers twice. They were fragile and damaged easily although they added to her always-elegant allure. As Princess of Wales, and certainly later as queen, Alix infuriated dress designers by insisting she knew better than they how their clothes would best suit her body. No designer cut clothe for the queen unless she had first discussed with them how best she thought their design would suit her. Long before there was an annual *best-dressed list,* Alix and Minnie led their social set in fashion and design. Minnie took the same attitude in Russia and with the unlimited funds at her disposal; her costly creations often caused a sensation. In the end, both Alix and Minnie took away from their early training a great talent for presenting themselves to the best advantage.

Not only did the sisters master the domestic skills taught by their mother, they also mastered skills most young aristocratic women were never exposed to, certainly not in Britain. Simply said, the girls became proficient scrappers. Alix and Minnie could handle both of their brothers at home. More than once, one or the other boxed Freddie or Willie's ears when the boys had irritated them. Never were their brawling talents more evident than when the family was at Rumppenheim. Rambunctious fun was the order of the day there and Alix was particularly quick to scrap with her cousins. Once while visiting Wolfsgarten, the country estate of the Darmstadt branch of the Hessian family, Alix and Minnie got into an entanglement with their Mecklenburg cousins. The two girls gave the male Mecklenburgers as good a hiding as the boys had ever received.[22] it caused such a ruckus the family never let the girls forget it. Year in and year out they were always reminded of their battle skills during subsequent Rumppenheim reunions. Of course Minnie was always ready to join in, but she was not the instigator. Alix was. When family honor was at stake, nothing stood in the way. Minnie was different. She possessed a much more vivid personality as well as a determined, hardheaded obstinacy. Her cousins knew not to anger her to the point of furry or the price to pay would be far too high.

Through her teens, Alix's spirits were usually high, too high to suit her father. She was cheerfully incorrigible and often found herself the recipient of her father's wrath, but she was the favorite of both parents. Outsiders saw her as perfect, and as she grew older, news of this lovely creature spread. The Glucksburgs were probably the most handsome family in Scandinavia. Alix and Minnie were tall and graceful and were watched closely by the Danes. It was as if the people of Denmark knew these two girls had become the nation's best assets. And they were! They could speak to foreign visitors in their own language, always in a flawless way, and their lack of shyness was so refreshing that men of all ages fell hopelessly in love.

As was also the norm within the British Royal family, the Danish family's routine followed a strictly regimented annual cycle. In winter they would come to Copenhagen whenever the king held Court. Happily this was infrequently, but Louise and the girls used this time for shopping, for visiting tearooms, or for charity work. Copenhagers were amazed to see members of their royal family walking the streets like common folk without the accompaniment of guards or attendants. This had never been seen before in Denmark. Previous to the arrival of the Glucksburgs, the Danish royal family had always been removed from the people. Louise's genuine affinity for her fellow Danes engendered a new public style which remains the hallmark of Danish royalty to this day.

In winter, when freedom from duty permitted, the family enjoyed cold weather sports. In summer they would go for day trips to Klampenborg, a three-mile journey from Bernstorff where they enjoyed the sea and sands late into the night. Every other year they found themselves back at Rumppenheim. The rest of the time the Glucksburgs lived quietly at Bernstorff. Often when in Copenhagen, King Frederik would summon the four oldest children to perform a musical piece or two for his assembled guests. As the king aged, he also mellowed and he eventually grew fond of the Glucksburgs, especially the children. King Frederik was one of the first to openly encourage marriage prospects for both Alix and Minnie. He saw them as young adults while their parents tried to keep their children young well after the approach of adulthood. King Frederik took great pride in the girls; especially knowing through them prestigious marriages would come and cast a fine light on Denmark after decades of territory loss and poverty.

Frederik hosted a ball for Freddie and Alix the evening after their confirmations. He was present. The Countess Danner was not. Afterward he proclaimed that Alix had officially come of age. One of the few perks of a princess achieving adulthood was she no longer slept in a shared nursery with her female siblings. And so Alix was given a bedroom of her own at both

Bernstorff and the Yellow Palace. The night of her confirmation was the first time Alix slept alone. Her new room was fitted with a single iron bed, a table, a shelf for books and mementoes, and a chair. It wasn't very different from the rooms she had shared with Minnie.[23] Her solitude was a heady feeling for her, but she missed Minnie's presence. Danish politicians realized what a prize Alix had become and soon after they began to speculate which foreign prince would finally win her.

Queen Victoria and her husband Albert had already heard through the royal grapevine about Christian and Louise's daughters. By the time Alix was fifteen, Albert was already considering both sisters as future wives for his two eldest sons. He would not live to see his plans come to fruition, but he suggested them to the queen before his death. Victoria did not initially share her husband's particular enthusiasm for a Danish match. After all, the family was more Hessian than Danish and their continued presence at Rumppenheim and other raucous events put Victoria off the idea. She, at any rate, was determined to continue the German marriage bonds which had marked the British royal family for two hundred years.

When Victoria and Albert's eldest son Bertie turned sixteen he was sent down to White Lodge in Richmond Park ten miles southeast of London. The queen and Albert wanted to keep Bertie isolated in order to remove unwanted distractions, especially any possibility of sexual awakenings. His tutor and a military adjutant accompanied him. During his stay Bertie was invited to a dinner party at Cambridge Cottage, his cousins' home in nearby Kew. This would be Bertie's first adult dinner party and he was anxious to attend. The Cambridge's were Victoria's first cousins. Their father and Victoria's father were brothers. Both older men were the younger sons of George III. The Cambridges included the three adult children and their mother, the dowager duchess. The old duchess was a Hessian and it was through her that these branches of the English family were also cousins of the Glucksburgs. Victoria liked her Cambridge cousins and she was particularly close with the dowager duchess despite her Hessian origins. Victoria hated this rambunctious family who had allowed many unequal marriages which she felt diluted royal bloodlines. Yet, she could be quite fickle at times. Where her Cambridge aunt was concerned, she overlooked her anti-Hessian feelings altogether although Victoria was not keen to permit a still very immature and unpolished Bertie any social freedom whatsoever. Eventually she relented and Bertie was finally permitted to attend the Cambridge's dinner party. Before they were all called into dinner, the family and their guests congregated in the house's large drawing room. Standing next to the fireplace was a side table on which were placed samples of the newest invention—photography. This table displayed several portraits of various members of the extended Hessian clan. Bertie stood at the table for a very long time examining one specific photograph with keen interest. When questioned about it, he attempted to make some rather purposely disinterested comments about the beauty and charms of the girl in the photograph, which fooled no one. That girl was their young cousin Alix of Denmark; the photograph taken at Rumppenheim the year before. It was actually the first photograph ever taken of Alix and in seeing it, the first time Bertie learned of the existence of the beautiful princess from across the sea who would one day become his wife.

CHAPTER TWO

A PRINCESS FOR BERTIE

Great Britain: 1860-1863

PRINCE ALBERT'S DEATH PLUNGED QUEEN Victoria into a deep sense of mourning that would last for decades. She was 42 years old. Her eldest daughter, Victoria, was already safely married to the Crown Prince of Prussia. Her second daughter, Alice, was preparing to marry the heir to the Grand Duke of Hesse-Darmstadt, a sizable but unimportant German state. Both daughters would play their part in Albert's plan for an eventual unified Germany. Victoria and Albert's eldest son, Bertie, heir to the British throne, however, remained a source of great torment and disappointment. Although at the time of his death Prince Albert was only in middle age, he long had suffered from various ailments. He shared the queen's responsibilities of state and also managed her estates.

These burdens along with the recent deaths of several people very close to him took a heavy toll on the prince-consort. His deep-seated melancholy and depression, which many courtiers had noted, produced in him a sense of approaching doom. Albert had always been a micro-manager. He assumed control of the queen's palaces, as well as their private residences in Scotland and on the Isle of Wight where they had built Osborne House as their principal family home. He also attempted to manage affairs of state in Germany through his daughter Victoria, the newly minted Crown Princess of Prussia, and also through his dissipated, yet compliant, older brother Ernest. The death in March 1861 of the queen's mother, the Duchess of Kent, that of his own doctor soon-after, as well as the deaths of the king of Prussia (which advanced his young daughter Victoria one step closer to the Prussian throne), and also the sudden death of his favorite cousin from typhoid, produced a change in the prince's appearance. Albert's health began an unmistakable decline.

Albert and Victoria made the decision early on that Bertie should undergo more extensive training in the British military. Bertie had always had a difficult personality. He often appeared to be dense and exasperating more than discourteous, but try as he did, Bertie simply could never master traditional subject matter. His parents were convinced the military would finally make a man of their son and hopefully bring him to a point where he would be able to do his duty to the nation. With considerable discussion amongst such leading figures of the day as the Duke of Wellington and the queen's cousin the Duke of Cambridge, it was decided Bertie should be posted to the Grenadier Guards in Ireland where he would, at the very least, master the art of military ceremonies. Bertie was ignorant of his father's declining health, his mother's increasing depression, and the effects of stress on them both. He took up his post with the Grenadiers at Curragh[1] where his shortcomings were quickly evident. It was not only his poor education and lack of military experience that drew attention to him; it was also a surprising lack of social ease with his fellow officers which caused them to openly mock him.

Prince Albert had arranged for his son to live in private accommodation a safe distance from the officer's barracks in order to avoid close contact with ordinary soldiers. In fact, the residence of General Sir George Brown, the commander of Ireland's forces, was commandeered to house Bertie and his entourage. Because Bertie craved friendships with other young men his age, handpicked senior officers were invited twice each week to dinner, and once each week he was permitted to accept invitations as the guest of honor at regimental events. Prince Albert's plan called for Sunday evenings to be spent at home in quiet solitude with Bertie's governor, General Robert Bruce attending him. Bruce had been instructed to do everything possible to improve the prince's intellect. Despite this restrictive regime and Bertie's general seclusion, he came to love camp life and reveled in interaction and camaraderie with his fellow officers, many who became life-long friends. After all, most of these young men were the sons of the great nobles of Great Britain, men he would rely on later in life as king. In short order, however, it became evident that Bertie was far more immature than his actual years. A lifetime of seclusion within palace walls surrounded only by his parents and siblings and devoid of any normal outside contact with men his own age had retarded his development. Whereas his fellow officers were men in every respect, Bertie was still juvenile in many ways.

While Bertie was slowly emerging from his cocoon in Ireland, Alix and Minnie moved closer to adulthood. The Glucksburgs had not raised their children in isolation as had Victoria and Albert. The girls were often seen in the shops of Copenhagen and strolling down the city's fashionable avenues in late mornings. They preferred dry goods emporia where they were now able to purchase the best quality of clothe for the wardrobes they continued to create. Minnie, always determined to have her way, searched for cloth that suited both sisters' skin and hair tones so the two could continue to dress alike. Alix had tired of the practice, but never objected too strenuously. She drew the line at wearing identical hats, however. By the time Alix was sixteen, Christian and Louise's income had improved sufficiently for the girls to exchange straw 'boaters' for new hats in the current fashion. Since the girls could not create these themselves they patronized the city's milliners. Alix was always certain to select a hat that flattered her but did not suit Minnie's facial structure. In this way, she was able to exert some independence. Shopping and mischief making were the sisters' favorite pastimes. Even in teen years, both girls were pranksters. They loved nothing better than to sneak up to the front door of a neighbor's house, ring the bell, and quickly hide behind trees to see who would answer. As staff had to answer the call bell no matter how many times it rang, the two, sometimes with brother Willie in tow beside them, would continue to ring the bell for hours' on-end. Time and again a servant came to the door to receive an unexpected caller only to be dismayed when no one was waiting at the door.

It was at this time that Prince Albert added a seventh name to his short list of approved princesses for Bertie's consideration. The first six were German. None were particularly attractive. Prince Albert entrusted the selection of each to Vicky, in Berlin, who now insisted he add Alix of Denmark to the list. Vicky's favorite lady-in-waiting was Countess Walburga von Hohenthal. She was engaged to Walter Paget, a British diplomat of promise who was about to be transferred to Copenhagen. Vicky entrusted Walburga with the task of befriending the Glucksburgs with the secret intention of making Alix's acquaintance.

With a letter of introduction from the Prussian crown princess, Walburga was immediately able to achieve an audience with Crown Princess Louise. Louise invited her to tea at the Yellow Palace. Countess von Hohenthal's diary entry relates how the day unfolded:

> *"Her Royal Highness had asked me to come quite informally, as she knew my husband well, and she had often allowed him to visit her in the same way. She was still a very pretty woman, with fine blue eyes and a pretty figure. Prince Christian came into the room while I was with the princess. There was a delightful charm and kindness about him which won all hearts and the patriarchal and unostentatious setting of the family life of this royal family was most attractive."*[2]

The countess continued:

> *"After I was with the princess a little time I said that my husband had so often spoken about Princess Alexandra that I hoped that I might be able to see her."*[3]

Louise sent for Alix who made a lasting impression on the countess.

"She was like a half-opened rose bud, so simple and childlike in everything,"[4] Walburga told Vicky that once she had met all the children, she realized at once that the still youthful Glucksburgs and their children had formed a truly loving and united family. Once this was reported, Vicky insisted Alix's name be placed at the top of the marriageable candidates' list.

What neither Vicky nor her father realized was that Bertie had already become enchanted by Alix's photograph, which he had carefully studied at Cambridge Cottage two years before.

Meanwhile, Walburga grew close to Crown Princess Louise and undoubtedly the two women began to plot on Alix's behalf. Louise had been planning prestigious marriages for all of her children for years. Her plotting for Alix was about to bear fruit. Only a few years separated Walburga and Alix. Soon the countess became friends with both girls. Walburga joined them on their daily shopping excursions and it was Wally (as Alix and Minnie called her) who attempted to foster an individual personal style in Minnie. It was also Walburga who first suggested Minnie as the best choice of a bride for Queen Victoria's second son, Alfred.

Vicky was not due to visit her parents for some time. She knew that the Pagets were set to honeymoon in England. She arranged for Walburga to meet the queen and Prince Albert. When Albert saw the photograph of Alexandra, which Walburga presented to him, he exclaimed:

"She is so lovely. I would marry her at once!"[5]

Queen Victoria smiled at Albert's exclamation, but Walburga understood that the queen was not as pleased as her husband. It was after this visit the prince-consort embraced Alix as the right choice as a bride for Bertie.

With his fellows at Curragh as unofficial tutors, Bertie began to mature soon enough and his general outlook slowly widened. It wasn't long before he was introduced to all the dissipations young officers have long been fond of. At this time it was considered quite normal for some of the more adventurous Grenadiers to keep a woman of ill-repute hidden somewhere in the camp. Soon enough Bertie's sexual innocence became well known and eventually the subject of ridicule. After one drunken night in the company of new friends, Bertie discovered a vivacious young actress by the name of Nellie Clifton in his bed; she had been slipped into Bertie's quarters by his companions. Bertie's first sexual experience was naturally thrilling, but it would not remain secret for long. Rich, aristocratic officers with too much time on their hands naturally took part in camp gossip and soon enough Bertie's lost virginity was the talk of London.

Within short order word reached the palace by way of all places, Coburg, where the much-trusted confidant Baron Stockmar had recently retired. Stockmar had heard of Bertie's affair through several of his old friends in the British aristocracy. Always quick to criticize Bertie, believing him to be thoroughly unfit to eventually succeed Queen Victoria, Stockmar wrote to Prince Albert telling him of his eldest son's indiscretion. Initially Victoria and Albert refused to believe the much-trusted Stockmar. Of the two parents, Albert was by far the more prudish. In sexual matters Victoria was really a typical Hanoverian—a woman driven by stoic pragmatism. She had been reared with the knowledge that men in her family kept mistresses and fathered children out of wedlock. As an adult she tended to accept, but not embrace, this behavior as fact. Albert never would. Because of his own parents' failed marriage, infidelity was a sin greater than all others in his view. Nevertheless Victoria feared that her son would adopt the proclivities she hated most in her uncles: laziness, lethargy and lecherousness. When Victoria's favorite London advisor, Lord Torrington, confirmed Stockmar's reports, the queen demanded, out of fear of her son's moral decay, that Bertie be severely reproached. Quite typically, Victoria flew into a rage when Bertie returned home. He was forced to stand for several hours while she ranted in German and English about the damage that similar behavior by his great-uncles had done the monarchy. The queen instructed Bertie's tutor to firmly explain the consequences of sex outside of marriage and the damage it could do to the Crown. Bertie would, in time, also have to suffer through a long dressing down by his father. Prince Albert's lecture was calm yet riddled with an infusion of guilt and sorrow.

Albert worried more about potential scandal and damage to the crown than he did any damage to his son's character. This is not to say that Albert wasn't dejected by his son's now corrupted morals. For Prince Albert, the implications were too terrible to contemplate: would a child be born of this deplorable union with a tart? Or had Bertie been infected with syphilis or gonorrhea, a common occurrence in military camps? Once politicians knew about the prince's indiscretion, Albert worried they would make it difficult for Bertie to succeed to the throne, particularly if the queen died young. Albert was also worried the Nellie Clifton affair would one day open Bertie to black-mail! Most of all, he wondered if any respectable princess would wish to marry his dissipated son. Realizing all of these scenarios were possible, Prince Albert was especially apprehensive about the deterioration of the Crown's image were all of this to become public fodder. He kept most of what he knew about the affair from the queen who was prone to fits of rage at the mere mention of Bertie's name. Albert no longer slept well nor did he eat much. His health suddenly seemed to be in serious jeopardy. At this time, the typhoid germ which contributed to his ultimate death had already entered Albert's body and was now in its incubation stage. His judgment was beginning to be impaired. Although many young men of Bertie's age and station had numerous affairs before marriage, in Albert and Victoria's judgment, princes were to be held to a higher standard. Of course Bertie had already fallen far below his moth-er's expectations and Albert piously claimed God would judge Bertie for his pre-marital liaison. He wrote his eldest son, ridiculing the young man.

> *"If you try and deny it,* [the affair] *she can drag you into a Court of Law to force you to own it, and there with you, the Prince of Wales, in the witness box, she will be able to give before a greedy multitude disgusting details of your profligacy for the sake of convincing the jury; yourself cross-examined by a railing indecent attorney and hooted and yelled at by a lawless mob!! Oh, horrible prospect, which this person has in her power—any day to realize—and to break your poor parents' hearts!"*[6]

London society sarcastically referred to Nellie Clifton as the 'Princess of Wales' and a great many Londoners knew of the prince's fall from grace. Meanwhile at Curragh in Ireland, Bertie continued to have sexual relations with Nellie who also shared a bed with several of his fellow officers. He had found freedom and cared little for what his parents, or London society, thought. Secret reports began to reach Prince Albert at Windsor of Bertie's behavior. The prince-consort was now suffering many advanced symptoms of the onset of the typhoid virus, including insomnia and joint and muscular pain. He was also deeply depressed and some courtiers believed, true to his morose nature, that he was privately courting death.[7] He continued to carry out royal duties, including a visit to the Royal Military Academy at Sandhurst where he was soaked to the skin during a hour's-long military review during torrential rain. He returned home shaking with chills.

Fever developed later that night. His physicians advised bed rest. But two days later, fearing news of Bertie's continued affair would finally leak to the general public, Prince Albert boarded a train for Cambridge against doctor's advice where Bertie had now begun studies. Albert believed the Curragh affair needed to be thrashed out in person as a matter of moral correction. The prince did not yet know that Nellie Clifton had followed Bertie to Cambridge. Although it was a stormy day the two men took a long walk where observers noted they seemed lost in conversation. Distracted by their intense discussion, they lost their sense of direction and were out in the rain far longer than anticipated. Prince Albert returned to Windsor Castle by train that evening without first changing his clothing. Soaked to the skin for a second time, Albert felt very ill by the time he reached home. The next day he found it difficult to get out of bed. But later that afternoon he kept his commitment to go shooting with the visiting Prince of Leiningen.[8] Ernst of Leiningen could not help noticing his uncle's illness and told the queen so. Although Albert insisted on being present at dinner, he could not eat and his skin color was poor. Victoria's own depression left her unable to notice any of the signs of decline in her husband's health. She had had no specific warning from the palace doctors who routinely kept her in the dark anyway about her own health, as they also did that of her family.

As this was unfolding in England, gossip was reaching Courts across Europe. Vicky learned the lurid details of her younger brother's sex life from table chatter at dinner at the Berliner Schloss. Christian and Louise also heard stories, as well, but Denmark was a quiet place and Court life, although it had its share of gossips, tended not to concentrate on foreign royalty unless war was eminent. The Glucksburgs did not worry nor did they show any real interest in Bertie's affair. Walburga Paget was not consulted and Crown Prince Christian seemed to take the position that this was normal behavior for a young man, especially a prince. Although Alix would come to know about Bertie's affair before she accepted him (because Louise was intent that her daughter should not enter into a marriage with her eyes closed), it is doubtful that she knew anything at this time. Empress Marie of Russia had likewise heard stories. She secretly wanted Alix for her eldest son, the Tsarevitch Nicholas Alexandrovitch.

Prince Albert's health continued its downward spiral. He suffered unattended for two more weeks, performing numerous duties, including meetings with cabinet ministers over the crisis in the developing American Civil War. By 4 December, the prince-consort could no longer eat solid food and was afflicted with severe diarrhea and vomiting. He became semiconscious late into the night of 5th/6th December. On the following day, the queen's doctors diagnosed typhoid but to shield the queen they referred to it as a fever. Bertie was called home from Cambridge without the queen's knowledge, but Vicky was too far away in Prussia to be summoned and was kept updated by letters and telegrams. The government, which knew very little about the state of the prince's deteriorating condition, knew enough, however, to try to keep this politically sensitive information from the Germans. Late on the night of the seventh, the doctors issued a public statement which appeared in the newspapers the following morning:

> "For some days His Royal Highness has been suffering severely from an attack of gastric fever and is at present much weakened by this disorder." [9]

This condition continued for another week. Shortly before 11 o'clock on the evening of 14 December 1861 Prince Albert died. The queen's wailing could be heard for hours throughout the castle. Many feared she was falling into the same madness that afflicted her grandfather, King George III who long-suffered from porphyria. This nervous affliction rendered its victims unable to function mentally. It was known as 'madness' in those days and was believed to be an inherited condition—present in the British royal family at that time. However, Victoria was suffering from profound depression aggravated by shock and sorrow. Nervous exhaustion would eventually bring calm, but the queen could not be consoled. Victoria departed almost immediately with her daughters for Osborne House, leaving Bertie and the male members of her family to bury the prince-consort.[10]

The Prince of Wales' personal grief was sincere and was particularly inflamed by his remorse over his behavior during the last month of his father's life. Victoria, for her part, sought to blame Bertie (whom she would never fully forgive) for his father's death at age 42. She told anyone who would listen that the shock of Bertie's sexual indiscretion, as well as the long hours Albert had spent in the pouring rain at Cambridge, had caused her husband's death. Of course, this was not the case. The typhoid virus had embedded in Prince Albert weeks before Bertie's Curragh affair had even begun. Modern physicians studying the case have since pronounced that advanced kidney disease would surely have been a contributing factor in the prince's early death if not the greater cause. Although the stress over Bertie added to Albert's suffering, it really did not cause his decline or his death. More likely, the origin of the typhoid germ can be traced to the deplorable design of the drains and sewage system at Windsor, which Victoria had never bothered to modernize.

When a senior royal family member died anywhere in Europe, the custom was for all the royal houses of Europe to go into mourning, as well. Typically, foreign Courts would dress in mourning for a month, and during this period public entertainments would be cancelled. And so when Prince Albert died in December 1861, the Danish Court joined all the others in Europe observing a period of respectful mourning. Louise and her daughters went into black and the entire family kept to the privacy of their home. They were seen in public only for formal engagements.

Christmas in Copenhagen that year was more subdued than usual, but observing formal mourning did not preclude having fun behind closed doors. A Danish Christmas was fundamentally a family affair. The staff was given token gifts early in the afternoon on Christmas Eve. Typically, these were hand-made items: scarves, mittens, or needlepoint. Louise, Minnie and Alix were charged with making these during the course of the year and then the gifts were stored away until Christmastime. A large decorated Christmas tree stood in the center of the main drawing room. Prince Albert may have introduced the Christmas tree to England, but the Danes had incorporated it into their celebrations a century before. Damasked covered trestle tables encircled the room—an individual table for each family member—and on each stood a small tree and presents by the score.

There were gifts from the king, from the government, from the Hessian family and from ordinary Danes. Hans Christian Anderson was a personal friend of the family. Most of his fairy tales were originally written for the Glucksburg children. He never forgot Christmas, always bringing along a new story as well as small gifts for all. The family, of course, gave gifts to each other. Most of these were hand-made, sentimental presents. The sisters also made gifts for their pets, especially their dogs. No one important to them was forgotten!

The family opened their gifts at teatime on Christmas Eve. The oldest went first followed by the next oldest, continuing until the entire family had finished unwrapping their gifts. Afterwards, they would gather around Louise's piano singing hymns, Danish folk songs, and Christmas carols until a light dinner was served at ten o'clock. Christmas day was sacred. The family spent the better part of it at church. Late on Christmas afternoon, the Glucksburgs would visit charity wards or old age homes, something both Minnie and Alix would continue to do when in their adoptive countries. The current British royal family still celebrates Christmas in this way, the Danish way, as initially established by Alix when she and Bertie started their family.

Charity was important to Louise and her daughters. She would visit the aged and infirm in villages near Bernstorff on a regular basis, not just during the holiday season, taking both daughters along whenever possible. Minnie often drove the carriage herself in these outings. She and Alix were keen equestrians but Minnie was also an avid coach driver.

During his last year, Prince Albert had quietly made three arrangements which would affect his eldest son for the remainder of his life. The first was the expansion and refurbishment of the London palace known as Marlborough House, which would be inhabited by the Prince of Wales upon reaching the age of majority.[11] Prince Albert's second arrangement was in the selection of a proper country residence for Bertie and the third, and most important, was to secure the woman who would become his son's wife and Britain's next queen.

Marlborough House had been Queen Adelaide's dower house after the death of William IV.[12] This large red brick town mansion on Pall Mall, designed by Christopher Wren, was intended as a gift for the first Duke of Marlborough, hero of the Battle of Blenheim in 1704. After the duke's death, it became the home of numerous lesser members of the British royal family. For a time it was the London base for Princess Charlotte and her husband Leopold, uncle to both Victoria and Albert. After Charlotte's death in childbirth, he was elected the first king of Belgium. Following Adelaide's death in 1849, (who had only entertained at Marlborough House while actually living next door at Clarence House) the mansion was finally designated as the future home of the Prince of Wales. On the old queen's death, the prince-consort began plans to both enlarge the complex and to refurbish its interiors.

Prince Albert made headway with the second task. Every great gentleman at this time possessed both a city residence and a proper country estate. Albert visited several potential country properties before deciding on the Sandringham Estate in Norfolk, which was then available at the price of £220,000.[13] It included 7,100 acres with a dilapidated manor house needing substantial attention to make it suitable for the heir to the throne and his future wife. Prince Albert arranged for the asking price to be paid out of the Duchy of Cornwall's funds and work began in earnest. The neglected house was immediately improved (although eventually torn down to make room for the construction of a new stately manor house), stables and kennels were added, roads were constructed, a chapel was erected, and numerous cottages for workers and guest accommodation were built. More than 5,000 new trees were planted and formal gardens were laid down. The improvement of the Sandringham Estate seemed to be the only thing that drew the attention of the wayward Prince of Wales. In the month's following Prince Albert's death, Bertie traveled to Norfolk as often as possible to monitor the work at-hand, often changing his late father's initial plans to suit his own. Sandringham sat near no other royal property, and many thought the flat terrain ugly and barren, but it proved to be ideal for Bertie. The estate stood in the middle of some of the finest shooting country in England, and once ensconced there, the prince took every opportunity to entertain his friends far away from the criticizing gaze of his mother.

Prince Albert's third challenge, the most difficult of all, was to initiate Bertie's engagement to Alix of Denmark. It was this arrangement which most troubled Albert at the time of his son's affair with Nellie Clifton. However, most nineteenth century royals fully understood a young prince was expected to form relationships before marriage and in the end the Curragh affair proved no hindrance at all for the Danish royal family who were delighted with the prospective prestigious marriage.

Of all the queen-consorts in English history, Alexandra of Denmark was by far the most beautiful and the most widely loved. The country had never seen anyone like her before nor would they again until a future Prince of Wales would marry Lady Diana Spencer. During the last year of his life, Prince Albert and Queen Victoria scoured Europe for a suitable bride of royal birth. The desirable choice would not only have to be beautiful, given Bertie's insistence upon it, but she had to be intelligent-enough to both stimulate and calm the restless prince. Victoria and Albert initially preferred a German princess, but the few available did not meet Bertie's demands. He was certainly not a great catch in terms of his own looks, intellect or personality, but he was 'the' catch of Europe all the same because the British throne came with him. Christian left the matter of his daughter's future marriage in the hands of his capable wife Louise (still known formally at this time as Princess Christian) who was, like Prince Albert, also worried the scandal surrounding the Prince of Wales would ruin her daughter's chances of becoming an English bride. Louise feared, (incorrectly as it turned out) that Queen Victoria would instead select one of her Hanoverian relations as Bertie' bride, which would be Victoria's way of keeping the extent of Bertie's scandalous affair out of foreign courts. At the same time, Empress Marie of Russia began a search for a wife for her own first-born son, the Tsarevitch Nicholas Alexandrovitch, and Alix was believed to be her first choice. Princess Louise much preferred an English life for her eldest daughter because, in her opinion, the Russian Court was filled with corruption and licentiousness. She was a pious Lutheran and had instilled in her children its particular exemplar of Christian life. Nevertheless, Louise kept the heir to the Russian throne in reserve in case Bertie was to somehow slip through her fingers. It was Wally Paget's efforts to secure an engagement between Alix and Bertie that turned the tide in the Dane's favor.

While the British queen and the Glucksburgs attempted to complete initial arrangements for the engagement, a meeting between Bertie and Alix had to actually take place. So a plan was hatched for an "accidental" encounter. The Hesse-Cassel family, to which Louise belonged, was scheduled for their bi-annual reunion at Rumppenheim Castle. While they were there, the Danes would visit nearby Speyer Cathedral.[14] Bertie would be simultaneously dispatched to Prussia for a private visit with his older sister, Vicky, who with her husband Fritz, would accompany him to Speyer on the appointed day. Bertie was well aware of what was to come. Alix, of course, was kept in the dark. Well-orchestrated by Victoria and Louise in advance, the two small groups entered the cathedral from opposite doors and meandered about as if they were simply admiring the beautiful architecture. While visiting the side chapel dedicated to Saint Bernard, the two groups converged. The meeting was brief. Afterwards Bertie wrote that he found Alix less than beautiful with a long nose and too low a forehead to suit him. He thought her hands were too large and out of proportion to her body. Alix did not seem to him the great beauty the photograph in his cousins' drawing room had projected. In contrast, Crown Princess Victoria, however, wrote glowingly to her mother after the visit. Later in life, Alix reminisced about her first encounter with Bertie:

> *"He was shy and did not look directly at me. At the time, I thought that he did not like me. I certainly did not realize that I was meeting the man that I would soon marry."*[15]

A day later, the two families again met 'by chance' at a hotel in Heidelberg where both groups were spending the night—also secretly pre-arranged by the two mothers. Before saying goodbye the following morning, both Bertie and Alexandra exchanged signed photographs, a custom in those days for people of rank. No other promises were made. Alix confided in her mother that she found *"the Prince of Wales handsome and quite manly."*[16] Louise was pleased her eldest daughter had seen something special in Bertie.

Vicky diplomatically massaged her brother until he finally admitted Alix's so-called defects were in no way averse to his liking. Other parties, however, were visibly opposed to any Danish match, once word of the clandestine rendezvous leaked out. First amongst these was the Duke of Saxe-Coburg, the queen's own brother-in-law, who did not wish to see a Dane on the British throne. Other German royals, especially the Prussians, felt the same way and many detrimental rumors began to spread across Europe about Christian and Louise and their family. Ernest of Saxe-Coburg was the first to spread blatant lies, putting it about that Princess Louise had secretly given birth to several illegitimate children outside of her marriage, and that Princess Alexandra, despite her young age, had also had numerous affairs with Danish, as well as, foreign officers. The duke knew that sooner or later these rumors would make their way into the British press. Once public, Ernst hoped the wedding would be called off in face of public outrage. Queen Victoria certainly had not been pleased with Princess Louise's family, believing she descended from a far too licentious clan, but she fiercely defended her when these rumors made their way to London. Victoria was particularly aghast at the various unequal marriages within Louise's family, including that of her aunt, Augusta of Hesse-Cassel, who had married the Danish Baron Blixen. It fell to Sir Charles Phipps, the Keeper of the Privy Purse and a close advisor to her late husband, to remind Victoria that Bertie was not marrying Princess Alexandra's Hessian or Danish families. He was marrying Princess Alexandra herself, who was assuredly above reproach. Phipps was learning how to best handle the mourning queen and wrote to her saying:

> *"It is of the first importance that the Prince of Wales' wife should have beauty, agreeable manners, and the power of attracting people to her, and these Princess Alexandra seems to possess in a remarkable degree."*[17]

Phipps also realized that Victoria was now leaning towards her late husband's prudishness and so he artfully added:

> *"With a virtuous and well-educated girl, the ill-repute of some members of her family usually adds to the ardor of that advice."*[18]

This addendum reassured the queen who finally accepted Princess Alexandra as the chosen candidate for her son's hand. Nevertheless, she worried about the Prince of Wales. Victoria feared Bertie was only entering into this marriage for sexual gratification. In the end, it was the queen's eldest daughter's assessment which mattered most.

> *"I never set eyes on a sweeter creature. She is lovely...a good deal taller than I am, has a lovely figure...a complexion as beautiful as possible, very fine white regular teeth, and very large beautiful eyes. Her voice, her walk, her manner are perfect, she is one of the most ladylike and aristocratic looking people I ever saw! She is simple and natural and as unaffected as possible...she is 'the' one a <u>thousand times</u> over!"*[19]

As marriage negotiations began, Bertie was sent on a military tour of the Near East under the close supervision of General Bruce. The queen was determined to make certain Prince Albert's wishes in life would be honored after his death.

In addition to Bertie's marriage, the queen's second daughter Alice was pledged to Prince Ludwig of Hesse-Darmstadt, heir after his father to the grand ducal throne of this small Rhenish duchy. The marriage took place at Osborne House on 1 July 1862, resembling more a funeral than a joyous wedding day, with the bride's mother presiding over the occasion in folds of black crepe. After this wedding, Victoria's attentions returned to Bertie once more whom she was determined to see finally married to a proper European princess. En route home from the Near East, Bertie stopped in Paris where he not only sampled the more raucous pleasures of nightlife in the City of Lights but also spent days purchasing numerous gifts and trinkets for the wife he was about to accept.

Obstacles still remained. Danish King Frederik VII was by now a thoroughly cantankerous figure and led a private life that greatly offended Queen Victoria; particularly his two divorces followed by his unsuitable marriage to his mistress. Denmark was also at loggerheads with Prussia and other northern German states over the duchies of Schleswig and Holstein. Victoria, entirely German by both blood and sensibility, as was her late husband, had sympathies with the various German states and their monarchs who were also closely related to her. Her eldest daughter Vicky was already the Crown Princess of Prussia and her second daughter had just married the heir to the Grand Duchy of Hesse-Darmstadt.[20] In face of growing familial opposition, Victoria was no longer as eager to invite the prickly Danish political question into her family circle. Suddenly Victoria again seemed opposed to the marriage. This fluctuation of being for and then later against the Danish marriage greatly upset the governments in both Britain and Denmark.

Ultimately, Alix's beauty as well as her flawless character and a subtle, but firm, reminder that Prince Albert had wholeheartedly approved her before he died finally won Victoria's formal assent. A now more mature Bertie also repeatedly assured his mother that he would never marry an ugly woman or someone he did not actually love and so, he said: "*It will be Alix or no one.*"[21] To everyone's surprise, Bertie now considered himself madly in love with the beautiful Danish princess and insisted the marriage go forth with haste. Alix had already told her family that this would not be a marriage of convenience. She professed a mature love for Bertie that surprised no one. The princess was a passionate creature by nature. She gave her heart with care, but on those she loved, she showered affection and sweetness. Bertie was reserved but wrote to his uncle Ernest after the honeymoon:

> "*Alix is so sweet and loving. I hope to earn the love she shows me. Our time together has been enchanting.*" [22]

As Queen Victoria was about to make her first visit to Germany since Prince Albert's death, both to see her daughters Victoria and Alice and to visit the Rosenau (Albert's favorite childhood home), she also arranged to meet Alexandra. The destination for this rendezvous was set for the home of Victoria's uncle, King Leopold of the Belgians. Laeken is a palace compound sitting in the far north of the Belgian capital and where the queen's uncle came to live when he was first elected independent Belgium's first monarch. To assure the meeting between the queen and the Danish royal family would appear to be coincidental, it was arranged for the Danes to vacation at the same time in Ostend, very near the palace at Laeken. The queen arrived in Belgium on 2 September, the Prince of Wales arrived on the continent the day before, but he was careful to stay away from Brussels until the appointed day. The meeting was set to take place on 3 September. The two mothers met alone—Victoria, awkward without Prince Albert by her side, and Louise particularly shy and hard of hearing due to her congenital condition. Louise told Victoria that her daughter was a good child, but not brilliant, and certainly one with a will of her own. She described Alix as being always eager to please. When Alix was later summoned to meet Victoria, the young princess showed no trepidation or shyness, which greatly pleased the widowed queen. Alexandra was tactful in both her appearance and manner. She wore a black skirt and a white blouse in deference to the queen, who remained in perpetual mourning. She wore no jewelry and her hair was pulled back into a tight chignon. The overall effect was one of breathtaking simplicity and youthful loveliness. Victoria was won over completely. She presented Alix with a sprig of white heather that had been picked for her by Bertie at Balmoral, saying she hoped it would bring her much luck. Alix was moved to tears by the queen's tenderness and the freshness of her emotion radiated across her face. Enchanted by Alix's genuine sweetness, Victoria praised her in the finest terms.

As pre-arranged, Bertie arrived at the palace the next day where he met with the Danish royal family for a second time. He went with them while they visited the sites of Brussels and he took an opportunity which presented itself to tell Prince Christian of his intentions to marry Alix. On 9 September both parties met again at Laeken. Alexandra had also charmed the aging King Leopold who, like all the Coburgs, was originally against the match. Alix used these days *en famille* at Laeken to further charm her future mother-in-law. When the young couple was left alone in the palace gardens, Alix showed Bertie the sprig of white heather he had picked for her in Scotland, which she was wearing partially concealed under her shawl. At the site of it, Bertie fell to his knees formally proposing. Alexandra immediately accepted. Surprisingly, Bertie urged Alexandra not to be hasty in accepting his proposal. Alix, however, replied that she had long ago decided to accept him if she were asked.

Writing from Brussels on the very day that he proposed, Bertie wrote *"it should be absurd to suppose that a real feeling of love could exist as yet for a person,"*[23] but it was clear—Bertie was ready and eager to fall in love with the girl he had just selected as his bride. Both the prince and princess lived in a time when they knew they would have to accept choices made for them by their parents. This was particularly true in royal marriages. For Bertie, the choice of a future bride was very limited and he was delighted to find a girl who suited his tastes. He was also clearly pleased by the enthusiastic praise of Alix meeting him everywhere he went. Although Bertie had only recently experienced lovemaking for the first time, he already had a connoisseur's eye for a pretty woman. In Alix he knew that here was a lovely girl already anxious to marry him. She was not only beautiful, but she was also warmhearted, ready to give him the affection he so badly needed. Alexandra's own feelings at this time are much more difficult to assess. The royal family reported that she was very taken by the prince and it seemed to them, she was much more in love with him than he at this time was with her. In the days following the engagement, the young couple went riding through the parks of Brussels and dined together quietly in the king's palace. Although it was unusual at the time, Queen Victoria permitted the two to be alone in a room together. However, that room had to be next to the sitting room allocated to Princess Louise and her door had to be kept open at all times. The couple was only permitted a few short days together. By 14 September the party broke up and everyone returned to their own homes. Alexandra invited Bertie to come to Denmark, but Victoria forbade a visit because of the Schleswig-Holstein problem which was growing more acute every day.

Prussia was intent on seizing the two duchies, which Denmark would never willingly surrender. War was eminent. Political opposition to the coming marriage now began to rapidly increase, especially in Germany where Prussian Crown Princess Victoria's role in arranging it had become so unpopular that people hissed at her in the streets of Berlin. For her part Queen Victoria insisted that Alexandra travel to England for a proper inspection; privately considering it a means to stall what might become a politically unpopular marriage. Victoria declared that it was a necessary period of introduction for a future British princess. Bertie was dispatched on a Mediterranean cruise to get him conveniently out of the way. Despite opposition from Prince and Princess Christian, and from Minnie who stated her sister *was being paraded like a zoo animal before the queen,*[24] Victoria adamantly demanded her future daughter-in-law come to England for several months. Prince Christian refused to permit his daughter to travel alone. He accompanied her as far as Osborne House on the Isle of Wight, but once there, he was told frankly he was only permitted to stay two nights. He would have to find accommodation elsewhere if he was determined to remain in England. When intended, Victoria could be very rude. In regard to Alix's required visit, the queen would brook no opposition, not even from the young woman's parents.

After Prince Albert died, Osborne House resembled a mortuary more than it did a restful, seaside retreat. The queen had left everything exactly the way it had been when Albert was alive. Bertie's sisters Helena and Louise initially befriended Alix and made her visit much more relaxed and enjoyable than it otherwise could have been. During this time Alix worked hard on her English, which she already spoke fluently, but she was unable to lose her strong Danish-Germanic accent. After dinner, she sat alone beside the queen, listening attentively to Victoria's tender reminiscences about Albert and their life in England. Alix, for her part, did all she could to make the queen like her, including appearing sincerely interested in the daily repetition of these morbid tales. Because of this attentiveness, in the end, the queen proclaimed Alix both a blessing and a perfect gem.[25] An unexpected benefit of Alix's presence at Osbourne was the visible change in the queen's mood.

For the first time since Albert's death, Victoria began to smile again and she even chuckled occasionally. Alexandra had brightened Victoria's gloomy existence and both the queen's family and Court were delighted by the princess' good influence. Despite general goodwill on all sides, the queen coldly informed Alix that she would not be permitted to speak Danish again after she married Bertie. Victoria wanted her son to understand everything his wife said and he had no facility whatsoever in the Danish language. Like most royals at that time, Bertie picked up languages quite easily and was already totally conversant in German, so learning Danish would not really have posed a great difficulty for him had he wished to master it. He did not!

Even so, Victoria would not entertain the idea. She further decreed that Alexandra could not bring private staff—ladies-in-waiting and personal maids—to help her in the transition ahead. Victoria informed the Danes that English women would be provided for her.

Queen Victoria intended for this first visit to be open-ended, but in her typically high-handed manner, she had not told this to Alix's parents when the visit had been first proposed. The queen was therefore greatly insulted when Prince and Princess Christian insisted Alexandra return home to spend her eighteenth birthday with them. Victoria had to relent, but this added to her growing disdain for Alix's parents. Christian dutifully returned to Osborne to collect his daughter since the very irritated queen refused to return her to

Denmark in the royal yacht. Nor would she receive Christian out of spite when he had arrived at Osborne.

The prince and his daughter passed through France on their way home and there they met Bertie who was on his way back to London from his recent Mediterranean cruise. He travelled with them as far as Hanover before he broke away to return home. The couple was not to meet again until their wedding, which was now fixed for 10 March 1863. The choice of this date fell in the middle of the solemnity of the Lenten liturgical season, which shocked both High Anglican officials and English Catholic churchmen alike. Each hierarchy made their displeasure known both in the press and in parliament, but the queen would not be moved. Victoria had already vetoed the month of April as a possible date for the wedding because Princess Alice was expected to give birth to her first baby, although the queen had no intention of traveling to Darmstadt to be with Alice. May was also out of the question because the British royal family had always been superstitious about the success of marriages entered into during this month. Several deaths in the royal family in the past century were of persons who had married in May. From this superstition came the adage: '*Marry in May, and rue the day.*' Victoria feared Bertie would not remain celibate if he was forced to wait too long and so it was decided the wedding must take place in March, regardless of the Lenten solemnity and the two churches' opposition to the chosen date.

The months leading into the marriage were full of difficult trials. The Danes believed they were being treated with disrespect and a lack of consideration simply because they were a small, indebted nation. Queen Victoria had not even sent an official delegation to their king in Copenhagen to formally request Alexandra's hand in marriage as protocol actually demanded. This procedural oversight had been intentional on Victoria's part because of her genuine disdain for King Frederik. Invitations to the wedding were yet another difficulty. Victoria refused to have any extended family members on either side in attendance. Because she remained in mourning, the wedding was to be an intimate family affair at Windsor Castle. Victoria saw it as a thoroughly British event, the very best fête she felt she could endure in her continued saddened state. This decision meant very few of the queen's German relations would be invited, not even her cousin the Grand Duchess Augusta of Mecklenburg-Strelitz.[26] None of the Hanoverian royal family would even be considered. The queen's decision also meant the Danish king would also not be invited, which greatly offended his countrymen, especially since Frederik had grown so fond of Alix.

Victoria also insisted that Prince and Princess Christian and their daughter should make a grand tour of northern Europe en route to England with special stops in Hanover to soothe the irritated family there, and also to Brussels. Even Uncle Leopold's name was not included on the wedding invitation list. Princess Louise vetoed Victoria's demands, insisting that a two-month journey would be too costly and too trying for her family to undertake. Louise wished to keep Alix (and indeed all of her children) as long as possible, particularly since Alix would live in distant England after her marriage. Queen Victoria's innate maternal feelings were less fervent than those Louise exhibited with her brood and she would not relent. All manner of demands were made by the queen that Princess Louise simply ignored or pretended not to have received. This clearly rubbed Victoria the wrong way. Her growing dislike for Louise, however, in no way affected Victoria's newfound affection for her future daughter-in-law.

Meanwhile wedding presents were pouring into both Copenhagen and London in anticipation of the royal wedding. Alix's possessions here-to-fore had been few and simple, filling less than one small closet in her parent's home in Copenhagen. King Frederik sent a magnificent necklace, a copy of the historic thirteenth century Dagmar Cross, which had always been the most revered jewel in Denmark's treasury. It was to remain the centerpiece of Princess Alexandra's jewelry collection thereafter. Every conceivable gift came from Alix's Danish and German relations, as well as from many of Europe's royal families. Meanwhile in England a magnificent array of gifts awaited her arrival. King Leopold presented his future grandniece with a bridal gown and veil worked entirely in rare and costly Brussels lace. Bertie provided her with an entire trousseau which awaited her inspection at Kensington Palace, including a grand pearl and diamond necklace and earring set as well as a magnificent matching diamond filigree and Fleur de Lys diadem.

Alix and her family arrived in England three days prior to her wedding. Despite Victoria's admonition that she be thoroughly English, all of the finest qualities of Danish heritage followed Alix across the sea. She embodied centuries of Danish history. Its many difficulties and hardships influenced her outlook and her loyalties. Her natural simplicity, so serene and innocent, and her innate charm were the result of her unassuming Danish upbringing. Her tastes and her habits, as well as the delightful warmth with which she could make every man and women feel immediately at ease were a hallmark of the Glucksburg family. Louise and both her daughters, Alix and Minnie, shared these unique qualities which drew people close to them. The Danes were a fiercely patriotic and loyal people and the Glucksburg children were likewise imbued with these sentiments. A virulent hatred of all things German was also inculcated in them at an early age. This hatred stayed with Alix, Minnie and their siblings all of their lives. Alix exhibited lifelong faithfulness to the nation of her birth and to her family. The tenacity with which she fought all their battles and championed all their interests sprang from deep family feelings characteristic of Danish home life. Such were the personality traits imbedded in this statuesque girl as she stepped upon English shores at Gravesend to a rapturous welcome, never before seen in the United Kingdom.

CHAPTER THREE

WINNING ENGLAND'S HEART

1863-1865

T HE GLUCKSBURGS ARRIVED ON-BOARD THE royal yacht
«*Victoria and Albert*», which the queen had ordered to land at the
ancient coastal village of Gravesend in northwest Kent. It had been
dispatched to Antwerp to bring the Danish family safely to England. The final
leg of the passage was relatively calm for winter waters, but Alexandra was
suffering from a severe cold and kept to her cabin for much of the journey.
Bertie rushed to Gravesend to greet the Danes but arrived thirty minutes after
the family had already landed. Charging aboard the yacht, he met Alix at the
top of the gangway where he publicly embraced and kissed her in full view of
the public who had been waiting for hours in the bitter cold to greet their new
Princess of Wales. It was the first time in living memory a British prince had
showed any sign of public affection and the gathered crowds responded with
wild enthusiasm.

The road to London teamed with crowds delaying the party's arrival at
Paddington Station from where they would begin their final train journey to
Windsor. Once at the castle, Victoria warmly welcomed Alix at the foot of
the great staircase before she suddenly withdrew again to her own apartments.

Victoria's welcome of Louise and Christian had been cordial and pleasant, but not warm-hearted. The Danes found the queen's behavior odd and off-putting. Victoria recorded the moment in her journal stating that she had fled to the quiet of her rooms because she was suddenly overcome by intense sadness:

"I was too desolate, without darling Albert, to be present."[1]

After an hour's rest, Alix asked to be received by the queen. She wanted private time with her future mother-in-law, falling on her knees at the foot of Victoria's chair once the two women were alone. In the privacy of the queen's sitting room, Alix and Victoria were able to show their genuine affection for one another. Victoria later wrote that she was so moved by Alexandra's humility she kissed her again and again.[2]

On the morning of the wedding, 10 March 1863, the queen appeared before her gathered family in full black widow's mourning dress brightened only by a white Mary Stuart cap and veil and by the brilliant cornflower blue ribbon and the diamond star of the Order of the Garter.[3] It was the first time she had worn the insignia of Britain's premier order of merit since Albert's death. Victoria announced to her family that although she would attend the wedding, she would do so only from the seclusion of the Catherine of Aragon Closet. This richly carved box was suspended high above the chancel of Saint George's Chapel and was the site from which Catherine of Aragon heard daily Mass centuries before. To access the Closet, Victoria had to walk up a winding stone staircase and over the roof of the deanery below. The chapel itself was packed to capacity. Despite claims this was to be an intimate family wedding Victoria had invited her entire Household which left little space for seating the few dignitaries who were present from abroad. The groom was only permitted four friends as his personal guests, while the bride was limited to her immediate family. Minnie mentioned this restriction to the queen when she and Alix had a private audience with her the afternoon before the wedding. Victoria took no offence at Minnie's impertinence. In fact, she found her to be very clever. As Victoria appeared in the Catherine Closet all present rose. Women curtsied deeply and the gentleman all bowed as the queen acknowledged their reverence with a gentle nod. As each procession entered the nave, they paused briefly before the queen to pay similar homage. Victoria pretended not to take note of them as she concentrated her attention upon the choir. Vicky, the next to enter the chapel, was magnificent in white satin trimmed at the edges with double ermine. As she made her way down the nave, she also dropped into a low court curtsy with an accompanying look of respect upon her face, which her mother also seemed not to take note of.

Soon after, Bertie entered the chapel wearing the uniform of a British general; freshly promoted to this rank the day before. Over his tunic he wore his deep blue and red velvet Garter robes and the order's gold and enameled collar fastened at each shoulder by white faille bows. He was flanked by his brother-in-law Crown Prince Frederik and his wayward Uncle Ernest of Saxe-Coburg, both chosen for him as groomsmen by the queen for political reasons. Despite Victoria's persistent claims this was to be a thoroughly British wedding, all of the principal participants were German. Bertie looked both pale and nervous throughout the ceremony. True to her nature, Alix was late, even on her wedding day. Her tardiness later became the fashion, women all over England adopting it for their own wedding day. Alix's inability to keep to a schedule soon became universally accepted as a privilege for all brides on their wedding day.

Because of Alix's tardiness, Bertie was irritatingly kept waiting in the chancel. As each late moment passed, the more visibly agitated he became. Alix wasn't just a few moments late. She kept Bertie and the queen waiting for more than twenty minutes. It was a foretaste of the hundreds of irritating delays Alix would cause them in years to come.

Instead of the magnificent wedding dress of rare Brussels lace presented to her by her husband's uncle, Alexandra wore a gown made of silver tissue and white English silk embroidered with Honiton lace.[4] The emblems of the English rose, the Irish shamrock, the Scottish thistle, and the Welsh daffodil were worked into the lace (beginning a tradition in the royal family that continues with each bride to this day). It was draped with garlands of fresh orange blossoms as an added flair. The gown, the veil and Alix's jewels were all gifts from Bertie. Alix arrived at the great doors of Saint George's trembling and red-eyed. She had been weeping at the thought of leaving her mother and sister Minnie forever. Minnie had helped Alix dress. The two sisters lingered over tender reminiscences from their youth and soon each realized a permanent separation now loomed over them.

Before Alix was ready to leave for the chapel, the two girls dissolved into tears.[5] Farewell and the brilliance of the ceremony itself were overwhelming for her. Alix was not used to such pageantry. Her wedding day introduced her to British pomp in full measure: richly vested high-churchmen, jewels that blazed and sparkled on every woman's head and neck, brilliant orders and decorations on colorfully uniformed officers, officials of state in tabards of ancient tincture and historic design, the gold of the herald trumpeters, the scarlet of the Queen's Guards, the Tudor era Yeoman Warders, and the Military Knights of Windsor in their brilliant finery and massive bowls of flowers of every type and color tucked into every nook and corner.

Queen Victoria was overcome at various moments during the service, particularly during the singing of a chorale Prince Albert had composed himself. She nodded sentimentally as the couple gazed up at her and from time to time she kissed her hand and waved it at Alix as a particular sign of affection. None of Victoria's family had seen her make this gesture to anyone before, several of her relations passing astonished glances as she did so. At the ceremony's conclusion, Bertie and Alix dined in the Waterloo Chamber with thirty-eight royal relations from both sides of the family while more than five hundred other guests were entertained in Saint George's Hall. Victoria did not make any further appearances that day, lunching privately instead in her own apartment with her youngest daughter Beatrice who was six years old at the time. After the wedding festivities had concluded all the guests had to crush into the one train destined for London since oddly no special transport had been arranged for them. Meanwhile the bridal couple departed for a tranquil honeymoon at Osborne House. In mid-nineteenth century England, honeymoons lasted only a few days and so within a week Bertie and Alix returned to the queen at Windsor.

Three weeks later, Bertie introduced Alix to the Sandringham Estate. Although unlike other regions of England, the Norfolk countryside being bleak and without lovely views, it immediately appealed to Alix because it reminded her of Denmark's flat plains. The estate workers and the people of the surrounding countryside anxiously awaited their arrival. Hundreds were there to greet them. Most were anxious to meet the much-heralded, beautiful Princess of Wales. Alexandra found the house comfortable and cozy and not at all too large; considering that the original house was only a quarter of the size of the house which would soon replace it.

Although no correspondence survives between Alexandra and Bertie, a great deal is actually known about their first months of marriage. Queen Victoria had set up a network of spies to report to her on a daily basis about the couple's activities. At first, Victoria found her son much improved by this marriage and she wrote to her daughter in Prussia about how satisfactory things were with the couple, but the queen's hopes for the marriage's positive impact on her son's behavior soon were dashed. Before long, she was reporting to her daughters and other relations as well, that Bertie had let her down and already had returned to his old ways. She further let it be known that she considered Alix's education accomplishments to have been misrepresented by Princess Louise. Victoria also did not appreciate Alix's shyness, which she felt was also underplayed by her mother. Rather than present herself to British society as she should, Alix spent each day writing long letters to her family in Denmark. This annoyed the queen, especially when she learned that these letters were written in Danish rather than in English as she had demanded. Victoria also complained that Bertie no longer did anything useful. She claimed he never read a book and knew little of international affairs. In her opinion, the future king was still too frivolous for his own good and never gave thought to the role he was to play as heir to the throne. She shuddered to think of *"the poor country with such a terrible unfit, totally un-reflecting successor! Oh! That is awful! He does nothing!"* Within six weeks of the marriage, the queen pronounced her opinion that Bertie was totally unfit to become king. Queen Victoria's honeymoon with her son and his new wife was already over!

In London, the Prince and Princess of Wales were installed at Marlborough House, which had been modernized at an additional cost of £60,000 in anticipation of the wedding ($1,219,000 in today's currency). Prince Albert had made careful plans to enlarge it before his death. Sir James Pennethorne carried out the work. The spectacular saloon, or grand reception room, originally decorated with scenes from the Duke of Marlborough's victories at Blenheim, and the grand painted staircase were preserved, but most of the remainder of the house took on a fresh, modern look. Prince Albert's intent was to create a place where Bertie could entertain London society at a single gathering. Once the mansion was remodeled, a lavish enfilade of drawing rooms, reception rooms and dining rooms were created in the styles of the Louis XIV and Directoire periods. Holland and Company, London's most popular interior design firm at that time, was commissioned to decorate the state floor. The private and household rooms were executed under the direction of Sir William Knollys, who politely listened to Bertie's ideas, but then closely followed Prince Albert's original plans in the end.

No sooner had Bertie and Alix unpacked their wedding gifts when the London season began. Night after night, the prince and princess hosted lavish dinner parties at home, attended colorful balls and formal diplomatic banquets in London, and appeared at the opera and other events, while at the same time they received local and foreign deputation's congratulating them on their marriage. Alix represented the queen who remained in seclusion during drawing room ceremonies at Saint James's Palace. These rituals were nothing more than traditional presentations of debutantes so noble young ladies afterward could formally take their place in society. Alix's Drawing Room schedule coincided with the start of the London season which traditionally began after Easter. Two or three days each week would be set aside for presentations. One to two hundred girls would march past Alix each day. When Prince Albert died in 1862, all such Drawing Room events had been cancelled. They were once again cancelled in 1863 as the queen continued her mournful seclusion.

After her marriage to Bertie, Alix was forced to receive more than two thousand guests at the first few rescheduled Drawing Room receptions in order to relieve the backlog caused by the queen's cancellations. From two o'clock in the afternoon until six o'clock in the evening on these occasions Alexandra curtsied in response to each act of homage made by these unfamiliar strangers. After this these ceremonies had been accomplished, the following week Alix was obliged to lead the royal procession through three state rooms at Saint James's Palace, rooms heavily crowded with British dignitaries and foreign diplomats. These formal diplomatic receptions had also been placed in abeyance by Victoria and now it fell to Alix to hold Court in the queen's name.

"In every room," she wrote to her mother, *"I had to make a deep court curtsy and then walk on through the room greeting each face to the right and each to the left! It was a terrible ordeal for me!"*[7]

Alix was only eighteen years old, she was new to the country, and had no formal training in Britain's elaborate form of protocol, and yet she was immediately called upon to become the leader of British society in the queen's absence. Despite her inexperience and youth, Alix represented Queen Victoria so flawlessly no one could fault her performance. Bertie was only twenty-one but because of his mother's absence from public life, he was simultaneously forced to assume his share of the leadership of London's society. It wasn't long before Victoria despaired that there would be no children from this marriage and she continually scrutinized Alexandra for signs of possible pregnancy. In this she was a true Hanoverian, openly discussing the sexual life of her heir and his young wife at Court. In Victoria's opinion, a bride with a twenty-two inch waist and a thirty-two inch bust could hardly be considered ideal for childbearing. One might ask why the queen had not considered this before she had sanctioned the marriage. Alix's youthful figure was in no way an obstacle to producing children. In contrast, Victoria, who produced nine children, had a short and stocky build. Further exasperating the queen was the exciting life led by the Prince and Princess of Wales. She did not believe anyone should be happy when she was so desperately sad. Bertie and Alix went out together each evening at ten o'clock and did not return until four or five o'clock the next morning. They were living a glamorous, exciting life which the queen resented most of all.

In addition to secretaries, ladies-in-waiting, and gentlemen chamberlains who reported to the queen each day on the couple's every activity, there were two doctors assigned to them who, in turn, shared the couple's most intimate medical conditions with the queen. Sir William Jenner had served Victoria and Albert for years and now served as primary physician to the Prince and

Princess of Wales. In addition, Sir Edward Sieveking visited them once each week. In an age where privacy in medicine was unheard of, especially when the monarch was also the parent, the queen was routinely informed about everything these two physicians saw and heard at Marlborough House. They reported that Bertie was hungover at least four days each week after long nights of raucous drinking. Jenner also told Victoria that Bertie had the sexual prowess and appetite of a bear. Bertie, for his part, was curious about medicine and sexual matters and undertook a study of the female menstrual system, closely watching his wife's own, reporting to the doctors whenever Alix's cycle was two or three days late.

After six months of constant, invasive observation, Alexandra began to bring her complaints to the queen telling her mother-in-law she could never conceive while everyone was so closely watching her. At the same time, Alix was often nauseous and suffered symptoms similar to morning sickness which repeatedly became a constant cause for hope. It was not until late August, nearly 6 months after the marriage, when doctors began to suspect Alix might finally be pregnant, but it was not until late September when her clothing became noticeably tight that Bertie joyfully attributed it to pregnancy. Victoria refused to believe the Princess of Wales was pregnant until absolute proof could be given her. The problem was, despite this being a genuine pregnancy, Alexandra was extremely thin and gained very little weight throughout her term.

Meanwhile, events in Denmark were changing and these would elevate Alix's quiet family to more visibility and influence. The first of these changes, of course, had been her own marriage to the Prince of Wales, heir to the most prestigious throne of all. In time this princess of Denmark would become queen of England. Now, in addition, her first pregnancy meant that the Glucksburgs of Denmark would soon be the grandparents of a future English king. And so the Glucksburgs would never again be considered obscure and insignificant in the eyes of more prominent royal houses. A surprise event three weeks after Alix's marriage launched the Glucksburgs further along on the world stage. Alexandra's favorite (younger) brother Wilhelm was suddenly elected king of the Hellenes. More importantly, on 15 November 1863, King

Frederik VII died suddenly from a deadly attack of erysipelas, a severe bacterial infection causing high fever and red lesions on the skin. Fredrick died at age fifty-five while staying at Glucksburg Castle. Alexandra's father who thought he would not become king for another twenty years would rule as King Christian IX suddenly succeeding Frederik on the Danish throne.

Frederik VII had promulgated a new constitution in 1849 transforming Denmark from an absolute monarchy into a constitutional form of government, which enamored him forever in the eyes of the Danish people. Because he had died so suddenly, the king did not have time to sign additional changes to these laws, changes known as the November Constitution, which included clauses concerning succession rights to the dual duchies of Schleswig and Holstein. Many Danes initially rejected Christian as their new king because he was from a German line of the historic house of Oldenburg which had ruled in Denmark for four hundred-fifteen years. Those that did accept him were still suspicious of his partiality in the growing Schleswig-Holstein crisis. After all, Christian's own brothers supported German rights in the duchies and Louise was a member of a sizable German royal house besides. Days before the late king's death, the Danish parliament had voted to incorporate Schleswig, the northern of the two duchies. Christian's first act was to sign the new November Constitution as the constitutional monarch he had just reluctantly become.

As tensions in Denmark continued to rise, no one could expect Queen Victoria to support the Danes. She had made it clear Alix ceased to be Danish the day she arrived on English shores. Her eldest daughter, Crown Princess Victoria was at Windsor with her husband Fritz when news of the Danish king's death arrived. They remained there throughout the coming days as the crisis began to build. Fritz naturally was pro-German as Prussia had taken the lead against Denmark in this issue. Young Vicky wrote in her diary that her husband had been *very violent* in his opposition to Denmark's claims.[8] Queen Victoria believed Denmark had been the true aggressor. King Leopold wrote from Brussels: *for the good of her multi-national family, Victoria should forbid any discussion of this political issue at Windsor.* Complicating the issue even further, Victoria's older half-sister, Feodora of Leiningen, was the widow of the late duke of Augustenburg.[9] Feodora's eldest son was now claiming Holstein as his, seeking to become its reigning duke. He pledged to place the duchy within the German Confederation if the duchy passed to him, an eventuality which appealed to the queen. Therefore, Queen Victoria endorsed the claims of the Augustenburgs, stating that Christian IX and the Danes had brought the succession problem to head and must now be paid a lesson.[10]

Queen Victoria's private support of the Augustenburg claims soon became public knowledge. She found herself in direct opposition to the political posture of both her own Prime Minister (Lord Henry Palmerston) and the Foreign Secretary (Lord John Russell) who both urged the queen to mediate between the two sides and to show favoritism towards the interests of Denmark over Prussia. Palmerston steadfastly maintained the position that as Christian IX had not violated any international law, the succession question of the two independent duchies should remain a family or dynastic matter. A family council composed of senior dynasts, he believed, should settle the conflict and the Great Powers should agree to endorse the results. The British people for their part were thoroughly behind Alix's father; their love for their new Princess of Wales overshadowed the interests of the queen's own daughter who was both the current Prussian crown princess and also the princess royal of the United Kingdom. When Lord Russell attempted to deter actions by the German Confederation further, warning both Prussia and Austria that Britain would be obliged to intercede on the side of Denmark if it was invaded, Victoria became inflamed bringing the issue to her full cabinet, intending them to act as she directed. To her horror, she was respectfully reminded, in the strongest language possible, that the monarch in Great Britain was required to submit to the foreign policy of her government—not to attempt to direct it.

As these international events continued to dominate conversation in the queen's houses, Bertie and a heavily pregnant Alix were invited to Osborne to spend Christmas 1863 with the queen. The gathering was anything but convivial. Alix and Bertie could not hide their opposition to the queen's German sympathies. Victoria reacted to their determination with anger. The tense freeze between the queen and her principal guests was magnified by the arrival of a telegram informing the royal party that German troops had just marched into Holstein. Alix became completely inconsolable.

The level of her shock and anger surprised everyone. The queen wrote to her Uncle Leopold saying:

"Alix's altered appearance is the observation of everyone."[11]

Leopold pressed Victoria to urge Bertie to take better care of his wife. Alix's intense defense of her father and the Danish people won over some who had opposed her cause, while it only served to further infuriate the queen. When her maternal grandmother died, Alix went into full mourning, dressed from head to toe in black serge. After the appropriate period, when she should have gone into grey or purple half-morning, she did not. So long as war was raging in Denmark, Alix would wear full mourning. She absented herself from any further interaction with her guests. For the first time since her marriage, the princess directly entered into British politics by corresponding with members of the government about the issues harming Denmark. Alix shared what she knew about the complicated Holstein question and Danish claims to both duchies, reminding her correspondents of Great Britain's obligation to come to the assistance of a defenseless Denmark if a war broke out. Almost no one really understood the complicated Schleswig-Holstein issue and so Alix's clear and concise outline of the facts opened the eyes of many.

Just after officially welcoming the New Year (1864), and with the queen still not speaking to her son and his wife, Alix and Bertie quietly stole away to Frogmore House in Windsor Great Park, which had been consigned to them for weekend use. On a late bitter cold winter afternoon, 8 January 1864, Alix insisted on joining the fun at an ice hockey match held between Bertie, his brothers, and some of their close friends against the Royal Household's younger more athletic members. Alix had been living under great stress for a fortnight and so she was now eager to have a pleasant distraction. She arrived at the frozen lake by sledge. Against the bitter winds she was swathed in sable and warm woolen tartans and heavily buried beneath fur blankets. Lady Macclesfield accompanied her and while enjoying the sporting rivalry, at six o'clock in the evening Alix's waters broke. She was beginning premature labor and was quickly rushed home. Within an hour her pains became more severe. The doctors were summoned from London but it would take hours for them to arrive at Frogmore. Everyone was concerned as Alix was only in her seventh month of pregnancy. Bertie angrily blamed his mother and her supporters for callously putting a pregnant woman under so much stress. Alix began to panic. When it became clear that the baby would arrive before the doctors could get to Frogmore, a local Windsor physician, Dr. Brown, was sent for. He was the only medical professional attending the princess that night. Everyone was pleased by his presence, fully qualified or not to bring the heir to the throne into the world.[12] As the princess' pains intensified Lady Macclesfield continually assured Alix that the pain of childbirth would pass soon enough. Macclesfield knew all about the subject. She had given birth to thirteen children, none of them born with the aid of anesthetic. Naturally, Alix would have preferred her mother and Minnie to be present. No one else, especially not Bertie, could sufficiently comfort her. Trying to remain gracious as best she could under the frightening circumstances, Alix turned to Lady Macclesfield saying *"as long as I see your face, I am happy!"*[13] Dr. Brown dispatched servants to local shopkeepers to gather flannel to be used in assisting in the birthing process and to wrap up the child once born. Nothing had yet been prepared for its arrival. Brown also ordered the ladies present to turn over any clean cotton wadding they may have in their luggage to help stop Alix's bleeding.

At ten minutes to nine that evening, with no aid of chloroform, the Princess of Wales gave birth to a son who weighed in at only three and three-quarter pounds. Alix told Lady Macclesfield she thought her child was smaller than one of her puppies. The little prince was almost two months premature and few thought the fragile boy would survive. It was clear to Bertie that the doctor thought his son would not survive the night. However, the boy was strong and healthy for his wee size. Word was sent to Victoria at Osborne, but her first reaction was not the unbridled joy one might expect at news of the birth of the next direct heir to the throne. Rather, she was angry at not being summoned to Frogmore before the birth of this special grandchild.[14] As the baby came six weeks early, nothing had yet been readied at Marlborough House either and the staff at Frogmore, the birth place, was completely unprepared because the prince and princess of Wales were rarely there. No nurses had been hired, no baby clothes had yet been purchased, no wet nurse sought out, and no layette established in any of the royal homes, Sandringham, Marlborough House or Frogmore. The baby's unexpected arrival meant no government minister had been present at his birth either—which was then a requirement under the law. As Lord Granville was at Windsor Castle by chance, he was listed as the official witness to the birth, but in actuality he had never been summoned. Late the next day Queen Victoria arrived. She sent these words to her daughter Vicky in Berlin after seeing her first Wales grandchild for the first time:

> *"This dear little boy has a very pretty little well-shaped round head, with very good features, a nice forehead, a very nice marked nose, beautiful little ears and pretty little hands"* [15]

As she would later do with all of her male grandchildren, Victoria demanded the name Albert be included amongst the list of names given the new baby. She intended Bertie to one day reign as Albert I and this new baby to rule one day as Albert II. British history, however, did not support her determination. No English or Scottish king ever bore this name and Bertie had no intention of fulfilling his mother's plans. Both Bertie and Alix naturally resented this intrusion into their parental rights. When the time came, despite their antipathy, the parents dutifully named their baby son Albert Victor but he was always known within his immediate family as Eddy even though, officially, his first two baptismal names honored both Prince Albert and the queen as she demanded. [16]

Not long after the birth, King Christian IX nearly lost his new throne after Prussian troops marched into Denmark. Many Danes blamed their new king personally for their humiliation. Many of his subjects also still considered Christian to be German. In the end, the new king retained his throne, but Denmark lost the two duchies to Prussian aggression. Otto von Bismarck also reneged on his pledge to grant Holstein to the Duke of Augustenburg. Rather, he absorbed the two duchies into the Kingdom of Prussia. The Austrians were powerless to rectify the imbalance. Queen Victoria was furious, her government was outraged, and Alix and Bertie were devastated at the loss of Alix's family's territory at the hands of their own brother-in-law, Crown Prince Fritz who had led the charge. Britain did nothing in the end to alter the outcome. To deflect some of the blame heaped on her by the public (who were steadfast in their loyal support for Alix), Queen Victoria admonished Bertie *"to never become a Danish partisan, or to put yourself against your sovereign and family in support of your wife's family's claims,"*[17] In front of the Royal Household she repeatedly reminded him that every allegiance hereafter not due England should always then fall to Germany. Victoria never hesitated to remind Bertie that their entire family was German and he himself was also German by blood through his father and also through his father, he bore the sacrosanct titles (in Victoria's mind) of Duke of Saxony and Prince of Saxe-Coburg und Gotha.

With the premature birth of their first child and with the distress and division the Danish War brought within his family, Bertie and Alix continued to grow even closer to one another, forging a loyalty during these trying times which would endure between them for the rest of their lives, even when Bertie's behavior caused Alix great sorrow. Bertie now shared his wife's passion for Denmark. A new antipathy for Prussia likewise increased in him. In her sorrow, Alix found Bertie more tender and attentive. Princess Mary Adelaide (Fat Mary) recorded in her memoirs Alix's mention of Bertie to her at this time:

> *"He seems to have more concern for me and wishes me to be happy."*[18]

Queen Victoria publicly soured on Alix after this drama became public knowledge in Britain as the British no longer supported the queen's German family. Victoria spoke of having paid too high a price for the Danish marriage—an unwanted rise in discord within her family now torn apart by war.

She openly regretted the union. Writing to King Leopold she compared their niece, Marie of Leiningen, to Alix:

> *"Marie is quite like my own daughter, much more so than poor Alix, with whom I can never get more intimate, much as I like and love her. She comes completely from the enemy's camp in every way!"*[19]

Victoria sensed that Alexandra was not recovering quickly after the early birth of little Albert Victor (Eddy). She began to worry Alix would be unable to bear further children. It was not uncommon at this time for parents to lose several children to premature death and so numerous pregnancies, especially in royal families, were imperative. In response to her new concerns, Victoria appointed a committee of three additional doctors to aid Sir James Clark and the two others who already attended the Princess of Wales. All of these doctors were to regularly report on health conditions at both Marlborough House and at Sandringham. Through them the queen ordered Alexandra to retire by eleven o'clock each night and to have eight hours of continual sleep without any disturbances, including Bertie's amorous attentions. She also ordered Alix to take long walks each day and undertake regular exercise. Alix was also forbidden to ride or hunt; her two favorite pastimes. The young princess' diet was also strictly regulated so, in the event of another pregnancy, the baby would come to full term and Alix's health would not suffer as it had with her first confinement.

Despite the medical attention, Alix was clearly unwell. She complained of constant headaches in the weeks following Eddy's birth and she also suffered a sense of general exhaustion. Alix also experienced symptoms which today would be diagnosed as postpartum depression, an unknown condition at the time. Another of her complaints, a prolapsed uterus, also an unfamiliar condition in those days, eventually required surgery to repair. Alix yearned to have Minnie with her in these trying weeks, but Victoria would not permit a prolonged visit, believing the Danish family to be a bad influence. The two sisters corresponded weekly. Later when Minnie married they would correspond daily. For months at this time their letters only concerned the war and the trauma its consequences had on their father.

They also wrote incessantly about conditions in Athens where their brother Willy was now king. Willy's needs and his safety were always at the forefront of their thoughts. Alix's letters spoke of her new baby and her life at Sandringham. She never complained about the queen's dictatorial manner or Bertie's selfishness. Minnie would not have noted any difficulties at this stage at any rate. Her head was filled with dreams of Russia and her own independence.

> *"Darling Minnie,*
>
> *Today I took tea with the Double-Duchess. It was a lovely afternoon. We spoke of aggression by those hateful Prussians and the harm they shall bring to Europe in the end. Of course she is sympathetic to Denmark as are all our friends here. Louisa is always a delight. She asked after all at Fredensborg. I yearn to see you again and for you, mama, and papa to see our little one."*[20]

The subject of Alix's letter home was Louisa von Alten, a Hanoverian-born countess who first married the duke of Manchester and then after his death, the duke of Devonshire. She was a leading force in London society and because of her two prestigious marriages was known affectionately as the 'Double-Duchess.'

In early September 1864, the Danish war now safely behind them, Bertie decided that Alix very much needed her spirits lifted and proposed a visit to her parents in Copenhagen. Victoria was once more opposed, but dared not incite negative public opinion again. The British people wanted Alexandra to be happy and they would certainly applaud Bertie for taking her home for her first visit after their marriage and the birth of their first child.

The prince and princess of Wales sailed into Copenhagen, taking with them their infant son, despite the queen's vigorous private opposition. Victoria was morosely unhappy and found great satisfaction in denying joy to others whenever she could. Alix was determined her parents would meet their new grandchild. With them came their official household—Lady Macclesfield who had been assigned by the queen as Alexandra's lady-in-waiting, the baby's nurses and their physician, Dr. Sieveking. It would be Bertie' first visit to Denmark and he was looking forward to seeing his wife's country. The Danes had fallen in love with Bertie when he took their favorite princess as his bride, but those positive feelings had vanished during the recent war when Britain had failed to come to Denmark's defense as promised. Many Danes protested the visit. It wasn't that the Danes wished to block Alexandra's visit home, it was simply they believed the British royal family was partially to blame for the German invasion and for the bitter loss of Schleswig-Holstein. They held the British royal family responsible for their problems because of their close blood ties to the Germans. Alix would not be deterred by any of this criticism. She knew the Danes and knew they all would be welcomed once they arrived. She was resolved to go home and she was just as resolute in having her husband and her baby by her side. Of course, the always-polite Danes greeted them with exuberance. Bertie won over his wife's compatriots by his cordiality and his natural *bonhomie.* The visit was a huge success. Alix once more found joy with her family. There were picnics in the city's parks, which amused Bertie. He had never before experienced relaxation in full view of the public. The family went boating together and in evenings they gathered for sing-alongs after dinner, quite unheard of at Windsor.

Bertie and Alix returned home well-rested and healthy. Alix's homeland was on the mend after the war, much to her relief. Minnie was betrothed to the Russian tsarevitch. Exciting days were on the horizon for the Glucksburgs once again.

Winterhalter portrait of the new Princess of Wales, 1865

Alix as a bride, 1863

Bertie and Alix's Wedding, 1863

Christian IX and Queen Louise, Alix and Minnie's parents

Tsar Alexander II, Minnie's father-in-law, with *Mi'Lord*

Minnie with her first fiancé, Grand Duke
Nicholas, shortly before his death, 1865

Bertie, Alix and baby Eddy, 1865

Sasha, Minnie and baby Nicholas, 1869

Minnie at age thirty, 1877

Alix at age thirty-two, 1876

Minnie and baby Xenia, 1876

Grand Duchess Maria Alexandrovna, Sasha's only sister and
wife of Bertie's brother Alfred, Duke of Edinburgh, 1874

Alfred, Duke of Edinburgh, Bertie's brother and husband
of Grand Duchess Maria Alexandrovna, 1874

Alix and Minnie during the Fredensborg holiday, mid-1870s

Sasha, Minnie and family at Gatchina, 1882

Thyra of Denmark, ca. 1878

17. Minnie and Sasha, 1883

The Princess of Wales always setting a new style

Alix with her five surviving children: Eddy,
George, Louise, Victoria and Maud

Minnie in Court Sarafan and State gems (portrait by V. Makovsky)

CHAPTER FOUR

OUT OF OBSCURITY

WHILE THESE EVENTS WERE CAUSING great excitement for the British public, Denmark was experiencing an enormous rise in international prestige despite the drama of the Schleswig-Holstein question. First amongst the events turning every eye towards Denmark of course was Bertie and Alix's marriage. Next was the unexpected offer made to her younger brother, Wilhelm (Willy) who was invited to become the king of Greece, to reign as George I, a mere three weeks after Alix's marriage.

Modern Greece had been ruled since winning its independence in the war of 1830 by German born king Otto I[1] born in 1815 as Prince Otto von Wittlesbach of the royal house of Bavaria. Otto's father was King Ludwig I of Bavaria, his mother was born Princess Therese of Saxe-Hildburghausen. In due course, Otto married Amalia of Oldenburg. The couple remained childless despite their desperation to found a dynasty for Greece.

Otto was a well-meaning, quiet and generous monarch, but something more than innate kindness and good intentions was necessary to govern so volatile a people as the clannish and superstitious Greeks who found their new king to be lacking any Hellenic identity. Otto would never measure up to Greek nationalistic expectations. The first half of his reign was immersed in the dilemma of foreign domination as the young king depended entirely upon Bavarian advisors and upon Wittlesbach troops to protect him. His inability to assume a natural Greek identity, his lack of an identifiable direct heir, and the presence of foreigners in Athens alienated his people. An early revolution forced Otto to grant a written constitution providing for a formalized government along modern European models but it was not enough to satisfy the Greeks and a second more ardent uprising in 1862 forced him to flee to Bavaria on-board a British warship. He died there as an exile in the land of his birth five years later.

To fill the now vacant Greek throne was going to be no easy task: not to many comfortably settled princes were keen to accept so great a challenge as the unstable Greek throne. This reluctance in no way inhibited the provisional Greek government from staging a plebiscite with the aim of winning a powerful prize for Greece; they intended to promote Queen Victoria's second son Alfred as their new king. Prince Alfred was technically elected King of Greece by a rapidly organized election, the Greek people believing a British prince on their throne would mean Great Britain would become a serious-minded protector of their fledgling independent state. News of Prince Alfred's election was proclaimed across the country. Even the few Greek warships existing at the time fired a 101-gun salvo in unison across the Bay of Athens proclaiming the election results.

Despite exuberance in Greece, none of the politicians in Athens ever bothered to formally request Prince Alfred's acquiescence before the plebiscite had taken place nor to even inform him of his subsequent election. When they finally dispatched a delegation to inform the British government, Prime Minister Palmerston politely explained the clauses of the international agreement which had originally been imposed by the protecting powers when Greece initially received its independence in 1830 stipulating that no member of any of these protecting powers could ever be proposed for the Greek throne. It was for this reason that an obscure Bavarian prince had originally been chosen in the first place. So even if he wished to accept their invitation, Prince Alfred was legally unable to do so. This is not to say that Great Britain had no interest in the Greek throne. On the contrary she was deeply interested. As one of the guaranteeing powers of the new Greek state, along with the French Second Empire and Russia, Great Britain was only too anxious to increase her influence in the eastern Mediterranean and Aegean Sea region.

Prince Alfred may not have been eligible to assume the throne of Greece, but Queen Victoria had many other potential candidates in mind. Her first thoughts always ran to Coburg where there always seemed to be a spare minor princeling capable and ready to assume a new throne if offered. Both France and Russia likewise had impressive candidates which they wished to put forth. The Duke d'Aumâle, the son of the deposed French king, Louis-Phillipe, was proposed by France. The Archduke Maximilian, brother of Franz-Josef of Austria and later emperor of Mexico, was another. Queen Victoria proposed her nephew the Prince of Leiningen, but he gained no other support and so the proposal was dropped. In the end Napoleon III decided, for unexplained reasons, to give his support to whichever candidate Great Britain would nominate believing perhaps it would be Leiningen in the end, Lord Palmerston however only wanted Willy.

There was no doubt in anyone's mind that the Greeks would accept any British choice as they had already selected the queen's second son in the earlier election. It was not that the Greeks were particularly enamored with Great Britain, although the prestige of the British Empire certainly continued to grow throughout the world at that time, but rather it was that Greece could not help but be impressed by the might and power of Britain's massive Mediterranean fleet. Moreover, it was the hope in selecting a British prince, or a prince selected by Britain as their king, that the Ionian Islands then held by Britain might be returned to Greece if a British candidate won the day.

There are many versions of how subsequent events actually unfolded and how Willy was eventually elected Greece's new king. It is clear from all the histories later related that Lord Palmerston and Lord John Russell had already decided their new Princess of Wales' younger brother, whom they had just met in London at Bertie and Alix's wedding, would be the ideal candidate. He was a prince of one of the oldest monarchies in Europe and he was from a neutral nation. He was young and thus potentially moldable, while his father would soon be king of Denmark and his sister would one day become queen-consort in England. Queen Victoria was consulted, and as an independent Greece was currently no impediment to British interests in the region, she had no objections to a Glucksburg prince ascending the vacant Greek throne. Besides, Victoria was also politically savvy and recognized the popular acclaim throughout Britain for Alexandra and her Danish family.

Popular Danish legend relates how Willy learned of his selection as king when he opened a parcel containing his lunch on a break in his studies at the Naval Academy near Copenhagen. It has been said he found a newspaper clipping proclaiming Prince Christian's second son as the new king of the Hellenes. Willy was only seventeen and had planned to make a career in the Danish Navy but as he generally disliked his studies he was delighted at the thought of being elected a king in any country so he would never again have to sit for examinations. Alix, however, tells a different story. In her diary she relates how while Willy was present in London for her own wedding, both the Prime Minister and Foreign Secretary asked him if he would prefer being the new king of Greece.[2]

On 30 March 1863, having been informed by Frederik VII that he would permit his heirs' second son to accept election, the Greek parliament officially proclaimed Prince Wilhelm of Glucksburg king of the Hellenes. Otto had been imposed on the Greeks, they had no say in his ascension as king, but Willy was actually elected by the Greeks. Otto had held the title king of Greece. He never abdicated and so technically this title remained his. The choice of the title king of the Hellenes was a quite modern one as it translated in theory to mean king of all Greeks wherever they may be living including those in territories which had not yet been returned to Greece after her newfound independence. Napoleon Bonaparte had been the first modern monarch to be designated as sovereign of his people as a whole rather than as sovereign of his nation when he declared himself Emperor of the French. Similarly, when Belgium was declared independent from Holland, its first king was likewise entitled king of the Belgians rather than king of Belgium and so now as Willy was preparing to accept the throne of Greece he was proclaimed the first king of the Hellenes not as the second king of modern Greece. This tweaking of royal title boded well for his dynasty as Willy was now head of the Greek royal house of Glucksburg and not merely the new incumbent on the earlier established Wittlesbach throne.

Once again, the Danes rejoiced at the bright light of international favor which had befallen them; entirely through the unprecedented successes of the children of Christian and Louise. This is not to say the parents were entirely in favor of Willy accepting so distant a throne. Prince Christian correctly considered the Greeks a volatile people and referred to his son being offered *"a crown of thorns"*.[3] Christian knew his young son did not possess a suitable temperament, or the formal education required, to govern such a wild nation. Christian continued to press the great powers to delay in order to give the family time for further consideration. Princess Louise began a campaign through Alix to influence Palmerston and Russell against the idea. In response, Alix wrote *"the Greeks are a terrible people, brigands and assassins all."*[4]

Louise and Christian could not simply refuse the offer, as they certainly would have wished to do. With their monarch, Frederik VII, firmly in favor of acceptance of this prize, Prince Christian had to acquiesce but not before he and Louise negotiated specific conditions which would protect their son both while he reigned and in a potentiality of being turned out of Greece one day as Otto had been before him. They insisted the three great powers— Great Britain, Russia, and France—must guarantee their son an annual stipend of £50,000 as long as he reigned and the pledge of a pension of £25,000 a year for life in the event, like Otto, that he too would either have to flee Greece or if he would be kicked out of the country one day. In addition, Prince and Princess Christian demanded Willy not be required to join the Greek Orthodox Church. He did, however, agree to pledge to raise all children Orthodox. Christian and Louise also demanded for their son's political prestige that Great Britain had to promise to formally hand over the Ionian Islands as part of his official dowry which had always been the hope with an ascendancy of a new king. Finally Prince Christian insisted that the Bavarian royal family be consulted, and their approval granted, before Willy would be able to accept the throne since a prince of that royal house had so recently vacated the Greek throne. Each hurdle greatly annoyed Frederik VII who wanted to see his young cousin on a foreign throne because of the prestige this would bring

Denmark, but even this last demand Frederik readily accepted as a matter of necessary courtesy between monarchs.[5]

Even when all of these demands were accomplished Christian and Louise were still not pleased as they simply did not wish to see their young son installed a continent away. Momentum continued to mount, however, and when the Marshal of the Danish Court arrived at Christian's home to deliver King Frederik's demand for the offer to be formally accepted, he found the prince in a state of deep dejection. Louise knew Frederik VII would not alter his permission and so it was clear Willy would now have to accept the throne offered him. Christian's only recorded words from this meeting were:

> *"Do whatever you like. It is all one and the same to me. My only duty is to obey my king."*[6]

On 6 June 1863 in the formal receptions rooms of the Christiansborg Palace, and in the presence of the entire Danish royal family, with the government and all foreign diplomats present, the Greek delegation formally presented their government's invitation to King Frederik as head of the Danish royal house. Before they were presented to him, however, Frederik beckoned Willy to come forth: *"Before I raise you to the high position you will soon occupy, and while you are still a Danish prince, I will confer upon you at the foot of the throne a visible sign of your king's favor, by nominating you a knight of the Order of the Elephant."* Frederik then took Willy by his arm, turning him to the gathering, but still looking directly at him saying: *"receive the blessings of your king, and may God be with you always."*[7]

The Greek delegation was headed by Admiral Kanaris, who addressed King Frederik directly:

> *"May it please your Majesty; upon 18 March the National Assembly of Greece proclaimed that it had chosen Prince William George of Denmark as King of the Hellenes, under the title of George I. The Greek assembly has honored us with the mission to offer the prince the crown. While, therefore,*

Sire, we deposit the decree notifying this choice into your Majesty's hands, we hope that your reply will fulfill the wishes and expectations of the Hellenic people. This choice, Sire, is as much an act of homage to the person of the famous sovereign to whom it has pleased Providence to entrust the destinies of Denmark, as a proof of confidence in the talents of the young prince. The choice will further prove a bond of union between two nations ever distinguished for virtues and patriotism. Greece bases all her hopes upon the young prince, and, reckoning upon the support of the three protecting powers, is possessed with the conviction that she will one day see the fulfillment of her national desires."[8]

King Frederik accepted the Greek crown *"for our young relative, to which he has been called by the Greek people,"* reminding all those present that his acceptance of the Greek throne for his cousin stipulated a union between the Greek crown and the Ionian islands which here-to-fore belonged to England. Frederik continued: *"we feel pleasure in expressing our certain expectation that this union will soon take place, and we wish that the young king, when received by his people, should be hailed as bringing with him the fulfillment of this well-founded, long-cherished, desire and I admonish the Greeks to develop the rich resources of their country, and in conducting the kingdom of Greece to a splendid future."*[9]

Appearing now for the first time as George I, the two kings presented themselves on the palace balcony. Willy was dressed for the first time in a captain's uniform of the Danish Navy[10] with across his chest the crisp bleu-celeste sash and diamond star of the Order of the Elephant,[11] his homeland's highest honor. Addressing his kinsman, while pointing to the crowds gathered below, Frederik added:

"Before you leave this spot I give you this heartfelt and well-meant advice. Let it be your constant endeavor to gain and preserve the love of the people. Without boasting, I speak

from experience when I say to you that it is in this that true happiness is found for a king. Adhere firmly to the constitution of your country; strive constantly to procure its recognition; watch that it may be maintained intact. If you make this your role you and your people will prosper forever."[12]

At this the Danish and Greek kings again mounted the steps of the silver throne. Fredrick publicly embraced Willy for the first time. It was only then that Willy formally accepted the Greek throne being the first of the Glucksburg line to ascend to the rank of king by way of either marriage or election. The Greek delegation stepped forward to welcome their new king. Kanaris spoke on their behalf saying: *"Sire, I have lived long enough, after having seen this day, to exclaim with Simeon: 'Lord, now let my servant depart in peace.'"*[13] Filled with tremendous emotion, overcome by the magnitude of the moment, and realizing that soon he would be leaving Denmark and his family forever, Willy spoke his first words as king:

"I received the first greetings of the representatives of the Greek people with true joy. It is with profound emotion that I have heard them from the mouth of the man whose name is linked with everlasting fame to the regeneration of Greece. I am deeply impressed with the responsibility of the position which has fallen to me and will dedicate to it the utmost powers of my life. I rely upon the loyal assistance of the Greek people for their attainment of our common object—the happiness of Greece. I have grown up in a country where legal order is combined with entire constitutional freedom, and which is thereby attained large and felicitous development. The lesson I that here received shall accompany me to my new country, and I shall keep the motto of the Danish king as my own, 'the love of the people is my strength.'"[14]

With the deed accomplished, the young king's family let it be known amongst the press, and throughout royal circles that Willy (as he would continue to be called amongst his family for the remainder of his life) would be keeping his bags readily packed in the event his new people decided that they no longer wanted him.

Through no machinations of his own Prince Christian's family now included the future queen of England, the reigning king of Greece, himself and his eldest son as future kings of Denmark, and his effervescent second daughter Dagmar ready to enter the Royal marriage market.

Willy set out for Athens by way of the capitals of the great powers where he consulted their monarchs and prime ministers. He also had the opportunity to spend a few happy days with Bertie and Alexandra at Marlborough House while in London. Fourteen days after his son finally arrived in Greece, the father, Prince Christian of Glucksburg, suddenly became King of Denmark. As we have already seen, Frederik VII died of erysipelas at Glucksburg Castle on 15 November, 1863. His earlier reception of the Greek delegation had been his last important function as king.

Now king, Christian appeared on the balcony of the Amalienborg Palace, the main residence of the Danish monarch, where the president of the Council of State addressed the crowd below: *our beloved King Frederik VII of happy memory has died. Long live King Christian IX.*[5] As they had when Willy received the Greek delegation several weeks earlier, all the foreign diplomats accredited to Copenhagen gathered to watch the historic scene unfold. The French minister, Monsieur Dotezac, wrote a report to the foreign ministry in Paris saying that Christian IX was quite tall, dignified, handsome and elegant and has an admirable presence and the people applauded him for so long a period that the king had to show himself twice more on the balcony. Diplomats knew well that unsecured messages were widely read and therefore intended his message to be intercepted in Copenhagen (and thus it would please the new king), but he subsequently added in secret cipher telegram that the reception of the new king had not been nearly as enthusiastic as it could have been. In fact, Dotezac added that the king's reception had been less than adequate and that in his estimation Christian IX possessed only a mediocre intelligence, making for the type of king who should rule only in quiet times.

These were not at all quiet times for Denmark. Talk of war with Germany paralyzed Copenhagen. Christian's ascension to the throne inaugurated more than just a new monarch's reign. It finally brought to a climax the decades-old Schleswig-Holstein crisis as we have seen. The issue was an extremely complicated one, a feud between the territorial and historic feudal claims of Denmark and the German Confederation's intention to control the duchies of Schleswig and Holstein. Prussia which led the German Confederation was served by its chancellor[16], Otto von Bismarck, a militaristic German nationalist to the extreme. Bismarck was determined to wrestle the two duchies from Denmark once and for all.

With Christian ascending the throne this long-smoldering quarrel finally erupted. The most important issue facing the new king, and which was at the top of the agenda of the first State Council meeting Christian was to chair, was the issuance of a new joint Constitution that formally incorporated Schleswig into Denmark which was an act contrary to the terms of the Treaty of London. Christian was reluctant to sign the new constitution which had been authored by Frederik before his death. When word reached the public of Christian's hesitancy, the municipal authorities of Copenhagen assembled at the Amalienborg Palace to present an address to their new king begging him to promulgate the new constitution. Failure to act, they said, would bring 30,000 Danish troops to the palace square to demand it. In the end Christian was mindful of his obligations as a constitutional monarch and signed the new constitution into law. To have repudiated it, he would have permanently compromised himself with the Danish people and perhaps would have provoked an uprising which would have driven him from his newly acquired throne. So sign it, he did! Austria and Prussia immediately made their disapproval known. In Vienna, the Austrian prime minister refused to receive the legate sent from Copenhagen with the news of Christian IX's ascension and in Prussia Bismarck publicly refused to receive the Danish ambassador. To throw further fuel on the growing fire, Prince Frederik of Augustenburg used the instability of the moment to proclaim himself Sovereign-Duke of Schleswig-Holstein.

Bismarck, always the keen politician and champion of German ambitions, suggested a compromise of a new "personal union" between the Kingdom of Denmark and the two duchies to be ruled by one sovereign but as separate monarchies such as the existing union between Sweden and Norway as two kingdoms ruled by one king. Bismarck knew that the Danes would never accept this condition as the Danes were adamant both duchies should be Danish, never to be independent states. Although Britain also attempted to mediate with Prussia and Austria, the Germans flatly refused while France turned her glance elsewhere ignoring the situation entirely. On 1 February 1864 a combination of Prussian and Austrian armies marched through Denmark. The Danish troops quickly pulled out of Holstein and Lauenburg just as the Hanoverian regiment under Prussian control had taken it. Not a single shot was fired. The Danes retreated to Dannevirke which they had fortified with a frontier wall in 1850. The Danes successfully defended the frontier for four days until it was clear their position was no longer tenable and they retreated thereafter deeper into Denmark. News of the retreat was greeted in Copenhagen with great anger which was mainly directed at the new king whom agitators proclaimed a German traitor. Christian and his family had traveled to the castle at Sonderburg in Schleswig as the German forces moved on Denmark so as to be visibly closer to the front and to show the people they stood at the head of their nation in this crisis. Christian also wanted to be closer to the front with his troops. After the Danish retreat, however, when Christian returned to Sonderburg Castle, an angry mob followed him forcing through the castle's gates. Displaying great sense of calmness Queen Louise sent for the local chief of police to ask him what measures had been taken to ensure the peace of the city, the district, and the safety of the royal family while in residence in the castle. Attempting to make light of the angry mobs outside, the police commander gave his personal assurance to the queen that the castle would remain safe. Louise was unconvinced by his arguments and informed him if he did not call out the Civic Guard himself she would be forced to do so instead. Soon detachments of the Guard patrolled both the city and the grounds. Several times through the night the Guard had to draw swords against the angry mob. In Copenhagen, while driving home from church on the Sunday morning following Danish withdraws from the front, Crown Prince Fredrik and his sisters Dagmar and Thyra were spat upon by people.

Despite an admirable defense, the Danish forces were soundly beaten and both duchies were claimed by Prussia as spoils of war. Bismarck had won. Within a matter of twelve weeks from the day of his ascension, Christian had been forced to relinquish almost half of his new kingdom, hardly an auspicious beginning for a king. Christian was particularly angry with Sweden which had continuously spoken of a policy of the symbolic and political unity in Scandinavia but, in reality had not lifted a finger to come to Denmark's aid when needed most. Christian would never forget the first few months of his new reign.

A peace conference was called in London on 25 April 1864 at which armistice terms were proposed by Prussia demanding the complete independence from Denmark of the two duchies. Lord John Russell, British foreign secretary, proposed one half of Schleswig should remain with Denmark as it was predominantly Danish in culture and heritage as well as language. Both Denmark and Prussia refused this compromise. Bismarck wanted the entirety of both duchies to pass to Prussia. Denmark could not stomach any of Schleswig going to Germany and so the armistice abruptly ended, hostilities resumed, and by 29 June Prussia fully occupied Jutland.

In England the people and the government sided with Denmark showing tremendous support for Alix who publicly mourned the loss of half of her homeland to Prussia. A real fear of revolution in Denmark caused great consternation in Britain. Queen Victoria wrote in her journal:

> *"The poor king may be sent away which would make a very bad impression here. Unfortunately he had shown no great moral courage or energy during the crisis."*[17]

Final peace was achieved with the signing of the Treaty of Vienna in October 1864 in which the Danish king signed over the lost duchies to the

North German Confederation under the control of King William of Prussia and Emperor Franz-Joseph of Austria. In all, Denmark lost the duchies of Schleswig, Holstein, Lauenburg and the whole of South Jutland to Germany, leaving a mere thirty percent of what had once been the Kingdom of Denmark.[18]

The effect of Prussian victory over Denmark instilled in every Glucksburg hatred for all things Prussian, and later all things German. Feelings within the Danish family would be carried across Europe and which would affect political decisions in the decades to come in many nation-states. Intensely loyal to their loving father, the children of Christian IX, and later his grandchildren, refused to be reconciled to Prussia in particular and to Germans generally. This hatred for all things German had already evidenced itself in Britain at the start of hostilities against Denmark when Bertie and Alix openly defied the queen and her pro-German family in an emotional defense of Denmark's claims to Schleswig and Holstein.

At the time of his ascension, Christian was still largely an unknown person in Denmark. Those that did know him were grateful for his support of Danish claims throughout his life rather than supporting his native German family, and indeed this is one reason why the Danes had accepted him as heir early on, but in almost everyone's mind after the war, Christian was considered thoroughly German. It was said that he spoke Danish like a German Schleswiger, true or not, and his arguably brusque manner as an officer in the Danish army presented a more German personality than it did a kindly Danish one. His first months as king were surely turbulent and ushered in great disappointment for Denmark.

CHAPTER FIVE

FROM FREDENSBORG TO THE WINTER PALACE

Saint Petersburg: 1864-1865

IN LATE SEPTEMBER 1864, EMPRESS Marie Alexandrovna of Russia, sent a letter to her Hessian cousin Queen Louise announcing she intended to visit Copenhagen. She had never been there, she said, and had always desired to see that city and now all the more so since Alix would be coming to visit from England with her first-born son, Eddy. The entire Danish family intended to gather at Fredensborg Palace, which had replaced Rumpenheim as the destination for their annual reunions. The Russian empress was also a Hessian, a member of the Darmstadt branch, and so she felt entitled to participate at Fredensborg just as she had frequently done at Rumppenheim. Under the circumstances, her request could not be denied. Accompanied by a substantial entourage, including scarlet-coated Cossack orderlies and over four hundred pieces of luggage, Empress Marie decamped in Denmark. Minnie, who was then seventeen, had never cared for the empress. The older woman had always taken a disapproving view of the spontaneity of the Danish royal family. At past gatherings when the empress addressed Minnie, the older woman always grew anxious and stiff as if it were a chore to even be in Minnie's presence. And so, Minnie was surprised to find that Empress Marie seemed to like her very much, indeed. She had come to Denmark for a very special purpose and singled Minnie out for quiet, personal, and sometimes embarrassing conversations. It wasn't long before Minnie came to wonder aloud if the empress had traveled all the way from Russia just to interview her. Minnie's intuition was correct.

Included in the empress' entourage was her twenty-one-year-old, eldest son Grand Duke Nicholas Alexandrovitch whose unexpected appearance at Fredensborg surprised both Minnie and her family. The tsarevitch was known within the Russian family as Nixa[1] and was now of marriageable age. Nixa was the direct heir to the throne, the son of Tsar Alexander II. He was immensely rich in his own right and his mother was now clearly searching for a princess to become his wife. Marie was devoted to her eldest son. Of all her children he was the most like her. She had managed every aspect of his upbringing and had already eliminated many princesses whom she thought to be indolent or possessed qualities she believed insufficient to make Nixa happy.

Empress Marie's own marriage had been mainly loveless and so she was determined Nixa would find a royal bride he could truly love. With Alix's marriage to Bertie the year before, Minnie had become the senior princess in the Danish family. She knew what was expected of her in this senior role. Although only seventeen, Minnie was mature beyond her years and she understood the game which was being played all around her. For centuries the Romanov family had preferred German princesses as the wives of their sons and so this sudden turn towards Denmark was unprecedented, but not entirely surprising. Empress Marie had made quiet overtures to Queen Louise in the months before Alix became engaged to Bertie. At that time she had hoped to win Alix for Nixa, but her timing was off. And so, she turned her attention to Minnie, waiting for the time she would be just old enough for her parents to consider a proposal of marriage into the Russian family. The Danish king's daughters were the most beautiful princesses of their time. It was this reputation which now turned the empress' eye away from her native Germany and towards Copenhagen. As Hessian-born, Marie had seen the Danes at Rumppenheim on the few occasions she also attended these family gatherings. She had lost Alix, but she was now intent on securing Minnie for her favorite son. And so to Fredensborg she went to make her case.

Some of the finest features at Fredensborg, with its many bright oversized salons and expansive halls, were the tiny inglenooks and cozy corners tucked seductively out of the way. A hallmark in Nordic designed castles, these privy spaces were typically decorated in the Victorian manner with an abundance of palm trees and plentiful greens, adding to a general sense of seclusion. It was here, in one of these obscure inglenooks, Minnie often found herself deep in conversation with Nixa. He listened with amusement to her lively flow of ideas. Unlike most girls of her time and breeding, Minnie never shrank from talking about topics which intrigued her most. Never far from her thoughts were her horses, the latest racy novels she had read, designs she created for new clothes, or the stories written for the family by Hans Christian Anderson. She was also a keen defender of Danish interests. Minnie was simplistic, but never simple. Nor was she seldom silent or disinterested. Nicholas told her many fascinating things about Russia and life within the colorful Imperial Court, which totally captivated her. Nixa also explained the problems then facing Russia and what he would one day inherit as tsar. During these halcyon days together, Nixa confided in Minnie about many things and praised her intelligence and understanding. Within days, he had won her heart.

After dinner on the evening of 5 October, Nixa spirited Minnie into a quiet alcove, which naturally piqued the interest of family and guests nearby. Behind the foliage, Europe's most accomplished prince seemed unable to speak. After an awkward beginning, Minnie asked a question about Russia, a subject closest to Nixa's heart. It was enough to break the ice and suddenly he began to speak in rapid French. The tsarevitch spoke neither Danish nor English, but he was fluent in French, German, and Russian. Minnie had not yet learned Russian and so the two alternated between French and German when they were alone. Nixa's rushed delivery caused Minnie to miss the significance of what he was actually requesting. As he spoke of the need for a stable monarchy, he asked Minnie if she would like to become a future empress of

Russia. But Nixa's proposal had not come through clearly. When she had fully understood what he was proposing, Minnie responded with a question:

"Is it your intent for me to be a future Empress of Russia?"[2]

Nixa chuckled before struggling to make things more clear:

"Yes, of course, this is exactly what I wish for you. This is why I have come to Denmark!"[3]

Forgetting the rules of decorum imposed at that time, Minnie embraced Nixa, kissing his cheeks over and over as she replied with confidence:

"Then I shall, indeed, become the empress of Russia."[4]

If Minnie seemed self-possessed and confident when she and Nixa returned to their families, it did not last long. Later that evening when she was finally alone with Alix, Minnie dissolved into uncontrolled sobbing. Bertie found his young wife and her sister weeping and quickly grasped the situation and the political significance of his wife's sister marrying a Romanov. He was the first to understand that the wedding would have to take place in Saint Petersburg rather than Copenhagen. No member of the British Royal family had ever visited Russia. The Russians hated Queen Victoria and all of her politicians. The Romanov family encouraged that same enmity towards Victoria's children and all of her subjects, as well. For their part, the British had always exhibited a suspicion for all things Russian. Surely Queen Victoria would not be pleased by news of this engagement, most especially as she had no hand in arranging it.

When Nixa returned to Russia, Bertie's supportive and encouraging words at Fredensborg were quickly embraced by both the tsar and his government. Bertie's foresight into how this marriage would eventually change the alliances in Europe showed an understanding and talent for international affairs which would later become a cogent grasp of affairs of state. By this union between his wife's favorite sister and the young tsarevitch, Bertie's vision of a new balance of European power with England leading the way, took hold. This shift infuriated the Germans, as the Prince of Wales knew it would, simply because Russia now departed from her long-standing custom of always seeking a German princess as future empress. In point of fact, because of this centuries-old custom, the house of Romanov was actually more German than it had ever been Russian. A marriage alliance with Denmark (and Great Britain) would upset the longstanding balance of power in central and eastern Europe. When Bertie returned home a few days later, his glowing reports on a future Anglo-Russian entente were widely spoken about in clubs and political salons. Initially, few in politics took the Prince seriously. To seasoned British politicians, Russia was a treacherous, scheming, and perverse nation devoid of both common decency and diplomatic courtesy. How then, they openly asked, could a foreign royal marriage change all of that?

All the same, Bertie fully intended to be in Saint Petersburg when his sister-in-law married the heir to the Russian throne. His political insight was on target regarding Minnie's entrance into the Russian imperial family. Although decades would pass before his own perseverance, and that of his wife Alix and her sister, would finally see a productive alliance between their two empires, Bertie was intent on laying new foundations which would eventually bear fruit.

Life in imperial Russia would be an immense change for Minnie, who would have to leave the tranquility of Copenhagen behind forever. She was about to enter a fantastic world of untold wealth and extravagance. Minnie crossed into Russia by way of the majesty of the imperial train, which was sent to meet her at the Polish-Russian frontier on 5 January 1865. She had come at the invitation of the tsar to visit Nixa and to become acquainted with his family. As next-in-line to the throne, Nixa possessed a luxurious train of his own, which now awaited his fiancée at the Russian border. Minnie had left Copenhagen in a simple wagon-lit public coach. When she alighted at the frontier, she had no idea of the splendors that awaited her. At Tsar Alexander's order, the imperial train had been filled with flowers of every type, which he had especially shipped from his estates in the Crimea. Valuable gifts also awaited her in her sleeping compartment along with letters from the tsar, his wife and Nixa. Minnie could never have imagined the luxuries her future life with the Romanovs would bring.

Like so many other foreign brides who came to Russia before her, Minnie was suddenly frightened and troubled by the magnificence of the Imperial Court. The frontier station was dirty and overcrowded. Nixa's train was safely waiting some distance from where her's from Denmark had pulled into the station. Minnie had to walk through impoverished, unruly crowds before reaching the train waiting to receive her. So much of what she first encountered in her new homeland was both ugly and offensive. For one thing, despite the obvious splendor of the imperial party in the distance, Minnie was immediately assaulted by the real, deplorable conditions of the Russian people. The stench of death along with the ever-present smell of tobacco and decaying food, unclean and unwashed people, squalor, and the odor of general filth were everywhere. For the first time ever, Minnie found herself choking as she breathed in the abject poverty affronting her senses. She had never seen anything like it in Denmark or in her travels abroad with her parents. At home, even the very poor appeared to be clean and well cared for. Not so here in Russia. She locked her eyes on the splendor of the imperial party waiting for her, men and women draped in furs, decorated with the finest jewels, and bathed in the best French perfumes. It did not occur to her, still just a young woman, why the welcoming party had not come closer to greet her. Had it, she might have realized they would have had to expose themselves to the vile sensations which now assaulted her; something Russian aristocrats would never do. Hurrying through the destitute crowds as quickly as possible, she boarded the waiting train, distancing herself from this putrefied world in the same blind way as the aristocrats awaiting her. This chasm between the Imperial Court and Russian peasantry would live invisibly side-by-side for the remainder of her life.

The imperial train was far more luxurious than anything Minnie had experienced in Denmark. Its walls were inlaid with precious saddlewood and mahogany. Oriental carpets and plush rugs covered its floors. Damask and tapestries hung upon its walls to muffle the sounds of long rail journeys, and the softest leather covered all of the seating. French champagne and Russian caviar awaited her enjoyment, presented in precious crystal decanters and gold tureens. She was served meals on china from the Imperial Porcelain Factory, a dinner service rivalling the most exquisite Limoges china in Western Europe, and as the imperial train pushed eastward she slept nestled beneath elegant silk sheets and cashmere blankets.

At the emperor's order, every Romanov in Saint Petersburg was present for the train's arrival in the capital. After all, they were gathered to welcome their future empress. The tsar was present with his wife Marie Alexandrovna at his side, a rare honor normally only accorded to visiting monarchs. By tradition, Russian empresses received everyone except foreign kings at the Winter Palace. Joining them were the grand dukes and grand duchesses, far too many to count. After Minnie embraced each member of the family in turn, Tsar Alexander escorted her to a waiting carriage, passing through a phalanx of Cossacks in scarlet coats, each carrying a silver lance. The tsar was a tall man with gray, thick mutton chop whiskers beneath which was a small, almost feminine face full of kindness and imperial dignity. His warm welcome inspired a new confidence which Minnie badly needed in order to face the heady days still to come.

In Danish palaces and castles, as in all buildings in northern Europe at that time, winters were typically cold and the rooms were often uncomfortable and drafty. Porcelain stoves and open fires attempted to heat each room, but these rooms were all very large, with tall ceilings. Most of the time residents shivered from chill unless seated directly beside a burning fire. At first glance as Minnie passed through the portal of the massive brownish-red Winter Palace, Minnie expected similar conditions.[5] Russian winters were harsher than those in Denmark, and so Minnie must have expected unpleasant accommodation in the tsar's premier residence. As she stepped into its colorful entrance hall, however, Minnie visibly gasped. She was not so much overcome by its vastness and beauty which she expected, but by the unexpectedly hot and highly perfumed air within its walls. Entering from the freezing weather outside, with its intense biting cold and its penetrating dampness, Minnie slipped into a dreamy state of euphoria for several moments and did not fully return to her senses again until she finally settled into her allotted rooms. Later that night, she emerged from her suite both well-rested and ready to take her place beside the emperor in the palace banquet hall. Her first public event in her future country was to partake of the feast prepared to welcome her as the intended wife of the Tsarevitch Nicholas Alexandrovitch.

In a pale blue and silver three-story hall, as long as it was tall, (just one of the many within the Winter Palace), tables had been draped with creamy white damask coverlets woven with the imperial eagle. Gold plate gleamed at every seat and vermeil chandeliers dangled above as far as the eye could see. These burned brilliantly from thousands of tall white tapers, each flickering in the breeze caused by an army of footmen hurriedly rushing about putting finishing touches on everything from the decorations to the dinner service. The core of the Imperial Court, and all of the imperial family, awaited Minnie's arrival. Many of the Romanovs rose in turn to toast their future empress. The grand dukes, as always, were dressed in colorful full dress uniforms chosen from one of the many imperial regiments. Orders and decorations glistened on their chests like diamond starbursts. The women of the Court appeared in the historic court costume as custom demanded. These gowns comprised a richly ornamented underdress of silver tissue or white velvet only partly visible in the front. Over this, each lady wore the traditional style Russian greatcoat with long opened sleeves that dropped down to the floor. Each gown was highly embroidered and included a train so long and heavy that numerous pages were needed to carry it. Without these pageboys, none of these grand duchesses could move about freely except by removing the outer coat of her costume, which both custom and the tsar forbade. Tsar Nicholas I in 1834 had introduced this costume at the Russian Court. It was loosely based on earlier traditional Russian styles and cost a great deal to create.

The empress's court dress color could never be copied. She alone could wear it. Each grand duchess was assigned a color at her majority or when she married into the family. The empress was permitted to select the color which best suited her. The various ranks of ladies-in-waiting were assigned muted colors which quickly identified their rank of service. All ladies, regardless of rank, also wore the Russian headdress known as the kokosnik, a half-moon, satin circlet that stretched from ear to ear. The edges of this ornament were sewn with precious gems; the richer the grand duchess, the larger and rarer the stones. Behind each guest stood a uniformed footman and behind him a page—all in glittering uniforms unique to their rank and station. Gigantic Ethiopian guards in scarlet coats and white turbans, military pages in gold uniforms emblazoned with the black double-headed eagle of the house of Romanov, bearded Cossacks in scarlet, and Astrakhan soldiers in vivid blue and silver, all stood side by side next to the walls along the entire length of the great hall.

The feast of the Epiphany, 6 January, arrived the day after the gala welcoming Minnie to Saint Petersburg. This was one of the most important days on the imperial calendar. On this day, the reigning tsar received the blessing of the church with waters taken out of the Neva River through a hole cut into the ice. This ritual took place opposite the Winter Palace on the English Embankment[6] with the full complement of the Imperial Court eagerly taking part each year. Minnie was also included, but along with most of the women of the Court she was only expected to witness the festival from a tall window inside the palace. At the appropriate time, one of the tsar's chamberlains arrived to escort Minnie to her appointed place. They passed through numerous grand salons and large halls, walking between towering lines of palace guards before finally, just as she drew close to the emperor's private apartment, she passed through a phalanx of the elite Corps of the Chevalier Guard, the tsar's impressive personal bodyguards. This was the most prestigious regiment in the Russian Empire; membership was reserved exclusively for the sons of the high nobility.

On the morning of the Epiphany feast, processions began to form early in all quarters of the palace, since on ceremonial days the Romanovs went about with their full retinues in tow. More than once Minnie's journey through dozens of state rooms had to wait as larger processions passed. Every grand duchess had a Court of her own and these processions could be lengthy. Thousands of courtiers normally participated in state ceremonies and this day would be no different. The tsar's procession was the first Minnie encountered. Alexander II's retinue was always the most impressive. It included the senior grand dukes and the great officials of state, all of the à la suite generals and admirals and the great dignitaries of the Orthodox Church—each group vested in brilliant splendor—all following the tsar in a long, distinguished parade. Empress Marie's entourage set out next. No color of the rainbow was lacking in the array of her ladies' Russian costumes. White lace veils complemented their jewel-encrusted kokosniks. The empress wore white velvet with a long ermine-trimmed blue velvet mantle. Her ladies-in-waiting, all titled women themselves, followed behind her two-by-two according to the strict table of precedence of the Court (precedence in Russia had been established by the Emperor Paul I and had not been altered in any way since his death in 1801). Minnie could not help but reflect upon the day she would stand in the place of Empress Marie. When that day would arrive, all the glory and glamour Russia had to offer would be hers.

Once outside on the icy Neva, the Metropolitan Archbishop stepped forward. Bending down into the hole in the ice he quickly dipped a silver crucifix three distinct times into the cold water. Raising his arms high above the tsar he imparted the church's blessing. Cannons thundered from behind the walls of the Fortress of Ss. Peter and Paul. Bells began tolling from the cupolas atop all the cathedrals in the city. It was all over within twenty minutes, but this medieval pageant exuded such great splendor it imbued in Minnie an absolute need to belong to Russia. Scenes like this, and many others like it, defined what it meant to be a Romanov empress in Minnie's mind and she ardently desired to be a part of it all.

The tsar had timed Minnie's arrival in Russia to coincide with the height of the social season. A court ball was scheduled to take place two days after the Epiphany as was the custom each year. Balls at the Winter Palace included guests numbering in the thousands. Each was marshaled into specific rooms by chamberlains according to that guest's rank and position at Court. No one was ever out of place. Hundreds of officials carefully orchestrated where each guest was to stand. These balls were always opened by the tsar and his empress. Their arrival was heralded by the Grand Chamberlain, the Court official who carried a six foot tall ebony staff crowned by a silver orb topped by the double-headed eagle of the Romanovs. At the monarch's impending approach, the Chamberlain would tap its metal base three times on the glimmering marble floor announcing with great resonance the presence of the Tsar of All the Russias. A hush immediately rippled throughout the palace; a sacred silence reigned. Only then did the tall mahogany doors of the Malachite Hall swing open. Framed within its portal, stood Alexander II with Empress Marie Alexandrovna by his side.

Minnie viewed this spectacle for the first time as a guest from across the room. She would never let herself forget the electric charge which rushed through her body at that moment and as years went by, she would often relate to younger generations in the imperial family how many times she had been moved to tears that night. Writing to her daughter Olga in 1907, Minnie said:

> *"My dearest Olga,*
>
> *When I close my eyes to recall that blessed day in 1865, my skin still tingles with excitement. How could I not feel like a Russian, like a Romanov, from that very moment onward? I had come home and here I wanted to remain."*[7]

The Romanov Imperial Ball was always opened with a *polonaise,* a dance of tremendous rhythm and style which originated in Poland. Minnie had never mastered the polonaise and feared she would embarrass herself before Nixa's family. She also learned at the last minute that she and Nixa would have to follow the tsar and empress as they danced the polonaise through the palaces' many halls. She understood all too well that the eyes of all gathered, especially the critical eyes of the Imperial Court, would be centered upon her.

Before leaving for Russia, Minnie had asked her mother if she could go to Paris to purchase a ball gown at the famous House of Worth, at that time the most prestigious couturier in Europe.[8] The queen would not permit an extravagance the frugal Danes could not easily afford. Minnie knew every other lady at the ball, dressed in a beautiful Court costume, would have an advantage over her. She also knew all the wives of foreign Dignitaries present would be wearing Parisian gowns. Worse still, Minnie also understood each of them would instantly know the style of her dress was hopelessly out-of-date.

She hoped the great ladies of Russia would never know her mother had made her ball gown at home. The two days leading into the ball were restless ones for Minnie with all these fears plaguing her.

The morning of the party, Nixa failed to make his appearance at Court as expected. He was in bed with a fever and exhibited flulike symptoms, probably contracted at the blessing of the water ceremony two days before. Minnie was secretly delighted to learn the doctors demanded he remain in his room for several more days. She hoped his illness would permit her to quietly blend into the background rather than play a prominent role at the gala. Nixa sent a message to Minnie through his brother Vladimir, the third son of the tsar and at that time a nineteen-year-old officer in the famed Preobajansky Guards Regiment. Vladimir informed her that Nixa had arranged for their brother Sasha to serve as her partner at the ball. He wanted Sasha to look after Minnie since he was convinced that his fiancée could not possibly wish to miss the spectacle. Minnie protested, saying she would prefer to remain in her room, but Vladimir insisted she had to take part in the festivities because it had already been announced she would be present.

Vladimir possessed a tremendous basso profundo voice and when he spoke a sense of absolute authority accompanied his words. With nothing to do but to capitulate, Minnie thanked Vladimir and asked him to convey to Sasha her happiness over how things had developed. Sasha was the tallest of the tsar's sons. His tight red hussar uniform emphasized his thick frame, but he nevertheless appeared striking because of his size and his mannerisms. Of all the brothers, Sasha was the only one who had not engaged Minnie in conversation on the day she arrived in Russia. Although he was not bad looking, in Minnie's eyes Sasha reminded her of the giant from a Danish children's fairytale which had always frightened her. Minnie suspected Sasha did not like her and for his part Sasha was aware that Minnie was somewhat afraid of him. Vladimir tried to calm her fears, assuring Minnie that Sasha was simple and kindhearted. He asked her not to be put off by anything he might do or say as he could be unintentionally rude at times.

Alexander II had named this second son the 'bullock' because he was always pushing his head forward and hunching over his shoulders as a bull would do when he was about to attack. The men of Sasha's regiment referred to him as the 'bull' for the same reason. In reality, Sasha felt uneasy around the beautiful Danish princess. He was afraid of elegant women and so he feared the outcome of his evening with Minnie as much as she feared it with him. This is not to say Sasha disliked women or was afraid of them. In fact, he was known to be the accomplished lover of a great many gypsy women as well as several low-class dancing girls in the slums and music halls of Saint Petersburg. He simply preferred bawdy evenings with these women to the company of society ladies, although he had secretly fallen in love with one of the ladies of his mother's court; a relationship which would never be permitted because of her lower rank.

As day turned into evening Minnie's dread increased, and with each passing hour she began to emotionally prepare herself to attend the ball. When the time came to take her place with the imperial family, Sasha said nothing at all to help put her at ease. Minnie stood rigidly by in terrified silence. Not knowing what to expect, nothing comparable to Romanov magnificence had ever taken place in Denmark, Minnie watched the scarlet footman swing open the double doors of the tsar's private apartment. She nearly collapsed in fright as her gaze rested on the assembled crowds. At that moment, she longed for someone familiar to simply call her 'Minnie' once more. She stoically recalled her upbringing and how determined she was to never disgrace her parents or her beloved Denmark. Alone, surrounded by strangers, petite Princess Dagmar of Denmark felt supremely ridiculous beside this enigmatic giant of a man. She was certain all the guests would mock her inadequacies. After all, Russians did not have any difficulty ridiculing anyone who did not meet their expectations. Minnie saw her future parents-in-law tightly embrace each other as they glided forward into the gathered crowd with ease and grace. She had to force herself to forget the partner beside her and followed the gracious posture of Empress Marie as they all emerged into the first of several great halls. As the orchestra struck up the first strains of the night's music, Minnie's first polonaise began. She knew there now would be no turning back.

This was Minnie's debut appearance before Saint Petersburg society. The great landowning families of the realm had been invited as well. Far from displaying herself at a disadvantage, the young future empress of Russia aroused universal admiration and satisfaction. The Russian Court was equally as ready to exhibit delight as it was to openly manifest disapproval. So as Minnie passed through the midst of the thousands of guests gathered, she heard abundant clapping and cheering in every hall and salon. She had won-over the highly prejudiced Imperial Court within moments of her appearance at the ball. Although Minnie quickly felt at ease, Sasha was mightily uncomfortable. Sweat poured from his brow and instead of talking to her as was customary during the polonaise; he marched ahead of her with tense embarrassment, crushing her fingers by his strong grip as he pulled her along. Once the dance had proceeded through the palace, the imperial family took their places on a raised dais for the remainder of the evening. The emperor and empress sat upon crimson thrones. Russian custom did not require them to participate in any further dances, but the grand dukes and grand duchesses were expected to do so. Sasha sat glumly beside Minnie without offering any conversation. At midnight a magnificent supper was served. The Imperial Corps of Cadets, a special college composed of the teenage sons of Russian nobleman, collected tickets from each guest and in turn led them in parties of ten to circular tables from which sprouted full-size live palm trees from beds of colorful exotic flowers. These had been shipped north on the imperial trains from the tsar's Crimean estates as fragrant decorations for the night. The high ceilings of the supper halls were painted dark blue like the night sky and were sporadically flecked with golden stars which twinkled when the glow of the candles reached them. These palm trees rose like a summer forest and thousands of strung colored paper lanterns added a special mysterious aura throughout the public rooms that night.

For Minnie, this midnight supper served as a welcome diversion from her wordless companion; things would now take a more lively turn. At these circular tables Minnie could, and did, engage other people seated around her. These newfound acquaintances amply made up for the taciturn nature of her companion. Sasha's brothers Vladimir and Alexis, along with two other young guard officers and their four female guests, made up the table while Minnie enjoyed strange new delicacies for the first time. Sasha added nothing to the party atmosphere. He swallowed champagne with startling gusto. He smiled at Minnie from time to time and attended to her obvious needs, but he never spoke directly to her. Later on he addressed a few remarks to his brothers in Russian, but was otherwise silent throughout the entire evening, never asking Minnie to dance again.

The champagne eventually relaxed Sasha, but it also brought out a bravado in him that was more fitting for a barracks than for an imperial ball. He picked up a heavy silver plate, roughly brushed a few desert cakes off into the flowers, held it up in both hands for all to see before bending it between his thick fingers until the outer edges touched. Next, he pounded the plate between his enormous palms, reducing it to a perfect half-moon shape of sheet metal. Then starting with Minnie, Sasha winked at each guest at the table as if to show his pride in his ability to conquer steel. He next snatched up a silver fork and in a flash turned it into a corkscrew. Behind him stood his personal servant, an officer in the Hussars who always seemed to anticipate his master's every need.

Sasha was now in full performance mode. He ordered a deck of playing cards, which his aide quickly produced. With a ferocious jerk, he tore the packet in half and hurled the pieces like rose petals into a palm tree. The tsar, who by tradition was visiting at each table, had just arrived at Minnie's side as these shenanigans unfolded. He was visibly displeased by his drunken son's antics. Now very much relaxed, and ignoring his father's obvious displeasure, Sasha left the table without saying a word. He walked to the orchestra pushing his way past startled and bewildered musicians. Suddenly he took one of their instruments in-hand, as the instrumentalist immediately abandoned his chair to the grand duke. Sasha sat down and began to play. Just as suddenly, he rose and took another instrument as that musician also quickly vacated his seat for him. Soon Sasha tired of this instrument, too, moving on to another. To everyone's amazement, Sasha was a very good musician. As he continued on through the orchestra, taking up instrument after instrument, not once did he make a musical mistake. He had certainly acted the buffoon, but he did not play a single wrong note, smoothly blending into strains of the music being played. Before he had finished, Sasha had captured the attention of everyone in the hall, including his parents. It was the grand duke's way of showing Minnie that he possessed many more talents than his family had ever credited him with.[8] The ball finally ended, much to the guest of honor's relief.

Minnie remained with Nixa in Russia for three months. He had quickly recovered from the flu and the two fell deeply in love as they made plans for their forthcoming marriage. She was set to return home to Denmark in early March.

> *"Dearest Mama,*
>
> *I leave for Copenhagen Friday next. I shall dreadfully miss Saint Petersburg. It has become a part of my being. Nixa's family has been so good to me. I thank God for them all but of course I anxiously await yours and Papa's tender embrace.*
>
> *Your loving daughter—Minnie."*

Empress Marie and Nixa accompanied her in their private train as far as the frontier. Minnie switched at the Polish border to a normal passenger train bound for Copenhagen and returned home in the same humble manner she had departed for Russia months before. Her time there had changed her. She was no longer the simple dreamer from Copenhagen. She was now very much a future empress of the richest monarchy in Europe and this reality had altered her personality. She now possessed a bearing and gravitas which did not exist before her exposure to the Romanovs and to Russia. After they said their poignant farewells, the empress' train was then diverted through Germany en route to Villa Bermont, her home in Nice on the French Riviera. Nixa would enjoy several weeks in the warmer climate as his mother sought her routine cure from the harshness of the Russian climate and the general indifference of her husband. The wedding was scheduled for mid-June. April and May were to be filled with preparations both in Russia and Denmark. Queen Louise had at last agreed to make a visit to Paris to purchase a proper trousseau for her daughter. The tsar arranged for a chaplain of the Orthodox Church to be dispatched to Fredensborg to prepare Minnie for her conversion and to teach her the rudiments of the Russian language. She already spoke numerous languages fluently.

Despite this excitement and all the activities now swirling around her, Minnie fell into a mild depression having been transported from this dreamlike fairytale back into her mundane past. No one could imagine the shock which loomed before them.

CHAPTER SIX

I'VE COME HOME TO RUSSIA

1865-1867

EXCITEMENT IN THE DANISH FAMILY continued through March, but in the first week of April things suddenly changed. Early one morning Queen Louise entered Minnie's bedroom holding a telegram that had just arrived. The queen's face was drawn and pale. She told her daughter that word had just arrived from the empress.

Marie asked Louise to break the bad news to Minnie that Nixa had been injured. She did not tell Queen Louise the full extent of Nicholas's illness. Three days before, the tsarevitch had been riding in the hills above Nice when his horse threw him. He landed hard against a tree trunk and was rendered unconscious. He was carried back to his mother's villa where a few hours later he seemed to be recovering. It was only then the empress realized that Nixa could no longer move. At first the doctors declared he was suffering from both shock and a bruised spine, perhaps even rheumatism, but the correct diagnosis was cerebral-spinal meningitis in addition to grave injuries suffered from the accident. Queen Louise and Minnie left for Nice that same afternoon not realizing how dire things really were. The doctors feared Nixa would not live through the night. At the time they believed he had harbored this disease within his system since childhood since such maladies were inherent in the Romanov dynasty. The doctors were convinced that the severe blow earlier that week (and a bad fall during a previous wrestling match in amateur competition) had caused the illness to manifest itself. Marie discounted this diagnosis, saying Nixa had always enjoyed a healthy constitution. The tsar and his family were summoned to France, arriving several days later by numerous private trains from various points in Europe.

Crown Prince Fredrik accompanied his mother and sister to France. He had grown fond of Nixa when he first came to Fredensborg. The two young men had become friends and Freddie was genuinely worried for him. The empress met the Danish family at the station and said nothing, but her face spoke volumes. Minnie rushed to the bedside of her fiancé who was now semi-comatose. He had only spoken a few words during her time with him, but she held his hand and prayed. Suddenly a heavy knock at the door aroused them both and there in the open doorway stood Sasha. It was his way of breaking the tension. He was wearing civilian clothes, clearly not tailored for him. His suit hung clumsily on his immense frame. Sasha approached his brother's bed inquiring if Nixa had sent for him. When Sasha took his place beside Minnie, a somewhat more alert Nixa began to speak in a firmer, clearer voice. He asked Sasha to take Minnie's hand, telling the couple he knew each of them better than anyone else. Nixa believed Minnie would make an ideal future empress and told Sasha and Minnie so:

> *"You are holding the hand of the next tsarevitch who shall soon take my place. And it is my dying wish that you two should be married."* [1]

In embarrassment, Minnie instantly began to pull her hand away, but Sasha held it firmly in place, even pulling it tightly back into his. Nixa next asked the two to kneel. He prayed over both of them in Russian before asking Sasha if he agreed to marry Minnie. There was a pause. Sasha seemed to be hesitant, but when he did respond the reply was a resounding *yes*! Minnie was asked to respond as well. She also hesitated, but because it was Nicholas' dying wish, she too agreed, hoping not to be bound by her promise. Sasha and Minnie rose and quietly left the room together saying nothing to each other or to the others waiting outside in the hallway.

Within two hours Nixa was dead. He was only twenty-one.[2] Only Sasha and Minnie could tell the secret promise Nixa had secured from them. Minnie said nothing to her mother or brother about what had just transpired believing were it ever to become reality, word would have to be released from the tsar in Saint Petersburg. While all of this was unfolding in Nice, rumors were already rampant throughout Saint Petersburg that the tsar intended to appoint his third son, Vladimir, to be his new heir supplanting Sasha from his rightful place. The tsar, rumors persistently claimed, considered Sasha to be no more than a hapless brute. Meanwhile Queen Louise was dismayed, envisioning her sweet daughter married to an uncouth Lothario with a vicious reputation who might soon be repudiated by his own father and thereafter sent into exile. Many believed the much more sophisticated Vladimir would eventually succeed the tsar. All of this seemed too sinister for Louise to contemplate. She returned to Minnie time and again to inform her of these developments and to forestall any further promises yet to be made to Sasha. Minnie heard her mother out in silence, but when she had finished, Minnie told Louise she had already given her word to Nixa and would marry Sasha if the tsar desired it. Fundamentally, Minnie was a pragmatist. She understood no throne would now come her way equal to Russia. She knew at the same time she and Sasha did not love one another. For her, it would be a marriage of honor, not of love, although one of love would certainly have been the life she would have lived with Nixa. Minnie, like her mother Louise, was a woman of great resolution. For the moment the matter rested within the walls of the French villa where a state of grief prevailed. Elaborate preparations for the ceremonial removal of the tsarevitch's corpse were already underway and arrangements had to be made for the imperial family's return to Russia. The French government was determined this should all be accomplished in great solemnity, and so the grieving family also had to concern itself with the rigid protocol imposed by French authorities.

The rumor, that Sasha would be repudiated as heir, had reached the interior of Russia. As rumors tended to do, this caused nearly everyone of note to take a position for or against him. By the time the imperial train pulled into the station in Saint Petersburg six days later, talk of Vladimir's promotion to tsarevitch was widespread and believed by most. After all, Vladimir possessed the qualities of a tsar. Many who did not know Sasha believed he did not. Until his arrival home, the tsar remained silent on this topic. His grief for his dead son was profound and he was deeply depressed, but once back in Holy Russia he took matters firmly in-hand. Within the Winter Palace, delegations from across the empire were already gathering to pay their respects to both the body of the deceased tsarevitch and to his new successor—Sasha. Of these delegations, the Poles were the most troublesome. They had always maintained an uneasy, imposed respect for the tsarist regime. To prove to them, and to the rest of the empire, that nothing of significance had changed by Nixa's death, Alexander II ordered his new heir, Grand Duke Alexander Alexandrovitch (Sasha), to stand next to him while he received each delegation. With Sasha at his side, the tsar used this occasion to reprimand the Poles saying:

> *"Here beside me stands my heir. He bears the name of the emperor who formally established the Kingdom of Poland. I hope he will know how to govern his arrogance worthily and that he will not endure that which I myself have not tolerated."*[3]

The tsar's immediate public endorsement of his second son was now clear to all. Any ambitions Vladimir might have entertained were firmly suppressed. To his family, the tsar also made it quite clear he felt Minnie's charming personality and her intellect would help guide his brusque second son to become a great tsar in his own right. And so, it was announced; Minnie and Sasha would marry in due course.

The wedding took place in the chapel of the Winter Palace on 9 November 1866. Minnie was now eighteen-years-old. Some in Russia thought her to be already somewhat old. Sasha would soon be twenty-two. Danish author and friend of her family Hans Christian Anderson stood on the quay at Copenhagen to witness Minnie's departure. Afterwards he recorded his emotions. He recalled that sad morning, standing in a large crowd of Danes, as the king and queen escorted Minnie on-board the ship which would 'bring her home' to Russia. When she saw him, he later wrote, Minnie stepped up to him and took his hand warmly.[4] Like so many on the dockside that cold day, Anderson had tears in his eyes as their princess sailed away, just as Alix had, to the strains of «*In Denmark I was born*». For the Danes, Russia now seemed so far away, much farther away than London. To make matters sadder still, Minnie's entire family was saying goodbye to her on a public dock. Only her brother Freddie accompanied her on this journey to her new life and would remain by her side until after the wedding.

Once on Russian soil, Minnie received an enthusiastic welcome from her new countrymen. The welcome ceremony took place at the imperial pavilion inside the train station in Saint Petersburg. Cheering spectators crowded the platforms hung with the imperial standard and the *Dannebrog*, flags of both royal families. Abundant flowers were displayed everywhere. So numerous was the gathered crowd nearly every rooftop, window, and balcony along the route to the palace was overflowing with eager spectators. The welcome festivities included fireworks, illuminations, and various gala balls. Minnie was enthralled by this exuberant welcome. As much as Minnie brimmed with excitement, these ceremonies created a sense of dread in Sasha. Although few knew or really understood him, the Romanovs knew him well. Sasha possessed a truly mercurial personality. He could be kind one day and abrupt, even cruel, the next. Many in the family tried to avoid him at all costs. The Russian people neither knew Sasha nor really liked him, but they came to quickly embrace the effervescent Minnie and her popularity grew with each new public appearance. Russians, mystical by nature, recognized in Minnie a new beginning. They craved excitement and glamour, which had been lacking in the reign of her new father-in-law and his quiet wife. The charming extrovert qualities, already exhibited by Minnie, encouraged Russians hopes and dreams for a prosperous new era and a modern outward-looking country. For her part, Minnie intended never to disappoint. Her smiling face would warm the hearts and brighten the eyes of all who saw her. Minnie's simplicity, charm, and ease of manner, also offered a promise of happiness for the imperial family, which in those troubled times translated to peace for all Russia.

Prior to marrying Sasha, Minnie first had to be formally received into the Russian Orthodox Church. Her conversion was to be a very public one. It would also be the ceremony at which Minnie formally adopted her new Orthodox name; Marie Feodorovna.[5] She appeared at the ceremony in a simple white satin gown trimmed at the neck and at the hem with white swan feathers. It was devoid of all other ornaments. She wore nothing in her hair and wore no jewelry except for a gold Orthodox crucifix suspended on a chain around her neck. The conversion ceremony was an ordeal, but one Minnie eagerly embraced. It called for this once simple Danish Lutheran to abjure the dogma of her childhood. This was no hardship for Minnie since she had been prepared to do so ever since her initial engagement to Nixa. Facing to the east and then to the west, the officiating prelate asked Minnie to publicly repudiate her old religion's teachings:

"I renounce and reject them all"[6]

She pronounced these mandatory words in perfect Russian. Next as a convert to Orthodoxy, she was required to lie prostrate on the cold marble floor while reciting the Orthodox Church's *Ten Articles of Religion*—once again in perfect Russian. Minnie next had to endure the rite of absolution of all the sins of her previous life again prostrating herself. Upon rising she was anointed with holy chrism and was proclaimed the *True Believing Grand Duchess Marie Feodorovna of Russia*. At that instance, Princess Marie Sophie Frederikke Dagmar of Denmark vanished forever. In her place a full Orthodox member of the Imperial House of Romanov emerged with its accompanying privileges and with the exalted rank of Imperial Highness. She would enjoy this rank until the day Sasha became tsar.

The elaborate wedding could now proceed. The incredible value of the wedding gifts, and the beauty and expense of Minnie's new trousseau, overwhelmed all who saw it on display in the Winter Palace. It was difficult for Minnie to comprehend all she had been given; still a simple girl from Denmark at heart. She was astonished by the grandeur of gifts displayed in the great halls of the imperial palace. Those from the Romanovs alone filled a space more than a city block in length. Even the older, more hardened grand duchesses and seasoned ladies of the Court were awestruck by the magnificence of the treasures. The teenage bride studied the dazzling, massive gems which covered several tables, each reserved for the display of one specific gemstone.

There were tables with suites of rubies, others for the demi-parures of dazzling sets of emeralds and tables just for diamonds, many as large as hens' eggs. Others displayed the pearls she had been given, by far the most exquisite in Europe. Lesser gems were placed on display tables set up just for them. All of these treasures were just the gifts the tsar had given her. Many of the women in the imperial family laughed at Minnie's response when she naïvely declared that she would be dead long before she ever had time to wear half of them. Freddie was overwhelmed by the wealth of the Romanovs, something he had been warned about in advance. He could not fully comprehend the value of the gifts given to his sister until he was exposed to them firsthand. Just one of her new brooches was worth more than his soldier's salary for an entire decade at home. Freddie was both pleased and concerned for his sister. He now understood what her life would be like in Russia. He saw the dangerous dichotomy between the immensely rich ruling family and the extreme poverty of the masses so visible in the streets, if only one were to open his eyes to see it. This worried him and he feared it would translate to danger for his sister one day.[7] Like all unassuming Glucksburgs, Freddie worried most of all that Minnie would never again be happy when she returned to the simplicity of life with her family in Denmark. He need not have worried, as both Alix and Minnie continuously yearned for quiet home visits with their family in their beloved Denmark.

Minnie's amazing trousseau was given to her mainly by Tsar Alexander II. Custom required the reigning tsar to furnish a new grand duchess (especially if she were a foreign-born princess entering the imperial family) with all she would need to live well within the Imperial Court. As Minnie was also the new tsarevna as well as the daughter-in-law of the tsar, the grandeur of the gifts was all the more excessive. Superb furs of every type were on display. Costly sable coats, ermine mantels, mink jackets and capes, and every other form of priceless fur clothing then available were folded high on tables in one corner of the vast Nicholas Hall as if they were no more valuable than bolts of mere cotton. The tsar's gifts alone required eleven leather bound registers to list them all. Her new wardrobe included rare silk stockings, gloves for every occasion, articles of fine lingerie worked in hand-sewn laces from Paris and Florence, dressing gowns, fur and leather boots, colorful silk shawls, and scarves repeated by the score in every color and style.

Everything Minnie would ever need as the senior member of the Imperial House had been provided by her father-in-law both from Russian designers and from the finest couturier houses in Western Europe. Even an abundance of monogrammed lace handkerchiefs had not been forgotten. All of these were in addition to innumerable tables displaying jewels of inestimable value. Additional rooms were set aside for Minnie's gifts from the empress, including three new heavily jewel encrusted Court costumes. Gifts from Sasha of equal value were displayed in yet another hall as were those from Sasha's brothers, his cousins and their wives, as well as from members of the extended Romanov family. Added to these were the gifts from the ladies of the Imperial Court and from members of the Imperial Household, from wealthy Russian families such as the Yusopovs, from foreign royal guests present, and from ordinary Russians who sent in thousands of icons and prayer card memorials for the occasion. Perhaps Minnie's most cherished gift was the large Danish language bible presented to her by her parents. Except for the years during the Revolution, it would never leave her bedside table.

A wedding day for a Russian grand duchess was a harsh ordeal to endure, especially if she was a stranger to the imperial family and its intricate protocol. From morning to evening an imperial wedding was an entanglement of arcane Romanov ritual and tradition. Minnie was a prisoner of these rituals and had little comprehension of what she was about to face. In fact, she would go through the ceremonies yet to come without a single thought of what to expect. It was not until later that night, when she had time to consider the day which had just ended, that she fully grasped what she had just experienced. Buried in furs against the icy winter darkness with Sasha looming silently beside her, she began to give serious thought to the significance of her wedding as their sledge swiftly sped through the dark countryside and their honeymoon.

The wedding melodrama would have exhausted any bride. Early that morning courtiers escorted Minnie to the magnificent Malachite Hall wearing only a silk sheath. It was here she would be dressed for her wedding. The Malachite Hall stood adjacent to the private apartments of the tsar and empress. Its tall windows looked out over the ice-covered Neva River. It was in this hall that members of the imperial family and senior members of the Imperial Household gathered for every important state occasion. For liturgies, gala balls, weddings, funerals or any other occasion of state, the imperial family began its long processions through the palace from this hall. The selection of the Malachite Hall was not by happenstance. Imperial brides were dressed here on their wedding day to symbolize that they were now full members of the imperial family. In fact, unlike other monarchies, Russian brides were elevated to the rank of grand duchess by an imperial *ukase*, the tsar's formal decree, on the day before their marriage or perhaps on the day of their conversion to Orthodoxy, as was the case with Minnie. And so they entered into their marriage as equals to Romanov-born grooms. Minnie's elaborate vesting ceremony was intended to symbolize this new equality.

A Romanov wedding day was intentionally rich in symbolism. Everything had been explicitly decreed centuries before by Catherine the Great. The day opened with a three-hour-long vesting process. Most of this time was spent before the famous gold mirror of Empress Anna Ioanovena where Minnie's hair was to be prepared in the fashion of Catherine the Great.[8] Catherine's protocol demanded each bride wear her hair in long traditional (now false) curls attached behind each ear so they would drape down over the front of the bride's exposed shoulders. Marie Feodorovna, as everyone now addressed Minnie, stood motionless during this ritual because of her immensely heavy antique gown of genuine silver cloth. There would be no lovely Parisian white wedding gown for her. Her shoulders were pulled back by the weight of the sweltering hot ermine-lined gold velvet mantle, cascading in endless folds behind her. With each slight movement the heavy mantle pulled her forcibly backwards and its weight, and the heat generated by the fur, caused perspiration to soak her body long before the wedding began.

Clusters of ancient jewels were taken one-by-one from innumerable red velvet cushions already resting on tables nearby. These were placed on Minnie by the empress' Mistress of the Robes, one of the historic perquisites of her position at Court. Dames of Honor gently removed these in quick order to replace them by still other gems. This exchange of gems continued without rhyme or reason until these entitled ladies found the perfect set of state jewels to be worn. The honor of selecting a Romanov bride's parure was jealously guarded by these senior Court ladies who took great pride in this privilege. The jewels belonged to the state. They were not a part of Minnie's impressive new private collection. In addition to the robin egg-size diamonds in the necklace chosen for her, Minnie also wore earrings so heavy that without the silver frames hidden behind her ears which secretly supported them, they would have torn through the flesh of her earlobes. Atop Minnie's head sat the massive Romanov wedding diadem, an elaborate white diamond tiara which rose to a peak at the center. This row upon row of huge diamonds completely encircling her head intentionally presented the idea of a halo. Its centerpiece was the large famous Romanov rose-colored diamond. But this heavy diadem was not adornment enough for an imperial bride. Catherine had also decreed that every Romanov bride should arrive at the altar wearing a special nuptial crown. Like all of the state jewels, this crown was kept in vaults far beneath the Winter Palace and comprised four diamond arches affixed to a stiff red velvet frame. It was under the weight of this combined concoction every imperial bride, draped in seventy pounds of silver, ermine and diamonds, began her married life.

Understandably, Minnie was exhausted before the wedding had even begun. She felt physically sick having not eaten for hours as Romanov brides were also required to fast before their wedding ceremony. She also had a severe headache from the weight of all the heavy jewels on her head and around her neck. Minnie moved very slowly under this barely supportable burden. The procession required forty minutes to transverse the palace. Sasha awaited her at the chapel. His procession, included his brothers and most of the other grand dukes, all-male members of the Imperial Household, and Sasha's military aides who all accompanied him from his apartment to the chapel where it had been arranged for him to arrive just moments before the bride. The tsar and the empress would be the last to enter. By the time Minnie set foot inside the chapel on the arm of her brother, she was already very nauseous from lack of food as well as from the incense heavily dispersed throughout the palace by archimandrites leading each procession.

Naturally under the weight of her regalia, Minnie was unable to move by her own volition. So heavy was the ermine train which stretched twelve feet behind her, six pages were required to uplift it every time she shifted her body weight. Grand Duke Vladimir, a force to be reckoned with in his own right, held a gold crown over his brother's head. Freddie held a similar crown over Minnie's head for the duration of the ceremony. A true sorrow, however, was the absence of Minnie's parents who could not travel to Russia for their daughter's wedding. It was not that Christian and Louise could not afford the costly voyage. Rather it was they could not afford the ritualistic practice of mass gratuity disbursement required by Romanov custom. Monetary gifts of substantial value were expected by every member of the Imperial Court and by all those persons whom any high-ranking visitor to Russia might encounter. Everyone in the palace felt entitled to these gratuities, from the highest courtiers to the lowest staff member, and every person in between.

Such an extravagance could bankrupt the Danish royal house. So Christian and Louise remained at home and were represented by their eldest son, Freddie, who was not expected to grant gratuities of substantial amounts because of his tender age. Alix could not be present for the wedding either as she was in the late term of her third pregnancy, but Bertie insisted he be permitted to represent his wife. Except for Bertie and Freddie, no one of real importance to Minnie was present. Even Willy, as the king of Greece, could not attend for the same financial reasons that kept their parents away. Following the three hour-long ceremony, Minnie and Sasha stood for two further hours to receive their guests, two thousand dignitaries in all.

A villa in the grounds of Peterhof, perhaps the most beautiful of all Romanov palaces, had been chosen as the site of part of their honeymoon. It had served as one of two destinations for Romanov honeymoons for decades. The park at Peterhof was dotted with numerous dachas or villas. Some stood in gardens, others in wooded landscapes. The area where the villa stood was within a thicket of dense trees offering the remoteness Sasha desired. When this long day was finally behind her, Minnie found that, even at Peterhof, Romanov wedding rituals continued as prescribed by Catherine the Great long ago. The old palace in the forest stood empty and silent when the couple arrived. Minnie found herself alone in the bridal chamber for some hours. The room was lit only by dim candlelight and presented a spectral air with frightening shadows flickering around a massive heavily carved four-poster bed in which the tiny Minnie lie awaiting Sasha's arrival. Her maids of honor bathed her and they helped her dress for the night, but they had already departed. Queen Louise had not prepared Minnie for her wedding night nor had Alix, who had already undergone this physical surprise. Minnie could not have expected the ardent lovemaking which was to come. The villas darkened corridors hid chamberlains and maids-of-honor concealed in the shadows. Each waited for the tsarevitch to leave his dressing room in the bizarre costume known in the family as 'the wedding night uniform.' It too had been designed by the great Catherine and although bizarre even by mid-nineteenth century standards, it was still worn by all Russian grand dukes on their wedding night. The groom's costume comprised a high silver turban for the head with a tall, white aigrette feather standing high above the forehead. Sasha was dressed in a silver gown which covered him from head to toe and which gave the appearance of military armor. Upon his feet were silver slippers with long curling metallic points like those worn in Arabian Nights fantasies.

Sasha did not warn Minnie in advance of what was to come. Ever true to his peculiar personality he remained silent about the honeymoon as their sleigh departed the Winter Palace for the slow journey westward. This was actually the first opportunity he and Minnie had to be entirely alone since her arrival in Russia the week before. It was during this long journey, each buried deep beneath rugs and furs they could engage in intimate private conversation. Although Minnie attempted to talk with Sasha, he only replied in single, static statements and so most of the journey was spent in awkward silence. The only sweet sentiment which passed between them was when Sasha silently took Minnie's hand under the fur coverlets. Like all Romanov men before him, Sasha was well-versed in lovemaking, but he had never been with a woman of quality, an unbreakable rule in Russian high society. His paramours had always been low-born women, camp followers and prostitutes whom he treated brusquely and without care. Sasha had no idea how to interact with a princess in an intimate way and so this robust giant entered into his wedding night more frightened by what was to come than Minnie. For her part, Minnie had no concept of what would follow once they arrived. All that her mother and the ladies of the Russian Court had told her was to do whatever her husband asked of her. This was the strict advice given genteel women about their approaching wedding nights in every nation of Europe at the time.

Alone in her nuptial chamber, Minnie heard the creaking of an opening door in the distance and heavy dragging footsteps that slowly grew louder outside her bedroom. Suddenly the door swung open with great force as if some very angry person had pushed through in order to cause harm. Minnie sprang up in bed. She was frightened until she noticed the absurd vision before her. She collapsed into fits of hysterical laughter at the sight of her husband in his ridiculous silver habit.

Now fully alone, with the arcane Romanov rituals behind them, the bride and groom were able to finally relax with one another and consummate their marriage. Sasha wrote his thoughts in his diary the following day:

> "*God grant that I may love my darling wife more and more, she who loves me with all her heart, a love for which I am so grateful, and for the sacrifice that she has made by leaving her parents and her fatherland for my sake. I often feel that I am not worthy of her but even if this were true, I will do for my very best to be.*"

If the two were still strangers, they were no longer cold to one another. The honeymoon had brought them both closer. Minnie would always hold Nixa in her heart of hearts and Sasha had loved a noblewoman for years, but she had been forbidden him. It would take them both a long time to forget their first loves, but they were already building sentiments of affection for one another even in those early days before the honeymoon had ended. In short order, these two exceptionally different personalities would find they had fallen in love with one another. Minnie was now the tsarevna of Russia and quickly became a very positive influence on her headstrong, arrogant husband. She also had a similar positive effect upon all the individuals she met during her first year in Russia. Not long after her wedding, Minnie appeared at a nobleman's ball as the guest of honor. According to one witness, the young tsarevna was the most beautiful woman present. Dressed entirely in a white tulle dress, with a triple strand diamond necklace, one of her wedding gifts from the tsar, Minnie looked like any bride in Western Europe. She was in high spirits, her round cheeks flushed by both her excitement and by the dancing. In contrast to the rather staid Imperial Court, Minnie was freshness personified—a very rare sight in Russia during the reign of Tsar Alexander II.[10]

A hectic schedule of festivities followed the wedding, including a ball in the Winter Palace in honor of Minnie's brother-in-law the Prince of Wales. Long before the actual wedding, Bertie had promised Minnie he would attend her marriage when the time came. He was determined to keep his promise, but achieving this did not come without difficulty. Alix was bitterly disappointed that she was unable to accompany Bertie as she always intended to do. She was determined that nothing would keep her home, but the timing of her pregnancy and the date of the Russian wedding made this dream unattainable. Queen Victoria was unmoved, as usual, by Alix's unsuccessful pleas for Bertie to represent her. Victoria believed the British ambassador in Russia was representation enough. She also did not want Bertie to be placed in any danger in the Russian capital where assassins routinely attacked both resident and visiting dignitaries alike. In the end it was the prime minister's opinion which prevailed. Victoria acquiesced and, to Alix's immense joy, Bertie was dispatched to the wedding as the queen's official representative. Tsar Alexander was indeed flattered at so high a level of representation from England. Great Britain and Russia had enjoyed a rather frigid, mutually suspicious, relationship for more than a century. The advent of the two beautiful Danish princesses in each nation's capital began to melt the long existing frost between these two states, but a *froideur* still remained.

Bertie arrived in Saint Petersburg with a small retinue three days before the wedding. He was met at the train station by the tsar himself and by all the grand dukes who had already gathered in the capital. There could be no doubt this reception for the Prince of Wales would become the nucleus of a very successful rapprochement between Great Britain and Russia. Language difficulties did not exist as all the Russian family had been educated by English governesses and each member of the family spoke English fluently. The official language of the Imperial Court had always been French, which Bertie also spoke fluently in addition to his father's native German. Nearly every grand duke also spoke German because most of their mothers were German-born. And so the Prince of Wales could converse easily with everyone present. Bertie's boyish exuberance delighted the younger grand dukes. They were a rather rakish group. He also amused the older grand dukes, and he certainly charmed all of the grand duchesses regardless of their age. Carefully instructed by Queen Victoria to avoid all political discussions, Bertie's social success was an immediate sensation. He easily steered clear of thorny political issues. He also cheerfully made the rounds of Saint Petersburg's low-class night haunts with Sasha's younger brothers, Vladimir and Alexis. Formalities aside, Bertie was never one to overlook pleasure found in seedy establishments. At times Sasha joined them as well. Oddly enough the social underworld in the Russian capital was one of the greatest sources of pride for the younger grand dukes. They loved nothing more than to introduce princely visitors to it whenever they could. And boast they did! This mingling between gypsies and prostitutes, and the raunchy nightlife of the city, defined the Russian capital as the most depraved city in Europe. The Romanov grand dukes treasured this side of their social life and came to regard it almost as their personal property.

Sasha reveled in liaisons with low women who routinely frequented these haunts. After his marriage he continued to indulge in such pleasures, but in time, when he came to love Minnie, he laid aside this part of his life and never again, it is believed, strayed from her. For the moment, nothing could please the irreverent grand dukes more than introducing the heir to the British throne (and indeed the heir to Denmark as well) to the seamier side of Russian imperial life. Bertie of course thrived in a ribald environment, which appealed to his vivid imagination and his sexual appetites. Until Sasha married Minnie these were the only places in Russia were he truly felt at home. Now that his new English brother-in-law showed an eagerness to participate, Sasha felt closer to him than he expected. The greatest success of this visit was the manner in which Bertie and Sasha bonded in sincere friendship. It seemed that Bertie could bring out in Sasha a vibrant, yet relaxed, inner personality which had not been seen in him before.

Wherever Bertie went during his stay in Russia he was generously applauded by Russia's peasants. Bertie's ultimate success occurred at the British ambassador's ball on the last evening of his visit. He appeared in full Highland dress with Minnie as his partner. Alix was receiving daily reports from her husband, but neither she nor Minnie initially learned about the bawdy nights that both their husbands had been enjoying. Once he had returned to London, Bertie did present a colorful fairytale-like depiction of the new life that would be Minnie's as tsarevna of Russia. He likewise informed Queen Victoria of his optimism about the political good he had already accomplished and forecast improvement in the long simmering distrust between both nations. Bertie was convinced, as were Sasha and Minnie that this visit laid a new foundation for accord between the two monarchies, which both couples were determined to foster.

CHAPTER SEVEN

DREAMS FULFILLED

B Y THE TIME MINNIE HAD finally settled into life in Russia, Alix and Bertie had already begun a family. Eddy, their first child, was born in 1864. George followed the next year and Alix was pregnant with Louise during the Russian marriage festivities. Princess Victoria was born in July 1868 to be followed by Maud in 1869. Bertie and Alix's last child, Alexander John, named in part for Sasha, was born on 6 April 1871, but died later the next day at Sandringham. His death was an immense emotional shock to Alix, a blow which she really never recovered from.

In Russia, Minnie and Sasha were busy building a family of their own. Nicholas Alexandrovitch was born in May 1868. He would reign as Tsar Nicholas II in time. A second son followed the next year, baptized Alexander Alexandrovitch but the baby only lived from June 1869 until May 1870, dying at the imperial estate at Tsarskoye-Selo from spinal meningitis. It was said later that he was the child who Minnie loved the most. Certainly his untimely death emblazoned in her memory of a perpetual love she had for this lost child.

Just as did Alix at the death of her own baby Alexander John the following year, Minnie slipped into a depression which lasted many months.

Understandably, she was inconsolable. Her renowned effervescence was extinguished for some time while she distanced herself from court life. Her depression, however, was not appreciated by the Imperial Court. To them, it was quite normal to lose one or more children and it was then believed that the mother had to simply buck up and move on. The sisters were different. They came from a simple family where love prevailed. The loss of babies to both sisters was a tragedy they simply could not easily move passed.

George Alexandrovitch's birth followed the loss of baby Alexander. He was born in 1871. Minnie later confessed she worried about George's health as he had been conceived while she was still deep within a depressive state. She felt this might cause physical weakness in her child once born. Minnie may have been correct in her concerns as George would become the sickly child of the family and the first sibling to die as an adult. George was followed by the first daughter in the family, Xenia Alexandrovna, born in 1875, the year after the infamous Edinburgh wedding. Minnie's sister-in-law, Maria Alexandrovna (only daughter of Tsar Alexander II), had married Bertie's younger brother, Alfred, Duke of Edinburgh. The match was not successful and many problems arose from it, but Alix and Minnie had helped engineer it in order to further foster strong ties between Great Britain and imperial Russia. At home, Minnie gave birth to Xenia at the Anitchkov Palace, the home she and Sasha shared in the heart of the Russian capital. The two surviving older children had been born at Tsarskoye-Selo. Xenia was followed three years later, in 1878, by Michael Alexandrovitch, who also was born at the Anitchkov. The last of the Russian children arrived in 1882, a daughter named Olga Alexandrovna, who was born at the summer palace at Peterhof. Of all the children, only Olga was born after Sasha had already succeeded to the Russian throne.

The Anitchkov Palace became the official home of Sasha and Minnie on the day of their marriage. It had long been set aside as the official residence of the tsarevitch and tsarevna and thus it naturally came to Sasha and Minnie in time. They also had at their sole deposal the palace-fortress at Gatchina and in off-times they shared the use of the Alexander Palace at Tsarskoye-Selo with the tsar. When Minnie first arrived in Russia, Alexander II made the 'Cottage Palace' at Peterhof her own. She owned it outright which was uncommon in the Romanov family whose members typically only had lifetime use of a palace while remaining property of the state.

The 'Cottage Palace' was Minnie's only actual home, the only residence registered in her own name.[1] It stood within the 1,500 acre great park at Peterhof in a section known as the Alexandria Gardens, named for the wife of Nicholas I. This park was designed in the English landscape style with long lanes lined by English plain trees, heavily wooded, winding bridle paths and hidden follies with spaces dotted by beautiful fountains and just before at the crest of the property's hill, the expanse of the Baltic coast opening wide vistas out to the sea. This section of the Peterhof property contained numerous homes and villas including four larger ones used exclusively by the tsar and his immediate family; one of these being the 'Cottage Palace.' This home was more a large house than it was a palace; it was certainly miniscule by Romanov standards. Built in a mixture of neo-Gothic and Queen Ann styles in 1829, it was painted bright yellow and white, and by 1850 it became the routine summer dacha of the tsar and his family. This cozy house stood within a small flower garden of its own, nestled high on a hillside overlooking the Gulf of Finland far below; and once she came to Russia as a bride, and because of its fine vistas, it became the favored vacation home of Sasha and Minnie and their growing family. Minnie gloried in her personal ownership of the "Cottage Palace" which would remain until the revolution, her only legal residence in Russia.[2]

The Anitchkov Palace in Saint Petersburg is an "E" shaped five story, stucco and limestone building built in the baroque style between 1741 and 1750, but in 1854 neo-classical elements were added to give it its present exterior appearance.[3] It prominently stands to this day on the Nevsky Prospekt, the finest boulevard in Saint Petersburg. It was built at the intersection of the Prospekt and the Fontanka Canal as a gift of the Empress Elizabeth to her favorite lover, Alexis Razumovsky. It takes its name from Colonel Mikhail Anitchkov who erected a military compound on the site during the time of Peter the Great's building of the imperial city. The palace eventually passed to Catherine the Great who gave it to her paramour, Prince Gregory Potemkin, and after his death in 1791 it returned to the crown after which it was reserved exclusively for the imperial family.

Saint Petersburg is crisscrossed by canals as Peter the Great selected a vast swampland on which to build his new capital. He intentionally faced the city outward-looking towards Europe and the West. Because of its many canals Saint Petersburg is known as the "Venice of the North." Peter's great empire was western in all aspects, at least this is how Peter himself defined it, and his capital city was to contain no elements of traditional oriental Russia. The palaces that grew up in the new capital and on vast estates surrounding it were, therefore, thoroughly European and modern; most designed mainly of the Italian rococo or baroque schools to begin with; later additions were the finest examples of neo-classical and Palladian style architecture to be found anywhere in Europe.

All of the palaces built on the canals of the city faced the waterway on which they stood, not the adjacent public avenue, as access to each compound was traditionally by way of the water until ca. 1850. Therefore, the Anitchkov Palace was built so that the front facade was hidden from the road. The grand entry looked out onto the waterway rather than upon the Nevsky but later a massive gatehouse fronting the Nevsky Prospekt was added once access to imperial homes shifted from the canals to the new grand boulevards of the city. Although the palace was large, the grounds around the residence were minimal with only the open space between the banks of the canal and the palace facade available for walking and taking fresh air.[4] Alexander II made a lifetime gift of the palace to Sasha and his bride-to-be and it was here that Minnie came to live whenever they were in the capital. It was here also that their young family called home, where they lived as small children, where intimate family gatherings were always held, and where Minnie's Danish and Greek family came for occasional visits. Thus it was also to the Anitchkov that Bertie and Alix and their children came for their rare sojourns in Russia.

When Sasha became tsar after the assassination of his father in 1881, he and Minnie decided to move to the fortified Gatchina estate where they and the children could be totally protected from Nihilists who were attacking Romanovs and their ministers with great frequency, but when in the capital the couple continued to live at the Anitchkov, preferring it over the immense Winter Palace. Also, as the Anitchkov was more easily protected than the Winter Palace could ever be with its sixty or more separate entrances. The Anitchkov would remain Minnie's city palace in widowhood as well, calling it home until the onset of the revolution.[5]

After her marriage to Sasha, and the formal move into the Anitchkov, Minnie soon learned that dirt and disorder were the rule of the day in Russian imperial homes. Although the structures looked extremely impressive, and the staff that manned each palace was dressed in costly liveries of satin and gold lace, Russian household officials and staff thought nothing of the dirt and dust abounding in every corner of every room in every imperial palace. Dagmar set out at once to correct the malaise which infected her Russian staff and together she and Sasha began to create an official household structure to manage their official life as the heirs to the throne. Their closest collaborators became two young married couples, the Count and Countess Vorontsov-Daskov and the Count and Countess Obolensky. These two couples would form intimate friendships with Sasha and Minnie which would last their lifetimes. The two young men were officers of the same regiment headed by Sasha and both were well-acquainted with the peculiarities of his personality and his managerial style. The two young women were quite sophisticated and were well-bred women of the Russian Imperial Court. Each offered the young tsarevna many insights into the byzantinesque labyrinth of court life in Saint Petersburg. Tanya Obolensky was the livelier of the two women and soon became Minnie's closest friend in Russia. She bubbled with fun and mischief mirroring the tsarevna's own sense of humor and fondness for practical joking. Tanya was also a brilliant dresser and came to teach Minnie the fine art and great allure of couture at the Russian Court.

Tanya's effervescence was offset by the more reserved Tatiana Daskov who descended from one of the oldest and most aristocratic of the original Muscovite noble families. Tatiana presented herself with distinctive grace and a sense of majesty which only ladies born into historic families could ever carry off. Her innate dignity caused genuine awe in even the most cynical and jealous of Russian women. It was Tatiana's carriage and deportment, which

Minnie keenly observed, and which soon enough she perfectly mimicked, so as to create her own style. This deportment quickly became Minnie's own for the rest of her life.

While Marie Feodorovna was settling into her new role as the wife of the tsarevitch, learning everything that Russia had to offer her, Sasha was not particularly an ideal and loving husband at home. The fault, in part, lie at the feet of Sasha's wayward brothers, Vladimir and Alexis, who were known for their desolate and depraved lifestyles. The two younger grand dukes frequented notorious nightclubs where prostitutes and courtesans abounded. Such was the vile nature of the orgies in these nightclubs, and such was the quantity of vodka and champagne allegedly consumed by the young grand dukes, that it was said that Sasha's health had been ruined since his marriage by his nightly escapades with women of ill repute and with his comrades from the army who paraded untold numbers of willing lovers before him. It was a parade of women which Sasha was initially eager and willing to experience nearly every night of the week.

Although Minnie understood the rumors surrounding Sasha to probably be true, she never spoke of them to her husband, to her sister in England, or to her parents in Denmark. Of course her relatives learned of these matters soon enough by way of reports from their ambassadors in Saint Petersburg who were always willing to include torrid details of the imperial family in their reports home. It was soon clear that Minnie had married a belligerent and obstinate man with the personality of an enraged lion, but at home with his wife; Sasha was always tender, attentive, and loving. Tsar Alexander II, and the court officials surrounding him, realized that asha was not properly prepared to become tsar, but stubborn as he was neither the tsar nor his administration could convince Sasha to take on an educational regimen that would properly prepare him for the throne. It fell to Minnie, therefore, to undertake the task of preparing her husband to succeed to the throne. A tsar had to grasp the intricacies of Russian and continental history, he had to come to know the makeup of the many peoples that populated his empire, and he had to understand fully the economy of the Russian Empire, how the empire functioned, how his huge army operated, and how politics in the European sphere affected Russia and her interests.

For all intent and purposes, at the time of their marriage, Sasha was as ignorant as any Siberian peasant in all of these disciplines. His two youngest brothers, Serge, then ten years old, and Paul, then only eight years old, were already better educated and more prepared to be tsar than their older brother who had escaped all forms of formal education simply because his was too difficult a personality to be around and everyone, even the tutors, who had been hand-picked by Tsar Alexander II to train him, avoided the tsarevitch at every opportunity.

And so once married and luxuriously installed in Russia, with Sasha and his brothers celebrating in decadent nightspots outside the capital night after night, at her father-in-law's instigation Minnie prepared a regimen which would bring her new husband up to speed and well-prepared to inherit the imperial crown. The couple shared a large bedroom and a shared marital bed, which was more uncommon than common within the Russian imperial family. Despite his adventures at night, Sasha sincerely loved Marie Feodorovna, but in those first few months Sasha seldom arrived home before dawn, only shortly prior to Minnie being awakened for breakfast by one of her chambermaids. Upon rising Minnie typically found a huge snoring ruin beside her, unconscious and buried beneath fur blankets against the bitter cold Russian winter dawn. Permitting her husband only three or four hours to sleep Minnie had Sasha awakened each morning at nine o'clock ordering his servants to prepare his bath and his clothes for dressing before he was awakened, and then she insisted that he sit at the partner's desk that she had installed in their suite where she had already chosen several tomes for both to read through the week, each book in their own way describing histories or politics which he would need to master as tsar.

At first this educational process was cold and painful for the couple as Sasha could not commit his mind to what he was reading nor did Minnie herself find it of much interest as she had never been bookish by nature, but after two or three weeks' time Sasha began to discuss with Minnie various topics which they had earlier studied together. It was then that Minnie understood that her efforts were bearing fruit, something that endeared her further to the tsar. In time Sasha began to enjoy his daily sessions and soon after several experts were introduced to expound upon political issues, Russian and international law, diplomacy, and the history and religions of the diverse population of the empire.

One such expert would come to the Anitchkov to teach the tsarevitch and would remain thereafter at his side for the remainder of his life, negatively shaping policy in Russia for nearly four decades.[6] As a result of this new influence, especially as Sasha's mind could easily be molded if he enjoyed spending time with a tutor thus embracing what he had to offer Sasha, policies would develop that would darken Russian history as a consequence.[7] This particular bureaucrat began his palace career as tutor to all the sons of Alexander II, but he initially found the then-second son, Sasha, to be so dimwitted he paid scant attention to him. It was not until the death of Nicholas Alexandrovitch when Sasha became heir to the throne that this ambitious man found his permanent protégé.

Constantine Petrovitch Pobedonostsev was born in Moscow in 1827. In maturity he became an uncompromising conservative, indeed an arch-reactionary and staunch anti-Semite. After high school he entered the Orthodox seminary as a divinity student developing a diet of extreme views. His greatest hope was a return to a Russia of the fifteenth century when the church controlled every aspect of Russian life, standing at the side of an all-powerful, dictatorial tsar-autocrat. Pobedonostsev favored the absolute power of the tsar, opposed any ideas of a representative body for Russia, and showed a deep hatred for the liberal views of Alexander II. He boldly expressed his own extreme opinions which outraged most of the libertine courtiers surrounding Sasha's father. He was still young when he began to tutor Sasha and so his influence through the decades ran long and deep.

In time, after Nicholas died and Sasha unexpectantly became heir, Pobedonostsev returned to Sasha and Minnie at Alexander II's insistence regularly lecturing the couple three times each week. He soon re-emerged as the man who molded the next tsar's opinions and created in him a thorough xenophobic outlook. They identified everything which was not pure Russian as aggressively anti-Russian. Pobedonostsev was an uncompromising conservative, indeed an arch-reactionary in the extreme. He favored the absolute power of the tsar in Russia and most of all he held a virulent hatred for Jews, Germans and Catholic Poles. In his conservatism, Pobedonostsev absolutely refused to come to terms with any form of modernity.[8] Having observed Minnie and Sasha during those first six months spent lecturing them, the 'professor' concluded that his two 'pupils' lived *like children in the wilderness, like nothing more than sheep.*[9]

Sadly Minnie initially fell under the spell of Pobedonostsev, but not to the same extent of her husband. Nevertheless, Minnie was tainted all the same as she initially embraced these prejudices as fostered by Pobedonostsev. Whereas Sasha came to hate the Jews, Germans and Catholics as much as Pobedonostsev, a bigotry which never lessoned, Minnie's reaction was more of suspicion of all non-Russian, non-Orthodox elements in Russia. Her Danish upbringing would not permit hatred to take root, with the sole exception, however, of that for all things German. Sasha hated the Germans because they formed a threat to his empire. Minnie hatred of Prussia came with her from Denmark as a result of Prussia's invasion of Schleswig-Holstein. It could never be said of her that she came to hate other peoples the same way Sasha had but she never felt comfortable with any group within Russia which was neither ethnically Russian or non-adherents of the Orthodox faith. In addition to these prejudices, Pobedonostsev also fostered an obstinate adherence to the principal of divine right of kings, which both Sasha and Minnie were quick to embrace.[10]

With Minnie and Sasha under their tutor's spell, Tsar Alexander regretted reintroducing Pobedonostsev into his son and daughter-in-law's life. This change in the tsarevna ran against everything her liberal parents, and humanistic Denmark, had instilled in her. Alix noted these changes in her sister, as well, hoping they would disperse once Minnie had been exposed to a wider education. In time this would indeed come to pass but Alix and Bertie, filled with reports from the British ambassador about changes in the heir to the throne and his young wife, became deeply concerned. Queen Victoria thought Minnie frivolous and flighty and did not hesitate in saying so to both Alix and

Bertie. Although Minnie's earlier (somewhat) liberal grounding neutralized much of Pobedonostsev's teaching, in time the tsar and her British and Danish relations soon realized that Sasha could not live without Pobedonostsev by his side.[11]

The only seemingly positive influence of Pobedonostsev on Sasha was his insistence that Sasha move away from the decadent lifestyle of his bachelor days and away from a social mix led by his wayward brothers— Vladimir and Alexis. In this the tutor was successful as history relates that Sasha never again strayed from his wife, becoming a model, faithful and devoted husband and a good (if not foreboding) father by the close of his first year of marriage. Unfortunately, Bertie did not walk a similar path in his marriage.

Meanwhile the hoped-for marriage alliance between imperial Russia and Great Britain (that of Alfred of Edinburgh and Grand Duchess Maria Alexandrovna) would never prove the success which Alix and Minnie had planned for. The Duchess of Edinburgh, as Maria would be known after marriage, never came to like or appreciate England. She thought herself far superior in breeding and education to Queen Victoria's family, she found London unbearably dirty, the constant rain intolerable, and she never ceased resenting her precedence at Court beneath Alix and at times even beneath the queen's lackluster daughters.[12] Alfred was away as a naval officer for much of each year. His drinking and irritable personality persisted, further alienating both his wife and the British royal family and despite several children born to their union, the couple never grew to love each other as anticipated and they quickly grew apart.[13]

In August a great family reunion took place at Coburg where the queen unveiled the statue she had commissioned of her late husband, the Prince Consort. It was not a happy family gathering as most of the royal family did not wish to make the journey to remote Thuringia. Nearly all of the queen's relations were also at odds with one another at this time, hopes for a happy reunion impossible, and so this cantankerous family had no desire to reunite at Coburg. Alix alone showed good humor throughout the family visit even though she alone amongst them despised being anywhere in Germany. Her good nature made the occasion bearable for the queen who could no longer manage her adult children's moods and disagreements. Lady Geraldine Somerset, who accompanied the queen on this visit, described the family as *"constantly quarreling and close to fisticuffs with the exception, of course, of our dear little Princess Alix."*[14]

The year 1865 was indeed one of great bickering and disagreement amongst members of the British royal family because the queen's family was deeply divided over the proposition of Princess Helena (Queen Victoria's third daughter and fifth child) marrying a minor prince of Schleswig-Holstein-Sonderburg-Augustenburg. Prince Christian was fifteen years older than his bride-to-be but because of premature ageing, the British public actually thought him to be decades her senior. Princess Helena, known within the family as Lenchen, was no prize herself. She was the least attractive of the queen's daughters, not at all pretty by the standards of the day, extremely short in stature with a huge protruding bust; she lacked the charm and beauty of her sisters and certainly was outshone by Alix in every way. Prince Christian was neither good-looking, nor rich; he was neither young nor engaging and he lacked the charm necessary to fit well into English royal life. But he had one attribute which Queen Victoria favored; he was willing to leave Germany for a life lived within the queen's circle, residing by Lenchen's side while living in the queen's various homes so that Helena could remain her confidential private secretary. Queen Victoria was determined to get her way in this marriage. She already lost Alice in marriage to the Grand Duke of Hesse-Darmstadt and she would not lose Lenchen to another foreign marriage. And so as the queen saw it, Prince Christian was the best available option. Lenchen agreed. Christian badly needed an annual income, prestigious places to reside, and the security offered as a son-in-law of the Queen of England. In her own mind, Helena needed to be married and to have a home of her own although she agreed to remain close to her mother so as to continue to act as her confidential secretary. It was Vicky in Berlin who proposed Christian as he was a close friend to her and her husband Crown Prince Frederick. Nearly all of the younger members of the queen's family likewise endorsed the marriage but not so the Waleses, Alice and Louis in Darmstadt, or Alfred.[15]

Alice, who by this time had grown into mature independence, was the only one of Victoria's children to stand openly in defiance of her mother when she believed the queen to be wrong. She publicly declared against the marriage. A series of ruptures between the queen and her second daughter had already taken place since Alice's marriage and now Alice's open opposition to Helena's marriage to Prince Christian furthered the breach between the two women. Alice was convinced the queen was sacrificing her third daughter's happiness in order to keep her at her side as secretary and she found Christian to be far too old and inappropriate as a spouse for her sister. Bertie and Alix on the other hand vehemently opposed the marriage because Christian's family, as subdivision of Alix's own family, had sided with Prussia and Austria against Denmark in the recent war to seize Schleswig and Holstein. Christian himself had publicly proposed German annexation of the two duchies. Christian and Victoria's children were third cousins, both sides descendent of Frederick, Prince of Wales, father of King George III, but those opposed to this marriage would neither treat him as cousin or friend and certainly would not accept him as a new brother. Queen Victoria, vexed with most of her children, was expecting a visit at Balmoral by Bertie and Alix but she was apprehensive as to how the visit would go off because of the severity of the family rift, writing to her uncle King Leopold:

> *"I fear that when Bertie and Alix arrive the hubbub will commence, but I will not allow it to do so. I had much to go through with his marriage, which was disliked by all her family."*[16]

After the visit ended, Victoria was later pleased to report to her uncle that Bertie and Alix had now taken a natural liking to Helena's marriage and would cause no further difficulties. But this was not so as Alix would never come to warm to her cousin Christian or would Bertie forgive him the hurt he had caused her family. For Princess Alice and her brother Alfred they, too, had come to somewhat change their opinion of the marriage. Although they still believed that Helena was being sacrificed so that the queen could keep her as secretary, both realized that Helena saw this marriage as her only way of leaving Victoria's control. They came to realize their sister actually desired the alliance despite the great differences existing between her and Christian. As each member of the family eventually, albeit reluctantly, became reconciled with the idea of the inevitability of Helena's marriage, the same cannot be said for the government or the British people in general who saw Lenchen's marriage as an abominable, disgraceful act binding her to a miserable starving German princeling.[17] Great Britain in general showed a great distaste for the queen's constant importation of Germans as marriage partners for her children. This most recent marriage between the naive princess and an older, droll German princeling as well as Christian's age and apparent poverty only increased British opposition to the marriage.[18]

CHAPTER EIGHT

THE ALEXANDRA LIMP

ON 15 FEBRUARY 1867 A heavily pregnant Alix began to complain of severe pain and constant chill, but as was usual Bertie was sufficiently disinterested to break his schedule of engagements at Windsor in order to return to his wife in London. Alix had remained behind at Marlborough House while Bertie went out to Windsor for a few days of engagements. The doctors attending Alix additionally diagnosed rheumatic fever, the cause of the severe pain in her leg and hip. It was only after dispatching three urgent telegrams to Bertie, each worded with more urgency than the previous cable, each using a more severe tone towards him than the previous, did the Prince of Wales finally return to the capital. During the next five days Alix suffered acute pain radiating in her hip and down her leg. The doctors were unable to administer any known pain relief because of her advanced pregnancy.

On 20 February an infant daughter was born and was given the names Louise Victoria Alexandra Dagmar. When Queen Victoria arrived at Marlborough House on 25 February to inspect her new granddaughter, she was shocked and horrified to see how ill Alix really was. Bertie had sent his mother numerous telegrams downplaying the crisis and so the queen expected her to be bright and energetic by the time she arrived to see both mother and baby. Victoria's sincere affection for, and comforting approach to, her daughter-in-law was in stark contrast to Bertie's daily absences which was a genuine trial for Alix to bear. In Bertie's defense, however, it must be said that he was not really wanted in the sick room as he tended to get in everyone's way. Although he did have his working desk moved beside Alix's bed, so that he could respond to the piles of correspondence received each day, as well as to enjoy her company for a few hours every afternoon, Bertie realized that his wife was in good hands and so there was little else he could do for her. Restless by nature, Bertie was always easily bored, and time hung heavily on his hands.[1]

Lady Macclesfield, one of Alix's primary ladies-in-waiting, complained about Bertie's behavior on numerous occasions during Alix's long recovery from post-partum rheumatic fever. For instance, when King Christian's mother, Louise-Caroline died in Saxony, it was decided by the Princess of Wales' doctors that the news of her grandmother's death should only be broken to Alix at the most opportune moment. They feared the harm such sad news would cause her. That same day her doctors examined Alix's stiff knee, roughly moving it in every direction to ascertain the degree of possible permanent stiffness. The examination caused her great pain. Lady Macclesfield heard loud sobbing coming from the princess' bedroom but it was not because of the pain just brought on by the doctors. Rather, it was Bertie's tactlessness. Despite strict doctors' orders, Bertie callously informed Alix about her grandmother's passing. Once the deed was done, he brushed past Lady Macclesfield without a care as he exited the bedroom: *"he is really a child about such things and will not listen to advice,"* Macclesfield is known to have said to Alix as she tried to calm her mistress.[2] Although a husband, and already three times a father, at only twenty-six Bertie was still very emotionally immature. His insensitivity has been credited too many flaws in his personality but in reality it was Bertie's inability to tolerate boredom in any form that most often led to his insensitive and sometimes cruel treatment of his wife.

Queen Louise arrived in London to see for herself the extent of the health of her daughter. As planned, King Christian arrived two days later. The arrival of father and mother greatly cheered up their daughter but it did not cause improvement in her overall health condition. Not until 20 April did the doctors find any sign of improvement and it was not until baby Louise's baptism that Alix left her room for the first time. The christening took place on 10 May 1867. Alix attended the christening ceremony in a wheelchair as the rheumatic fever had now left one leg permanently stiff and prone to swelling. The onset of the ill effects of this disease simultaneously saw a worsening of Alix's growing deafness. As a consequence, the Princess of Wales now turned to a small circle of trusted friends and to her children for comfort as her growing loss of hearing became more and more problematic. She also surrounded herself with her beloved dogs and made a clear effort to avoid Court life and London society as much as possible. Inevitably, Bertie, who was never domestically oriented, looked elsewhere for companionship and camaraderie and for new sexual adventures.[3]

The same night their daughter Princess Louise was christened, Bertie set off on an official visit to Paris to tour the 1867 Paris Exposition but not all of his time was devoted to the official functions associated with the visit. Sir William Knollys, a senior A.D.C. accompanying Bertie on the trip, reported in his diary with a great level of disapproving indignation: *"we had supper after the opera with some of the infamous female Paris notorieties, etc., etc."*[4] From all reliable accounts, the Prince of Wales spent most of his evenings in Paris in dalliances with both women of society and women of far lesser renown and the City of Lights took note.

Despite her husband's rampant infidelity, Alix retained an inner serenity. She no longer paid outward notice to what others knew or said about her husband's nocturnal activities. The princess's discretion and serenity was absolute. It wasn't known if she had known of the Saint Petersburg prostitutes which shared his evenings, including bathing in champagne with several women at a time, during Minnie and Sasha's wedding festivities, or of all the Paris beauties during his all-too-frequent visits to the French capital in which he often engaged in a *ménage à trois* at the city's most exclusive brothel *Le Chabanais*, or of his relationships with fashionable aristocratic ladies of Britain or a host of other infidelities more or less in the public forum. However stoically Alix bore these hardships, the public humiliation of her husband's absence in Paris during her recuperation was the hardest for her to bear especially as her parents were with her and thus she could not hide Bertie's coolness to her. Now London and Paris society knew that while his wife lay sick at Marlborough House Bertie was indiscreetly amusing himself elsewhere.[5]

Some weeks after returning from Paris, as a show of his concern for his wife and as a way to tamp down unwelcome commentary, Bertie took Alix to Wiesbaden to help her find a heath cure, once again against the explicit wishes of the queen.[6] Victoria dreaded the proximity of Wiesbaden to the castle at Rumppenheim owned by Queen Louise and her family and she also disapproved of Bertie's gambling at foreign horseracing courses, which he surely would enjoy doing during the proposed upcoming visit. Victoria also complained bitterly about the cost of all of these journeys. Somehow she found an accurate accounting of the money that Bertie had already spent on the purchase of new jewels when outside of England. Of course not all of these jewels were destined for Alix, as the Prince of Wales loved nothing more than to present an exquisite bobble of great value to a favored mistress or new paramour. The queen naively believed all these purchases were intended for his wife wondering aloud to her ladies *"what woman could want so many pieces of new jewelry when she already had more jewels than she could ever wear."*[7] The queen's perverse interest in her son's financial excesses and his outlandish lifestyle was a small matter compared with Alix's insulting behavior towards the king of Prussia while Bertie was away from Wiesbaden for the evening. The king sent a telegram to their hotel announcing to the Princess of Wales he wished to pay a courtesy call upon her that evening or during the following day.

Alix ignored the telegram altogether as if she had never received it. Bertie did not learn of it until he returned to Wiesbaden later that night. As Alix, with hatred for all things Prussian, refused to even consider meeting the Prussian monarch, Bertie had to brush aside his wife's rudeness by informing the king that he would call upon him instead the following morning. He used as his excuse Alix's recent illness, writing that she was too ill to receive visitors. This would have sufficed, and a diplomatic gaffe would have been avoided, had Alix not defied Bertie further by leaving Wiesbaden in an open carriage early the following morning, appearing to all who saw her progress to the train station to be the personification of robust health. She and her ladies were destined for Rumppenheim so as to be present at Alix's grandfather's funeral. Victoria made her position clear; if Alix was well enough to attend the rigors of a public funeral she was certainly well enough to receive the King of Prussia. In what could best be described as merely a courteous diplomatic gesture on the part of the king, the princess denying the monarch's desire to call on her had become a negative diplomatic incident creating unwanted tension between Britain and Prussia. Bertie was furious with his wife for her public rudeness to the king, as was his sister Crown Princess Victoria as the king was her father-in-law. He hurried to Rumpenheim and the funeral, and while there Vicky dispatched a telegram to her sister Alice in nearby Darmstadt asking her to speak to Bertie and Alix as quickly as possible after the funeral in order to undo any affront Alix's actions had caused. Bertie saw this as a dressing down by his older sister, whom he greatly resented, but he unleashed his anger on Alix instead since she had been the source of all the trouble in the first place. Alix saw the two sisters' interference as yet another unacceptable intrusion into her personal life. For some time afterward she refused to communicate with either woman.

Naturally, neither Bertie nor Alice could persuade Alix to be conciliatory towards the Prussians. Ever since the Schleswig and Holstein wars Alexandra's antipathy for all things German never changed. In this her sister Minnie, her mother Queen Louise, her brother George I of Greece and many other Danish royals were likewise unbending.[8] Bertie turned to his mother-in-law Louise who was likewise at Rumppenheim for her father's funeral. He begged Louise to persuade Alexandra to lay aside her personal feelings, something Louise was willing to do despite her own personal feelings because as a queen she fully understood the necessities of diplomacy between nation-states. But while Bertie was with his mother-in-law discussing how best to undo the damage caused by his wife, a further telegram arrived at the castle. King Wilhelm informed Queen Louise that he now intended to call upon her the following day so as to offer Prussian condolences at the death of the queen's father. Louise initially agreed to receive the king despite her own serious misgivings and still lingering feelings against Prussia. She would do so for the good of Denmark, but when Alix learned of the Prussian king's intent to call upon her mother as well, she became incensed, considering King Wilhelm's insistence as just another brutal Prussian attack on her family. A heated argument ensued in the presence of Queen Louise and Sir William Knollys but a determined Alix would not yield to Bertie's attempt at reasoning. After digging in her heels with each of Bertie's arguments, rather than respond to them, she simply stood in silence, smiled at her mother, and leaning heavily on a her walking stick, she finally hobbled with great dignity from the room as if nothing serious had even been discussed. Furor overtook Bertie as a result which no one, including Queen Louise, could extinguish and so he too stormed out of the castle, disappearing for a time into the gardens not to be seen again for an hour. Politically, Bertie could not let the matter drop as it would reflect badly on his mother and on her government and so in response he sent a telegram to the Prussian king without informing Alexandra. Bertie invited the king to call upon them both at Rumpenheim the following day. Because the Prussian monarch was coming to Rumppenheim where many members of the Danish and Hesse-Cassel families had gathered for the funeral, both families grew anxious at this news. As a result, Alix's extended family, her vital support system, quickly packed their belongings and left the castle early the following morning before the wily Prussian king could arrive. Alix, now isolated from her relations, grew even angrier, anger that she now directed squarely at Bertie for orchestrating the unwanted visit.[9]

Despite hurt feelings, and realizing she had lost the diplomatic dance orchestrated by the adept Prussians, Alix had no choice but to be present when the king arrived.[10] She waited in the salon at Rumppenheim where Bertie intended to escort the king for their meeting. Also waiting in the room was Sir William Knollys who was again serving as Bertie's aide-de-camp. While others present were somewhat distracted, Knollys commented that the Princess of Wales looked extremely pale, asking her if she was ill. Alexandra responded as haughtily as she could manage:

> *"Maybe I am pale but it is not from cold but from anger at being obliged to see the King of Prussia. And what I mind most of all is that it is a consequence of those two old women,*

the Prince of Wales' sisters, interfering or I should not have been obliged to do so."[11]

Alix, now alone and without the support of her family, her household in support of Bertie and his mother, and Bertie still angry at her for her obstinate and careless actions, placed the blame for the necessity of her meeting the king squarely in the lap of her sister-in-law Vicky, whom Alix knew had telegraphed Queen Victoria demanding that Bertie and Alix receive the monarch. Alix's disdain stretched to Darmstadt, as well, and the three women—Alix, Vicky and Alice—would remain cool towards each other, never to be close again.

Queen Victoria was indeed involved as she should have been. To her Prime Minister, Lord Derby, [12] she expressed her feelings:

> *"The queen trusts that Lord Derby will take an opportunity of expressing both to the Prince and Princess of Wales the importance of not letting any private feelings to interfere with what are their public duties. Unfortunately the Princess of Wales has never understood her duties of this nature, making it her duty to follow Danish and Hessian advice. It is a great source of grief and anxiety to the queen for the future."*[13]

Returning home from the failed visit to Wiesbaden, and resettling once again into life at Marlborough House, Alix continued to recuperate from the damage done to her body from rheumatic fever. Initially she walked with two canes but eventually she was able to rely on only one for support. Her leg remained stiff thereafter and her off-balance walk became so admired by society ladies throughout Europe that in time it was mimicked as the most stylized manner of moving about. It became known as the *"Alexandra limp."*

Within five months of the Wiesbaden visit, and despite her permanent stiff leg, Alix had regained most of her muscular control. She could pick up her friend Lady Augustus Hervey and carry her from room to room and then laughingly fling her down onto a nearby sofa. Her sense of humor had returned and her sense of fun was intensified. She took up dance as beautifully as ever, always being the last, or near to the last, to retire each night, and in winter she again began to skate on the frozen lakes at Sandringham and Abergeldie.[14] Her gait was not normal but she was able to again enjoy the activities she loved most.

All fun aside, Alexandra was also determined to resume her official duties, particularly those at the side of her husband and she was most determined of all to accompany Bertie on his upcoming state visit to Ireland in 1868. Although motivated by a genuine desire to visit Ireland, something she had long wished to do, Alix was also concerned for her husband's safety as the previous year had been one fraught with disturbances by the Irish Fenian Brotherhood agitators who were fighting for a free Irish Republic and who typically fought for their new state by way of violent means. So violent where their attacks in Ireland and in England the previous year, that even at remote Sandringham, security measures had to be taken to protect the Wales family. Alexandra believed that her presence at her husband's side would mitigate any danger he may face while in Ireland, correctly as it turned out, for as she saw it, the Fenians would not harm her, or her husband when by her side. Queen Victoria wanted Bertie to make the journey but she was apprehensive about Alexandra accompanying him. Bertie and Alix sought the support of Prime Minister Disraeli who in the end pleaded Alexandra's cause with the queen:

> *"Is it not worth your Majesty's gracious consideration whether the good might not be doubled if His Royal Highness were accompanied by the Princess of Wales? Would it not add to the grace, and even the gaiety, of this historic event?"*[15]

Despite Disraeli's eloquence, Victoria was not convinced and this time the couple could not sway her. The press favored the Prince and Princess of Wales while the queen's family openly opposed Alexandra accompanying Bertie, but in the end it was Alix who once more won the day when she informed her mother-in-law that if she did not get official permission to stand by the side of her husband when he was facing real danger than she would go with him nevertheless and without official sanction. In her determination Alix wrote to the queen to plead her cause, saying:[16]

"I have a sort of very strong wish and feeling, if I may say so, to go with my Bertie this time to Ireland, and as three medical men don't see any objection, I feel I would much rather go than be left behind in a state of fever about him the whole time, which I don't think can be very good for me now. And as I really feel so well and my leg is so much stronger, I feel I can as well go to balls there than here and as for the journey I don't really much mind that. Besides, I know Lady Abercorn so well and she wrote me such a nice letter. I really think, and have a sort of conviction, that it will do me no harm and therefore have almost made up my mind to go with my Bertie. In these times, now I think one gets to feel more anxious about those loved ones most in the world and it makes me always feel anxious when we are obliged to be separated for a while, but in this case I confess I almost shudder to think of the possibility of his going alone, and I should feel dreadfully disappointed, if anything really were to prevent my going with him. I feel like a sort of call and wish to go. Please excuse this long explanation but I wish myself to tell you my feelings and wish about it and I hope dearest Mama that you understand all of this as I have not told my Bertie as I did not like to say anything about my private feelings for him, but to you dear Mama, who know what I mean, I could not help opening my heart to you."[17]

The Danes first invaded England in A.D. 1069, and now another Dane invaded Ireland, in turn, and with her the Irish people fell as deeply in love as had the English when Alexandra of Denmark first arrived as a young girl who had sailed across the sea to marry the British Prince of Wales. And at the side of Bertie during this Irish visit, he was not only safe from any danger as Alexandra knew he would be, but together they won over large numbers of Irishmen. Those that accompanied them on the journey attributed this success in large measure to the Princess of Wales knowing Bertie, with all his flaws, could never alone win-over the Irish people as she had done.

Alix's third child, Louise, was sickly and with Alix's prolonged convalescence, 1867 was a difficult year and yet by Christmas she informed Queen Victoria that she was once more pregnant. On 6 July of that year she gave birth to her second daughter and fourth child, Victoria Alexandra Olga Marie. Little Victoria was the queen's fourteenth grandchild and by this time the reclusive queen found the whole matter quite boring:

> *"This all becomes a very uninteresting thing—for it seems to me to go on like the rabbits in Windsor Park!"*[18]

By this time Bertie and Alix were married four and a half years and had produced two sons and two daughters thus securing the throne for the next generation. When Alix's leg stiffness did not improve with time, Sir James Paget, Queen Victoria's surgeon-in-attendance, suggested her rheumatism had been partially caused by the perpetual dampness pervading the original manor house on the Sandringham Estate, suggesting the Prince and Princess of Wales either remain in London or travel abroad for a time so as to avoid it. Bertie loved Sandringham more than anything else and wanted to make his home there the showplace of England and so he commissioned experts to study the original house and the damp conditions said to pervade there to see what could be done to correct them. He was advised that the premises were indeed infected with serious mold and mildew and that the house had to be demolished with a new replacement house built were this problem to be successfully corrected. As the project would take more than a year to complete Bertie secured permission from the queen to spend the winter abroad.

At this time, Bertie found himself deeply in debt and yet Sandringham had to be rebuilt. The Wales' did not have access to the open treasury of Russia as did Minnie and Sasha where their slightest whim or desire instantly became reality no matter how extravagant nor did they enjoy many tens of thousands of extra pounds sterling per year in added income generated from Marie Alexandrovna's dowry which she and Alfred enjoyed enthusiastically. Bertie was in heavy debt and Alix's spending and charitable giving continued to go unchecked.

Neither the princess' lack of money-sense nor her husband's gambling excesses where the real cause for their financial troubles. The drain on their income was almost entirely due to the enormous expenditures required at Sandringham where an elaborate program of improvements had been embarked upon well in excess of the actual value of the estate. Without counting the money spent in rebuilding the house itself, which was believed to be at a cost of £80,000,[19] the Prince of Wales spent on improvement projects on the estate between 1863 and 1867 more than his annual income from the Duchy of Cornwall created; sums at least £20,000 more than he had earned.[20] The original Sandringham House and the surrounding estate, in time built up to include twenty thousand acres, in no way could be considered suitable for a royal residence, and yet the Waleses spent so much of each year there, it clearly being their favorite home, that the royal household had to add the estate to the formal list of residences of the royal family. It was at unfathomable expense, therefore, money that Bertie and Alix simply did not have that the Prince and Princess of Wales eventually transformed their unacceptable quiet country retreat into a massive, full-fledged royal palace.

Despite identifying substantial amounts of mold and mildew, which substantially contributed to Alix's rheumatic fever condition, and despite a firm commitment to rebuild, the original Sandringham House was still standing in 1865 because Albert Jenkins Humbert, the architect of record, had not yet succeeded in producing a satisfactory design for a new home which pleased both Bertie and Alix.[21] The two could not agree on the original floor plan designs. Despite this, work had already begun in creating new kitchens with service corridors and several other grand rooms which were initially freestanding structures but which would be incorporated into the new residence once the plans had been approved and once building began in earnest. Besides the kitchens, the new billiard room and an indoor bowling alley were two of the structures begun at once.

The estate itself was in no better condition than the house at this time and required another fortune to be spent to bring it up to modern English standards. New farms in the area were purchased so as to increase the total acreage held by the estate, old farms were repaired and housing across the property was either newly built or generally improved.[22]

What Bertie did care keenly about was the great numbers of pheasants and partridges which abounded on the estate. Sandringham's game warden preserved these numbers with great determination which caused talk even in a generation when landlords as a whole were fanatical on the subject of game preservation. This was not so as to populate the various species; it was to produce enough numbers of each to be killed in shoots staged weekly at the estate. This form of game management at Sandringham made Bertie very unpopular amongst his tenant farmers. That unpopularity, however, never touched Alix who was adored by the people of Norfolk as much as she was by all in London.

At Sandringham in those early days hunting was almost as important as shooting.[23] Foxhunting at Sandringham was a major past-time, one that Alix herself very much enjoyed but which Queen Victoria found a horror for a lady of her high rank and standing. At one point Queen Victoria actually forbade her daughter-in-law to hunt at all arguing that everyone would be shocked at the spectacle of seeing a Princess of Wales mounted on a horse running a fox into the ground. At first Alix was distressed by the queen's order but soon enough she had her own way and was soon back in the saddle; the queen being wise enough to let the matter drop. When it came to her daughter-in-law, the queen was learning to pick the fights she could win. When Alix was pregnant and could not hunt she drove herself in a small carriage to meet with those who had earlier ridden out. Typically, she drove her team and carriage so recklessly that this too caused the queen to complain to Bertie.

Despite the luxuriousness of a visit to Sandringham once the new house was finished, which would not happen until they returned from a six month long stay abroad, guests still had two major causes for complaint—the bitter cold Norfolk climate which Alix loved because it reminded her of home, and Norfolk's dampness which did not seem to bother either the prince or the princess. Most difficult of all for the guests, however, were the extremely late hours kept by their hosts. Bertie and Alix were night owls and in monarchies, then as now, it is considered ill-mannered for guests to retire for the night before their hosts have slipped away, most certainly before the senior royalty present had departed for the night. After a typical meal consisting of between nine and eleven full courses, often more, and lasting up to three hours, guests would retire to the billiard room for a night of cards and genteel gambling; whist or poker were typically played Monday evenings through Saturday while charades or other games without gambling would be the fair on Sunday evenings.[24]

Although Bertie was always downstairs at a reasonable hour each morning, Alix never appeared before eleven o'clock at the earliest, having taken her typically Danish style breakfast in her suite before summoning her maids to help her to dress.[25] Very thin her entire life, Alix actually enjoyed a very hearty appetite and ate far more than a woman wishing to remain thin and healthy would today. The country air in Norfolk seemed to only increase her robust appetite.

So exacerbated by both Alix's late rising and her unpunctuality at events held later in the day, Bertie secretly moved forward every clock on the estate by thirty minutes, a custom which would become known thereafter as 'Sandringham time' and which would remain in effect until the day Bertie's grandson King Edward VIII assumed the throne in 1936. This was also the forerunner of the American Daylight Savings Time as this practice added thirty minutes each day to the active time offered Bertie and his guests outdoors and as such they had more daylight hours in which to shoot.[26] As a hostess at Sandringham, as at all her royal residences, Alix was unparalleled. Her personal charm and wit won over even the most temperamental of guests and Bertie's penchant for the finest foods and wines made Sandringham, indeed Marlborough House, as well, the finest tables in Great Britain.

The British government decided that the Prince and Princess of Wales should travel on a diplomatic mission to Egypt stopping enroute with Alix's parents for a holiday in Denmark before moving on to Berlin and then Vienna before embarking at Venice for the crossing to Alexandria. Alix was thrilled at the opportunity of spending time with her parents who had not yet seen her youngest two children, Louise who had been named for her Danish grand-mother and the youngest, infant Princess Victoria.[27] True to her nature, Queen Victoria later decided that Bertie and Alix could only bring their two eldest children with them, princes Eddy and George, and only as far as Denmark, insisting that they return to England under her care while Bertie and Alix traveled on to Egypt. As for the girls, Queen Victoria refused to permit them to leave England at all pronouncing they were too young and too fragile to be spirited away from England because of a selfish whim of their mother. Alix collapsed into floods of tears at the news Queen Victoria would not permit the family to go as a group to visit her parents in Denmark. Alix believed her mother-in-law was acting out of spite because of her near psychotic dislike for King Christian and Queen Louise, which may very well have been the case. Bertie for once stood by the side of his aggrieved wife, writing a tactful letter to his mother explaining the reasons why they felt it necessary that all four children should accompany them to Copenhagen. He cited the frequent visits to England by his sisters Vicky and Alice who always came for visits with their mother with all their children in tow:

> *"It seems to me rather inconsistent not to accord to the one what is accorded to the others."*[28]

As the queen openly favored Vicky and Alice and their children, Bertie was wise in his approach. Therefore, having brilliantly prepared his argument in a thoughtful way, Queen Victoria had no choice but to change her mind but she did so with a great amount of rumbling to her ladies for days on end.

Rejoicing in their success with Queen Victoria, the Wales family set off for Paris in mid-November and afterwards spent six weeks in Copenhagen with Alix's parents. After a delightful family Christmas at Fredensborg, Bertie and Alix's saw their children off at Hamburg; the children, Dr. Paget, and the children's nurses sailed home on board the royal yacht, H.M.Y. *Osborne*, while Bertie and Alix continued on as planned to Berlin, Vienna, Venice, and ultimately Egypt. Bertie and Alix did not return home to their children in England until mid-May but when they did arrive it was full of memories of the wonders of the Orient that would hold Alix's fascination for the rest of her life.

That autumn Alix continued to seek treatment for her lame rheumatic leg and thereafter the family traveled north to Balmoral for a visit with the queen. The couple was now closer than they had been since their marriage, mainly because during these many months abroad Bertie had limited access to other women with whom he could continue his customary dalliances. As a consequence of this closeness during that winter abroad, on 26 November, their third daughter was born. She was given the name Maud.[29] The Waleses returned to Norfolk and a new, palatial country home at Sandringham[30] and there Alix's final confinement followed in late 1870 which brought on in her great bouts of depression and all-too-easy exhaustion. The queen became more and more concerned about the health of her daughter-in-law and that of her unborn infant. Despite this change in her mental health condition Alix continued to keep up with her public schedule, being certain to be present for all shared public events with Bertie, quite possibly to keep a closer eye on his activities.

On 6 April 1871 Alix gave birth at Sandringham to her third son and fifth and final child. As with all of her children's births, the new baby arrived early and with ease, but it was clear to the physicians in attendance that the child was not whole. The vicar from St. Mary Magdalene Church on the Sandringham Estate was quickly summoned to baptize the infant who died very early the following morning.[31] Both of the infant's parents were bitterly distressed at this family tragedy. Alix's grief surprised nobody, she was a gentle woman deeply wounded by the loss of her child as any grieving mother would be, but the household were moved by the profound reaction by Bertie who always remained aloof from the intimacy of family life, with tears rolling down his cheeks, sobbing audibly as he put his child's tiny body into the coffin, carefully arranging the white moiré pall around its body and the banks of white flowers placed upon the lid. Alix was not thought well-enough to attend her dead child's funeral, as was quite common in those days, and so she watched the somber procession to Saint Mary Magdalene Church from her bedroom window, Bertie walking hand-in-hand with his two eldest sons; the three princes dressed in matching grey kilts, black crêpe scarfs and stockings and black gloves.[32]

Despite the sad loss of his child, the British press was already weary of the Prince of Wales' extracurricular activities and troubled friendships and therefore showed him no mercy in his time of grief. One newspaper in Norfolk took great satisfaction in informing its readers of the baby's death:

> *"The infant prince died shortly after its birth, thus relieving the working classes of England from having to support hereafter another addition to the long roll of state beggars they at present maintain."*[33]

Rumors abounded that Bertie had sired numerous bastards and many children in his aristocratic circles seemed to resemble him quite distinctly. For Alix, the death of her last child heralded the end of marriage relations between her and Bertie and thereafter the Prince of Wales felt no compunction in seeking his pleasures outside of his marriage.

The Prince of Wales' affairs were becoming scandalous. What had been an open secret amongst his own social circle and in time amongst the wider British aristocracy was now being discussed with open disdain and condemnation in the public press and as a consequence in every public house and house party in the land. As Alix battled health issues, she continued to try to keep the fire of her husband's love alive, albeit now in a sexless marriage. It would prove to be a lost battle as months and years moved forward without any intimacy in the marriage at all.

In Russia, the fires of passion were still burning fiercely in Minnie and Sasha's marriage who were now seeing their own family grow. Although Minnie and Sasha's marriage was now a happy, stable one, Sasha having become a truly reformed and faithful husband, life in Russia for the tsarevitch and tsarevna was contentious and very dangerous. Change was soon in the air.

CHAPTER NINE

MINNIE THE TSAREVNA

Russia in the 1870s

IMPERIAL RUSSIA WAS RULED BY Alexander II for twenty six years. His reign stretched from 2 March 1855 to 13 March 1881 during which time the splendor of the Imperial Court was at its all-time zenith. The Romanovs had never been richer or more brilliant. On the one hand, Russia possessed ostentatious, fantastic wealth as epitomized by the ruling family; grandeur and splendor unmatched by any other court in Europe, including the prestigious Court of St. James in London. Under Tsar Alexander II, the Russian Imperial Court had reached the apex of its splendor.[1] The nobility delighted in glamorous displays. Every night in the social season saw a profusion of galas, balls, banquets, tableaux and colorful celebrations.

Sasha initially mirrored his father's political views. At the time of his marriage to Minnie, whose Danish upbringing was far more enlightened than most of her new Romanov relations, the tsarevitch continued to lean towards liberalism but Sasha was not well-educated and he could be easily swayed as a young man. Certainly he had not received the extensive education provided his late brother Nicholas, but both Sasha's father and his late brother's political outlook had influenced his own thinking as a young man. Minnie arrived in Russia with contemporary Scandinavian views, which were traditional but not reactionary. By Russian standards she and her family were quite libertine despite each of them viewing themselves as conservative. The first weeks of their marriage found the young couple squarely in line with the tsar's liberalization program. Their move towards conservatism, and later arch-reactionary autocracy, was still to come.

In 1872 a new and colorful personality entered Minnie's life. Born Duchess Marie of Mecklenburg-Strelitz in 1854, she married Alexander II's third son, Vladimir Alexandrovitch, Sasha's strong-willed younger brother. Vladimir was the most difficult and prickly of the tsar's sons. By Romanov standards, Vladimir had chosen well, but the way in which Marie of Mecklenburg came into the imperial family was quite unusual. She, too, was most unusual in every way. The duchess could best be described as being cocksure, nearly always acting accordingly. As a teenager Marie had seen Grand Duke Vladimir when he came to pay a visit to Germany and seeing the Russian entourage accompanying him in all its rich color and magnificence she decided then and there that a life as a Russian grand duchess should be her destiny. She broke off her engagement to a minor Austrian prince informing her father, Grand Duke Frederick Franz II of Mecklenburg-Strelitz that she desired to marry Vladimir instead.[2] And although Marie's determination was initially dismissed as teenage fancy, in time her father and his third wife agreed that a marriage to Vladimir would be a good match for Marie and a beneficial one for their family. As was the norm in those days in royal circles, Frederick Franz wrote to the tsar, sovereign-to-sovereign, suggesting the possibility of a marriage between their two children.

Marie Mecklenburg was tall, beautiful, and certainly possessed a commanding presence. Like Minnie, when she walked into a gathering, no matter how large or how small, the attention of those present immediately turned to her. Oddly enough, through her father's close rapport with the German chancellor, Marie also became friendly with Otto von Bismarck who was said to have praised the young woman for her forceful character and diplomatic insight. Bismarck knew high energy and superior intellect when he saw it and he was happy to have a new friend at the Russian Court, which was always ripe with intrigues against Germany. After coming to know Marie, Bismarck realized he could certainly rely on his young friend's continued support once she married into the Romanov family.

Vladimir was not initially impressed by Marie. His free time was filled with courtesans, great beauties and high-class prostitutes and as one of the richest men in the world, and one of the most entitled, he was not looking to settle down. In the end, however, Vladimir acquiesced to his father's demands as the tsar's word was law. Alexander II thought the marriage a good idea and so it was to be whether Vladimir liked the idea or not. Marie's beauty and her endearing personality eventually did come to attract Vladimir and so the tsar's plan for him to marry was not the difficult trial he thought it would be. Their wedding took place in Saint Petersburg on 28 August 1872. After an extended honeymoon, the newlyweds were quickly befriended by Sasha and Minnie who entertained them often at the Anitchkov Palace. First of all Sasha wished to keep Vladimir close at-hand. He always appreciated his younger brother's more forceful intellect, as well as, his vocal opinions. Secondly, the new Grand Duchess Marie Pavlovna,[3] as she was known after marriage, expressed a wish to take her place at Court beside the tsarevna. In the precedence of the imperial family Marie Pavlovna was now the third lady of the land; just one step below Minnie.

The empress took no part in society after 1865 because of her increased illness and the trauma resulting from the sudden death of her eldest son Nicholas which threw her into a deep depression.[4] In fact, she was rarely seen in public in Russia thereafter. And so, for all intent and purpose, Minnie became the de facto first lady of the empire. Marie Pavlovna did not wish to begin a rivalry with her sister-in-law but she did intend to become a force in Saint Petersburg society in her own right and the Vladimirs had the money and caché to pull it off. Vladimir for his part was much valued in Russia. He was a natural raconteur, a linguist of some note, he was lively at parties and at balls, he possessed a formal demeanor resulting in almost immediate respect from those meeting him, his was a strong military bearing, and he enjoyed society life in Russia which Sasha had never liked. But Vladimir and his wife were strongly pro-German and this Sasha could not abide.

From almost the outset, Sasha disliked Marie Pavlovna but as she and Minnie initially became friends, he tolerated her frequent visits at the Anitchkov. Sasha should have realized that his wife and new sister-in-law could never become true friends with Minnie's intense abhorrence for all things German. No one at the Imperial Court was more patriotically German than Marie Pavlovna. Minnie had an effervescent personality and quickly warmed to almost everyone—except, of course, Germans. As such, Miechen (as Marie Pavlovna was known within the Romanov family) soon grated on Minnie's nerves. Sasha only tolerated his new sister-in-law in order to keep peace in an already contentious family. He would never come to warm up to her, and after a year or so Minnie had also had enough of the socially ambitious grand duchess.[5]

In addition to his personal dislike for her, Sasha also had political reasons for wishing to keep his distance from Miechen. Although he had begun his adult life with more liberal political leanings, once Pobedonostsev became is closest advisor, it was not long before Sasha learned about the clandestine rapport between Marie Pavlovna and Otto von Bismarck. This inappropriate relationship between a Russian grand duchess and a foreign power was highly inappropriate. Moreover, Sasha actually considered it treasonous.[6] Sasha's innate hatred of all things German, despite his mother being born German, and Minnie's own abhorrence of Prussia soon caused tensions to rise between the two couples and the relationship between them rapidly deteriorated. Miechen took little public note of neither the tsarevitch or his wife's disdain for her and with Vladimir's support, she successfully broke out from under their shadow creating a brilliant Court life of her own at the Vladimir Palace on the Palace Embankment very near to the Winter Palace and the Hermitage. In short order the Vladimir's social circle rivaled the official Courts of both the tsar and the tsarevitch.[7]

With his favored, first-born son Nicholas now dead, with Sasha the brute now his legal heir, and the hot-tempered and fierce Vladimir, the more outgoing son married, Alexander II began to take stock of his life. The tsarina was slowly dying. For some time all intimacy between the tsar and his wife had ended. His beloved daughter Marie Alexandrovna had married Alfred and the two lived in distant London. His younger children amused him but there was no real closeness between them and their father.[8] With the tsar and empress living away from the public it fell to Sasha and Minnie to lead Russian society in their own image while Vladimir and Miechen drew an exciting, more cosmopolitan, set to their new palace on the Neva.

Russia with Minnie leading society was an exciting place to be. The brilliance of the Russian Court was unrivaled anywhere. But amidst its magnificent splendor, there also existed wrenching poverty. This dichotomy presented a disturbing contrast between the riches of the notable few and the misery of everyone else. The sharpest disparity could be found in Saint Petersburg, the most European of Russian cities, where "nowhere else could one see luxurious splendor so close to the most bitter poverty: men and women in rags among the carriages of the rich, and miserable wretches among elegant officers and uniformed officials. Here was the visible clash of Western civilization with the primitive life of Asia."[9] It was not uncommon in Saint Petersburg to see Russians lacking every necessity of life overlooked by not only the nobility who routinely stepped over them on the streets but also by the highest levels of the hierarchs of Orthodoxy as well. This dichotomy between fabulous wealth and profound poverty echoed throughout Russia's political scene just as it did inside Russia's military machine.[10]

For the Romanovs, a mighty Russia translated to a highly respected and wealthy Russia and so under Alexander II the empire continued policies of earlier tsars seeking to expand the nation's frontiers from Germany in the west to the Pacific Ocean and across to Alaska in the east. The empire stretched from the Arctic Circle in the north to the plains of once-independent Georgia and the Caucasus in the south. More than anything else, the Romanov regime craved recognition by their more powerful neighbors. This Britain was not yet prepared to do. To accomplish their goal, Alexander II embarked on a path to extend the empire beyond its already distant frontiers—to the north, south, east and west. This extension policy began by acquiring new territory in Central Asia during Alexander's Turkmenistan campaigns. In 1860, "Russia had wrestled from China the port of Vladivostok, which eventually grew into Russia's major city in the Far East."[11] Soon after this achievement the tsar ordered the building of the Trans-Siberian railway so as to connect his empire which now stretched from Saint Petersburg and Moscow in the east to Vladivostok on the Sea of Japan.

At the apex of the empire sat the tsar with Sasha and Minnie at his side. This high position suited Minnie well; she quickly assimilated into Russian imperial life and the many comforts this life afforded her. Minnie was now a rich woman in her own right. She certainly was wealthier than Alix and even more so than her parents. Although she came to Russia with little more than a few trinkets from her mother's jewelry box and a small Danish government dowry,[12] her marriage contract committed Russia to providing for her generously.[13] On the morning of her marriage 50,000 gold rubles were transferred from the imperial treasury into her personal account. She additionally was given the sum of 40,000 gold rubles for her official Household expenses and the tsar provided her with an additional trust of 100,000 gold rubles from which she could freely spend the interest generated each year. Her marriage contract also provided for widowhood. In the event Sasha died before her, in addition to any funds which he would personally bequeath to her, she would receive an annual widow's pension of 85,000 gold rubles, she would be provided a residence in Saint Petersburg suitable to her rank and standing in the imperial family, and all the costs to staff and operate this life were met by the crown treasury.[14] From the day of her marriage, Minnie never again had to consider the cost of anything. She never carried any funds on her person nor did she ever have to. No matter what she purchased, no matter how great or how little the value, the invoices were always sent directly to the Ministry of the Imperial Appanges Department for prompt payment. When abroad, invoices for Minnie's expenditures were sent to the local Russian Embassy. They paid them promptly before seeking internal repayment by the Appanges staff in Saint Petersburg. For lesser purchases made in small shops while abroad, her ladies-in-waiting paid for everything and they, in turn, would also be reimbursed later by the Appanges office. For the remainder of her life, even when during her exile, Minnie never again asked the cost of anything she desired to acquire. In fact, she, like all other Romanovs, was now so wealthy she never had to justify any purchases she made. In addition to the funds placed at her disposal because of her marriage contract, she also was showered with millions of rubles worth of jewelry, furs and a costly trousseau. She now wanted for nothing and if in widowhood she would desire a return to Denmark, or even to remarry and settle outside of Russia, her marriage contract stipulated that the Russian state would still be responsible for her annual salary (but it would be reduced to the sum of 42,000 gold rubles per year after remarriage).[15]

In the earliest days of their marriage, Minnie and Sasha quickly settled into the Anitchkov entertaining the younger members of the Imperial Court and the young military establishment in Saint Petersburg in what would come to be known as the Second Court. The Anitchkov was well suited to the young couple. Like all Romanov residences the palace was unrivaled in both beauty and lavishness. "Inside, an impressive staircase with bright green carpet and green marble columns led from the entrance hall to the lavishly decorated state rooms. Massive crystal chandeliers were suspended from the high classical ceilings, Venetian glass torchères and Chinese vases stood everywhere and there was a profusion of flowers and plants."[16] The Romanov estates in the Crimea cultivated many hundreds of acres of lush plants and flowers which were harvested as needed and shipped on private trains north to the capital. No Romanov celebration was complete without carloads of fresh cut flowers from the warm climate of the Black Sea basin. The palace's main drawing rooms, four in all, were decorated in precious silks and damasks. Minnie's music room was furnished in red and gold. The couple's formal reception room was hung in gold and blue and the Knights' Hall, where they entertained at their most impressive gatherings, was decorated with large painted panels depicting medieval knights in battle. There was a private chapel, a throne room, and a winter garden which stood above the projecting vestibule at the center of the façade serving as a covered portico for arrivals and departures. Minnie made the winter garden her own, decorating it with wicker furniture purchased for her by Alix at Maples in London. She filled this personal sanctuary with potted palms, expensive marble statues, and two odd additions—two large granite frogs which stood guard on either side of the winter garden's entranceway.

Sasha and Minnie settled into their private apartments on the top floor. These rooms were happily cluttered in typical Victorian fashion with an abundance of potted palms, hundreds of photographs of close family and foreign royalty, all in expensive gilded frames, folding screens providing a cozy corner here and there for intimate moments away from gathered crowds, overstuffed furniture, and thick heavy velvet portieres. Every available space was cluttered with porcelain knickknacks and inexpensive ornaments which they had collected in their travels; most of these of absolutely no real value. "The effect was homely and comfortable rather than elegant. A diplomat who saw the contents in 1917 described hideous Japanese screens, cheap pictures, stuffed monkeys under glass domes, and antique statues mounted on pedestals covered with cheap plush."[17] Minnie wanted her private rooms to be decorated in a style reminiscent of the private rooms of her sister Alix at Marlborough House rather than the profusion of high French elegance typical of other Romanov salons.

The Anitchkov staff was not used to the close attention which Minnie immediately paid to the working environment. No other Romanov lady in recent memory had cared so much as to intrude in the daily operation of her homes. Typically, Romanov women left the particulars of the administration of their palaces to capable housekeepers. Minnie, however, took uncommon interest and special pride in how the Anitchkov operated. She visited every room, even those hidden in the basements. She inspected the linen rooms, the silver vaults and the laundries and she was the first Romanov grand duchess to care enough to inspect the servants' quarters in order to assure that they were comfortable and well-appointed. And she insisted on the constant flow of fresh air in all palace rooms decreeing in her familiar Danish style that air must circulate each day through all the rooms to assure the healthiness of both the family and the resident workers alike. She found the Romanov preference for hot rooms very stifling. Russian palaces typically had locked windows which were normally kept sealed so the steam heat mechanism found in every palace basement assured intense warmth inside; fighting a never ending battle against the bitter cold outside.[18] The Romanovs loved this stifling heat. The ladies of the Court relied on it so that they might comfortably appear in reveling décolletage. They would arrive at the palace wrapped from head to toe in plush sables and warm ermine against the winter freeze but once inside they could exhibit a style of dress so revealing that only extremely hot rooms could support it. Male guests, meanwhile, were more concerned with the offerings of fine food, exotic wines and vodka offered by their hosts, but even gentlemen preferred dinning in warm comfort to cool draughts. Once Minnie was comfortably ensconced at the Anitchkov, however, the cold Russian air filtered through its halls several hours every afternoon in order to clean out the germs she believed lived within the palace's walls. By the evening's entertainment, however, the windows had been closed, the heat turned up, and the temperature in the salons again acceptable to visiting members of the Imperial Court.

Minnie loved the social life which marriage to Sasha offered her. She preferred going out to the opera, to concerts, and to parties more than staying home with her new husband who much rather preferred spending his evenings at the Anitchkov with his closest friends than to mixing at Court. Once he finally left behind the nightly orgiastic escapades encouraged by his brutish brothers, Sasha became the first modern Romanov to fully embrace marital fidelity and a cozy home-life.

For the first time in her life, Minnie could be as extravagant as she wished. In Denmark as a young girl, only two or three hand-sewn dresses hung in her closet. Her Danish trousseau had not been extensive and certainly it was not as lavish or as current as those of the least important grand duchess. Now at the Anitchkov several large rooms on the top floor were reserved just for the dozens of new gowns Minnie continued to order from Paris each month. She likewise patronized the best shops in Saint Petersburg on a fairly regular basis. Minnie's extensive new wardrobe and jewel collection was closely guarded by a staff of seven women charged with their care and in dressing her.[19] As for the jewelry that had been extravagantly lavished on her at the time of her wedding; Minnie now took great delight in wearing it all in public. She never had to wear the same diadem twice in any given month even when she was scheduled to attend two or more events on the same night. Her jewelry collection was so immense that Minnie thought she would never wear it all. Of course, she would wear every jewel in her collection, something she did with great style and delight. It wasn't long (certainly within her first year in Russia) that Russia society revolved entirely around Minnie and Sasha.

Minnie now purchased her richly embroidered gowns so that they matched her jewels. Couturiers came to her at the Anitchkov with their designs, she being the first to see each new collection twice a year. She chose the fabrics for each dress with a specific favorite jewel in mind. With white, gold and cream she wore pearls and diamonds. With every possible hue of blue she wore sapphires, with mauve or purple she wore her amethysts, reserving rubies, emeralds and aquamarines for the most daring and expensive of her court gowns. The grand duchesses and all ladies of the Imperial Court, including Minnie and Miechen, planned their new wardrobes far in advance of the forthcoming social season. It was necessary for each of these ladies, including many who had no substantial wealth to speak of, to order dozens of new dresses and outfits each year. "A woman might purchase perhaps ten or twelve tea gowns for afternoon social functions and luncheons; two dozen day dresses; at least five or six ball gowns; and assorted cloaks, evening gowns, nightclothes, and lingerie, as well as necessary accessories: numerous hats, shoes, boots, gloves, handbags, and parasols."[20] The greatest couturier of the age was the English-born, Parisian transplant, Charles Worth whose establishment on the rue de la Paix was the foremost couture shop in Europe.[21] Minnie and Alix both patronized Worth early on helping to boost his reputation worldwide. In addition to Worth, Alix and Minnie and the ladies of the imperial family also patronized the Parisian couture houses of Poiret, Doucet, Cheruit, and Paquin. But it was Worth who became the ultimate arbiter of couture in the last half of the nineteenth century even in far off Russia.

The Russians also ordered bespoke wardrobes from the more exclusive shops on the Nevsky Prospekt. Minnie in particular purchased a large percentage of her annual wardrobe needs in Saint Petersburg so as to patronize Russian artisans and craftsmen as well as to support those foreign shop owners established in the city and assimilating into Russian culture. "There were seven principal dressmakers in the capital, all catering to the elaborate needs of society. Anna Gindus had trained in Paris at the house of Paquin before opening her own shop, offering elaborate concoctions of silk, velvet, and tulle."[22] Chernyshevs specialized in richly embroidered gowns favored by the older generation of the ladies at Court. Olga Bulbenkova specialized in the creation of the official Court costume, the *sarafan*,[23] at her shop on the Nevsky Prospekt which every lady at Court regardless of rank was bound to wear on formal state occasions.[24] This costly costume took its design from the traditional medieval peasant dress known as the *kapot;* made in the caftan style. They were costly to acquire and each took many months to complete. The costume comprised three separate parts: the bodice which was the most richly embroidered, the coat which was worn fastened at the waist but split down the center to review a second gown beneath; and the train which fell behind it and which because of its weight required at least two cadets to carry it. The coat and long train were always heavily embroidered in gold thread and silver. "The underskirt was of white silk or satin, worn over layers of stiff petticoats to give the desired bell-shaped and embroidered with gold or silver thread in a variety of foliate designs."[25] The empress and the grand duchesses wore the most elaborate court costume, each sewn with jewels from the Imperial Treasury. They were thus heavy to wear and the most costly forms of modern clothing found anywhere at that time. The decorations of each costume became more elaborate the higher the rank of the woman at Court with imperial grand duchesses, the tsarevna and the empress each displaying more gold lacing than lesser ladies at Court. The closer the bloodlines of the lady to the tsar, the more elaborate the design. And so it was both the color of the garb and the amount of jewels sewn onto it that identified the ladies of highest ranks but even the lowliest of official maids-of-honor were required to appear in this mandated form of dress. By imperial decree each gown had to have long stiff sleeves which split open at the front from the shoulder and which permitted the lady's arms to be fully exposed so she might display a great many bracelets, although at Court, ladies always wore above-the-elbow length white kid gloves. A separate train, the length of which was mandated by an 1834 decree, fell from the waist. The empress' court gown had a train fifteen feet in length while the tsarevna's train stretched ten feet behind her and the grand duchesses wore gowns with trains nine feet in length. Ladies of aristocratic birth formally recognized at Court were permitted six feet long trains while maids-of-honor were required a costume with a three foot long train.

Minnie's mother-in-law preferred silver brocade and real gold thread in arabesque styling although she seldom appeared at Court events after the death of her eldest son. When she did appear her costume was encrusted with many of her private jewels sewn artistically throughout the rich cloth's patterns. Each grand duchess was assigned a color or hue distinct to her alone once she was old enough to appear at Court. Whereas the empress appeared in silver brocade, Minnie was assigned the colors periwinkle blue and lavender for her Court sarafan, always worn over a white silk or satin gown. She wore this costume as tsarevna but once she became empress in 1881 she was free to select any color she desired and her gowns reflected thereafter this new found freedom. Miechen was assigned a dark brownish-orange hue with silver and gold thread throughout (which she detested and would later have changed) while the Grand Duchess Elizabeth Mavrikievna wore dull yellow.[26] Another hue of yellow, a softer buttery color, was assigned to Grand Duchess Elizabeth Feodorovna while Queen Olga of Greece, born a grand duchess, wore a much deeper blue.[27] And so, gowns of these colors worked in rich silk velvets, brocades and embroidery, embedded with precious family jewels, became the centerpieces of every Romanov gala during the high social season each year beginning on Christmas day and continuing through to the beginning of Lent. It was not uncommon following a ball to see footmen scurrying about the Winter Palace in search valuable gemstones which had fallen from one or more of these costumes. Stones routinely worked loose during dancing, many of these worth more than twenty-five year's salary of most government bureaucrats.

When a grand duchess disliked the color assigned her sarafan, as Miechen did, she had no recourse but to wait until another Romanov grand duchess died. She could then petition the tsar to assume the deceased's color for herself, but if any other family members protested, or if another grand duchess made a similar request first, the tardier grand duchess was promptly denied. And when a change of hue was actually granted, the cost to the grand duchess was prohibitive as she then had to order several new court costumes in the new hue, each at great cost. Of course, the Romanovs paid scant attention to costs for anything and so when permitted to change her court color, a grand duchess simply instructed Olga Bulbenkova to create several court costumes in the new hue. And if the change of color clashed with the color of her existing jewels, new suites of jewelry in corresponding colors were purchased, as well. Costs be damned!

Olga Bulbenkova held the highly coveted official warrant as "Supplier to the Imperial Court of the Russian Empire" and thus had the right to display the tsar's coat of arms on the exterior frieze above her shop on the Nevsky Prospekt. Madame Olga, as she was known, also made the gilded uniforms for most of the male officials of the Court and she was called upon to create the sumptuous coronation mantles for Alexander III and Marie Feodorovna in 1882 and again for Nicholas II, Marie Feodorovna, and the new empress Alexandra Feodorovna in 1896.[28] These coronation mantles were made of gold double silk velvet onto which were woven the Romanov black double-headed eagle topped by the imperial crown. Each of these black insignia measured ten inches in height by four inches in width. On the eagle's breast was sewn the imperial coat of arms. The colors were vividly depicted in expensive silk threads; this heraldic emblem was repeated thirty or more times across the gold cloth of each of the robes of state.[29] The House of Sapozhnikovy created the embroidered insignia but Madame Olga's seamstresses wove them into the cloth. Each luxurious robe of state was twenty-three feet in length and each weighed in at sixty-eight pounds. "Gold buckles with cut emeralds, previously used to decorate previous coronation robes...were brought from the Kremlin Armoury to be sewn onto the new mantles."[29] It took eight hundred and ninety-seven ermine pellets, with some three hundred ermine black tipped tails, to cover the lining, borders and mozzetta of each mantle.[30] But time for a new coronation in Russia had not yet arrived.

The elaborate Court costumes created by Madame Olga, particularly those worn by the higher ranks of women of the Court, were extremely costly but even those required for ladies-in-waiting cost more than some minor noble families could afford. Despite this burden, nobles would struggle to meet the high cost of being appointed to the Imperial Court as this opened the family to eventual favors from the imperial family or from the chief ministers of the tsar's entourage; favors which more than offset any initial costs incurred. Baroness Agnes de Stoeckl spoke to this cost in a diary entry saying:

> *"She considered herself lucky to purchase a secondhand court gown for her daughter, who had been appointed as a [maid of honor] at court as it only cost the sum of 1,360 rubles."*[31]

To complete the court costume, each lady also had to wear a proper kokoshnik, a silk crescent-shaped headdress symbolic of medieval Russian peasant's folk headdress with a large satin bow at the neck. These modern kokoshniks were adopted by Nicholas I in his 1834 decree as a colorful nod to Russia's peasant past. Initially they were the exclusive headdress at Court and the grand duchesses typically had large rare gems from the Imperial Treasury sewn onto them when they appeared at state events.

At the Imperial Court (which always strove to keep up, or to surpass, England and Germany) the tiara became the norm for every woman of means particularly after 1850. By the end of that decade, European women regularly wore diamond tiaras regularly as well. In Russia they were typically designed in a style similar to the kokoshnik. This style was adopted for nationalistic reasons often taking the place of the time-honored silk peasant inspired headdress. In short order every Romanov grand duchess possessed at least one costly heavily jeweled diamond *tiara a la russe*.[32] Minnie had five of the new Russian fringe style tiaras in her private collection, one of which became her favorite jewel in her now priceless collection. This favorite diadem had fifty-nine individual diamond rays—the tallest of these, the center ray, comprised ten large diamond stones with numerous smaller stones filling in the ray's frame. The remaining rays graduated downward from the center on either side with a smaller number in appropriately smaller sizes. This diadem came from the official court jewelers Bolin and Company.[33] Between each of the fifty-nine rays was a twisting spindle comprising up to nine smaller diamonds each. The jeweler had inscribed a number on the back of each ray and each had hooks so that a seamstress could attach it to a kokoshnik if Minnie preferred. As such Minnie typically wore this tiara sewn onto a white velvet kokoshnik but she did appear wearing it without the Russian peasant headdress from time to time, especially outside of Russia. Two seamstresses where employed at the Anitchkov to attach Minnie's special tiara to the clothe kokoshnik whenever Court attire was required. Bolin and Company created this diadem from stones in Sasha's personal collection, most of the hundreds needed being fine-faceted Indian and Brazilian diamonds set in gold and silver.

The second enormous kokoshnik tiara in Minnie's collection was very similar in design, in fact some courtiers thought the two to be one and the same. It also was created for the imperial family by the House of Bolin. The second of the two diadems was actually the larger of the two in Minnie's collection. It contained eight hundred brilliant cut diamonds in graduated sizes in a silver and gold frame. Whereas the rays of the first of the Russian fringe tiaras were separated by diamond spindles suggesting a lighter feel, the second, larger *a la russe* tiara was more faithful to the historic Russian peasant design with each ray tightly fitted together so that the effect became that of a full crescent panel of uninterrupted diamond bars. It stood high upon her head— three inches in height by ten inches in length. There was also a row of small round diamonds across both the top and bottom which suggested the frame of the traditional silk kokoshnik. At the base of this massive tiara Minnie usually affixed a round stone, sometimes she wore a ruby while at other times the choice in this setting was a round emerald. This tiara was one of the heaviest in her collection and caused both a headache and neck pain, especially if it was worn throughout a long dinner or church service. As such, Minnie soon learned to only wear this treasure for portrait sittings and shorter social events. Sometimes, Minnie removed its frame so that it could be worn flat across the top of the breast as a corsage.

The third Russian diadem in Minnie's collection was again a Bolin creation. It was a gift from Sasha and was made for her as the new empress after her coronation in 1882. As the new tsar had at his disposal all the loose stones from the Imperial Treasury, Sasha used four hundred of these in various sizes to create a new tiara comprising a base row of square cut diamonds, each eight karats in weight which formed an enclosed circlet around her head. There were sixty-eight of these stones along the base in all. From this row of diamonds rose a stylized mirror-monogram in the letter "A" representing the double cipher of Alexander III. Each "A" entwined in a stylized flowing manner. This pattern, which gave the appearance more of the letter "X" than two co-joined double "A" letters was repeated around the diadem forming a full circlet of this motif.[34] Above each of these double "A" motifs stood a pearl the size of a grape. Each pearl was mounted on diamond settings. Upright pearls resting atop diamond pediments stood between the repetitions of each "A" cipher. There were nineteen rare pearls in all. Like many others in her collection, the frame of this diadem could easily be removed so as to convert it into a fabulous necklace. Minnie actually preferred it as a necklace and most often appeared wearing it as such while at the same time wearing one of her other tiaras.[35] Minnie only stood five feet four inches tall and so she made use of hair pieces to suggest the illusion of height, as did her sister Alix, and she always opted for the tallest of her jewels to add to this illusion. Despite her petite size, Marie Feodorovna very much carried herself as an empress and no one in her presence could ever think otherwise.

The heaviest kokoshnik tiara at Minnie's disposal was not her own. It belonged to the Imperial Treasury and by house law had to pass from empress-consort to empress-consort. It is known formally as the 'Marie Alexandrovna Kokoshnik State Diadem' and weighed in at two hundred seventy-five carats. The diadem was created by Bolin for the wife of Nicholas I around 1830 and it is believed to be the first diamond kokoshnik created in Europe. It was worn only on the most prestigious of events and did not pass to Minnie until the death of her mother-in-law in 1880. Although she coveted possessing it, Minnie almost never wore it because of its heavy weight and old-fashioned design. This design was twofold in nature; the bottom was solidly worked in diamonds, a fusion of sunrays which emanated from the center outward in every direction. Resting atop these rays at its center presenting the image of the sun was a ten carat diamond encircled by smaller brilliant cut diamonds. The design of the upper section was entirely different in style. There was an airy space between the solid lower, and the filigree upper, divisions which consisted of thirty diamond tear drops of graduating sizes, each suspended from an elegant frame of silver and gold. Mirroring the stones which dangled delicately from the frame above it, identical stones similar in number and shape stood upright along the crest of the diadem. At the center point, the headdress stood four inches high, all of it a pleasant concoction of extremely heavy diamonds. Traditionally each empress wore a complement of tall white ostrich feathers and a white lace veil with this tiara.

It is the last of the kokoshniks in Minnie's treasured collection which became her personal favorite. It was made for the Imperial Treasury by Bolin in 1841, and was thus not her personal property. It was known as the 'Diamond Pearl Drop Kokosnik.' This tiara encircled the head as did all kokoshnik tiaras but it had an added magic in its design which fascinated everyone who saw it. This diadem pleased Minnie most of all. She preferred it to all others. It, too, was worked in silver and gold and had two frames. The first of these rested atop the head and was lightly decorated in diamonds which were rarely seen as in those day fuller hairstyles generally covered the framing of a tiara's base. The second, top frame rose upward from behind the wearer's ears in a high arched manner. The arch was wide so as to suggest a halo leaving a full inch and a half of open space which provided an air suggesting the halo was floating above the head. The top frame was richly ornamented in large circular diamonds below which dangled twenty-five huge, matching, graduated pearl drops suspended from diamond encrusted gothic style arches.[36] The settings of the pearls permitted each stone to gently rock with the motion of Minnie's head and so these rare grape-size pearls of great luster twisted and bobbed as she moved her head graciously from side to side.[37] Minnie loved its effect so much that it was this tiara that she wore at most functions at Court. It was so beautiful that Miechen publicly envied it. In time Miechen commissioned the House of Bolin to create a kokoshnik tiara for her which would provide the same effect. It was designed as a two inch high diadem on a gold and silver frame with fifteen interlocking diamond circles. In the center of each of these circles, pearls similar in size and luster to Minnie's favorite tiara, dangled enchantingly. This new creation has gone into history as the 'Vladimir Tiara.'[38]

On the occasion of her twenty-fifth wedding anniversary to Bertie in 1888, the peeresses of Great Britain presented a copy of the larger Russian fringe tiara in Minnie's collection to Alix.[39] It consisted of seventy-seven upright bars, each containing between 8-10 brilliant cut diamonds of appropriate size, the top of each bar being rounded, the frame following the shape of the top diamond in each bar.[40] Because of Minnie and Miechen in Russia and Alix and the Duchess of Edinburgh in Great Britain amongst others who showcased this tiara design, the *tiare al la Russe* became the most popular style headdress in the 1880s with nearly every royal lady in Europe, including Queen Victoria, seeking to add one to her personal collection.[41]

In addition to the diadems at her disposal, Minnie owned twenty or more ropes of pearls, each larger than the next, with some of these pearls being as large as small plums. She also had state jewels at her disposal, these kept in a large vault in guarded sub-basements in the Winter Palace, which when grand ceremonies required she wore with great dignity and elegance. One such jewel was the exceptional *collier d'esclave*, a diamond necklace so large as to cover all of her exposed skin when dressed in the décolletage of the traditional court costume. It was "formed of a string of twenty-one cushion cut diamonds, mounted in silver settings with the channel in gold below held together by silk threads to make the necklace more flexible. Suspended from this were fifteen antique pear-shaped diamonds, each surmounted by a much smaller diamond: probably cut sometime in the seventeenth or eighteenth centuries; they were of Indian origin and had a total weight of four hundred seventy-five old carats."[42] Some of the diamonds in the necklace were pink while others cast a light blue tint producing an enchanting effect especially in the candlelight. The central stone in the necklace alone weighed thirty-two carats with the two large stones on either side weighing twenty-three carats and sixteen carats respectively. Minnie wore this necklace on state occasions most typically with the *collier de chien* (dog collar) choker which Alix had made fashionable in England. Minnie's choker was worked in diamonds with a row of pearls above and below and a gold clasp in the form of a Russian double-headed eagle at the neck.

The Imperial Court and Minnie particularly, never shone brighter than during the height of the social season. As tsarevna, Minnie reveled in the schedule of balls, parties, galas, and concerts, sometimes three each night. Prior to each event Minnie always returned to the Anitchkov for a complete change of wardrobe and jewelry so as not to appear at two or more events on the same evening in the same ensemble.

"Officially the Russian social season began with the Christmas bazaar at the Circle of the Nobility, organized by the Grand Duchess Marie Pavlovna, which lasted for four days—from two in the afternoon until midnight."[43] Each night from Christmas until Shrove Tuesday, Saint Petersburg hosted at least six balls and concerts. Unmarried girls attended highly chaperoned parties separately from the married nobility. These *bals blancs* were held strictly for the unmarried and were organized according to very rigid etiquette. At these gatherings young ladies formed a bank along one wall while young cadet officers stood opposite them against the other wall. There was no orchestra. Music was provided by one or two elderly pianists. Chaperones dressed entirely in black formed rows of nun-like judges scrutinizing their charges seated upon gilt and damasked armchairs, *face a face*, at both the head and at the foot of the ballroom. Alexander II considered all modern dance steps to be vulgar. He deplored modern forms of dance such as the two-step, and at any rate imperial etiquette forbade close contact between unmarried persons. The waltz and tango were likewise forbidden at the chaste *bals blancs* where only sedate dancing between the sexes was permitted. As such these gatherings tended to be very boring for both sexes, especially the randy young officers already exposed to the delights of society in the Russian capital.

CHAPTER TEN

IT HAPPENED
ONE COLD NIGHT

I F THE WINTER PALACE WAS the center of political life in Russia than the Nevsky Prospekt was the heart of Russian society's frenzied desire for European products of every type. The Nevsky housed most of Russia's most fabulous shops including Fabergé, Bolin (the crown jeweler's) Chernyshevs, Thonet (the Viennese furniture manufacturer), Adolph's Hairdressing (where the Romanov women had their hair dressed for special occasions), Yeliseev (the upscale department store), Steinway and Sons, and the American manufacturer Singer Sewing Machines. Entertainment in Saint Petersburg revolved mainly around the palaces of the imperial family and the nobility but upscale restaurants and private clubs began to spring up in the 1860s. By 1880 the middle classes could also enjoy dining out. "The restaurants of the capital were plentiful and popular, but there was no such thing as a bar or pub, although there were automatic buffets where it was possible to drink on the-penny-in-the-slot principle, and children were sent to the shops with empty bottles and *kopecs* to bring vodka home. Most of the restaurants offered entertainment of one sort or another, whether Gypsy singers or, less appealing, mechanical organs with drums and cymbals, which could be run by electricity and played raucously throughout the day."[1]

Russian social life was centered around religious seasons. Christmas opened the season which ushered in grand balls and galas night after night lasting until the beginning of Lent. These weeks were the liveliest of the Russian year. Celebrations were also permitted on solemn feast days and on the name days of the various Romanovs even during Lent. But during Lent the atmosphere in Saint Petersburg became more somber. Meat could no longer be purchased in the butcher shops as abstinence and fasting was the norm. Sweet shops shuttered their doors except for the name day celebrations. Alexander II and the empress left Saint Petersburg for Tsarskoye-Selo where they secluded themselves from public view until Easter. Sasha and Minnie spent Lent at Gatchina where they only received close family and the other Romanovs likewise scattered to their estates outside the capital. The nobility made the same exodus if they could afford to do so and social life inside the capital came to a quiet halt. All of the theaters closed and acts of spiritual preparation for the coming Easter festival, real or superficial, overtook the capital. Churches and shrines were filled as in no other time of the year and Saint Petersburg took on a holy peace which was normally non-existent during the remainder of the year.

On 2 May 1867 Minnie and Sasha traveled south to Moscow by train with Tsar Alexander. As wife of the tsarevitch, Minnie had to be formally presented to the Muscovite aristocracy and the time had come for her to make her ceremonial pilgrimage to the old capital. It would be her first formal event outside multi-cultural, polyglot Saint Petersburg and she was very nervous as to how the earthy Muscovites would receive her. Minnie never lost her Danish accent and spoke Russian strongly tinged by her Scandinavian heritage. The Muscovites were the most ancient of the Russian aristocratic families and also the most insular and critical. They were xenophobic to the core, imbued in a suspicion for all things, and all persons, foreign. Minnie had reason for concern but she won them over all the same. The imperial family spent their first night in Moscow outside the city at the Petrovsky Palace. This red brick oriental-style concoction with a huge gold central dome and four turrets crowned in gold leaf was built by order of Catherine 'the Great.' It was designed by the famous Russian architect Matvei Kazakov between 1775 and 1782 and was never intended as anything more than an overnight rest stop on the last night of the long journey from Saint Petersburg to Moscow. Here the Romanovs could rest for the night before a grand ceremonial entrée into Moscow the following day. And so, it was to the Petrovsky that the imperial party headed the afternoon prior to setting out for the Kremlin.

Alexander and Sasha led the procession from the Petrovsky on horseback while Minnie was driven into the city behind them in the carriage which she would also one day use for her own coronation. The visit to Moscow began with the *Te Deum*[2] sung at the *Uspensky Sobor*, the cathedral within the Kremlin used for tsars' coronations. For the duration of her time in Moscow, Minnie's days were filled with visits to other cathedrals, churches, and charities now under her patronage but her evenings were filled with gala performances and impressive balls with fireworks displays closing out each night. On the second day of her visit, the day on which she was actually presented to the senior nobles of Moscow, she wore a "blue velvet dress embroidered with gold and loaded with diamonds [and sapphires] to impress the Muscovites."[3] This visit south concluded with a visit to the Monastery of the Most Holy Trinity and Saint Sergius which was the center of Orthodoxy in the Moscow region. It stands at the edge of a forest about forty-four miles northeast of the city. The structure forms a massive white and gold Russian architectural delight with dozens of turrets and golden domes surrounded by a large wall in the style of the Kremlin. It has stood on this site since 1337 and remains to this day one of the most important spiritual centers in the country.[4]

Two weeks after her successful introduction to Moscow, Sasha and Minnie set out by yacht to Copenhagen to celebrate the silver wedding anniversary celebrations of her parents which was set to begin on 26 May 1867. It was Minnie's first return visit after her marriage and the Danes turned out in record numbers to welcome their princess home and to see for themselves the man she had married. She and Sasha appeared on the central balcony of the Amalienborg Palace, being called back by the excited crowds for numerous appearances. This was Sasha's first real experience with the casual lifestyle of the Danish royal family and their easy interaction with the Danes. It was also the first time in a long while that he could freely walk the streets in public, interacting with common folk, visiting the shops and speaking to Danes of all classes. He could never do this in Russia and so thereafter Denmark became the only place where he truly felt free and happy. It did not take him long to relax in this comfortable setting and soon he was playing practical jokes along with other members of his wife's family; a family known for its many pranks. These were also the early days of Minnie's first pregnancy but sadly this ended in an early miscarriage while in Denmark.

In their daily letters to one another, each filled with routine gossip about the various royal families of Europe, Crown Princess Victoria of Prussia wrote to her mother informing her of the miscarriage: *"Minnie has had a mishap and the Russians are much concerned about it."*[5] It was no surprise that young Vicky learned the news quickly for even in Denmark where the Prussians were hated, they had a very efficient spy network which always got word back to Berlin quickly. Alix learned of her sister's lost pregnancy from the queen by way of Vicky in Berlin long before Minnie sent word from Denmark. Sasha was desperate for a son and heir even though they were still freshly married and had every natural hope that they would have a large family before too long. "On 18 August he prayed that he and Dagmar [Minnie] would have children, or at least could be sure that they would be soon starting a family, a strange concern for such a newly married man unless there had been a problem already."[6]

When Minnie married Sasha, she also married into a nation bound to the mysticism of the theological and political dogmas of 'Holy Russia.' The tsar and his family, and most of his subjects, were bound together in one holy faith—Russian Orthodoxy—with the tsar as supreme head. Every law considered, every decree issued, every reform undertaken was first studied in light of how any changes or implementations would affect the religious life of the state and more importantly the sacred powers of the tsar-autocrat. The Pauline Laws governing life within the imperial family, including imperial family marriages, and the succession to the throne, were all structured with Orthodoxy at their core. Under Alexander II the concept of Holy Russia rose to mythical proportions and by the time Sasha had succeeded as Alexander III it would become both his mantra and the legal justification for all of his actions as

Autocrat of All the Russias. It was not Alexander II's dictum; however, as he saw Orthodoxy as a partner in his reign, not as the force driving it as Sasha would do when he became tsar himself.

Alexander II was the son of Nicholas I and Alexandra Feodorovna who was born Charlotte of Prussia. She was the daughter of Frederick William III and Princess Louise of Mecklenburg-Strelitz. Alexander became tsar at the early age of thirty-seven. He was the best prepared of all tsars before him. He studied with numerous tutors all of the important subjects of his time, and undertook a six-month long tour of Russia in which he visited twenty of the provinces of the country. He was the first tsar since Peter 'the Great' to tour extensively throughout Western Europe. He was also the first Romanov emperor to ever visit Siberia. After the end of the Crimean War (1856), in which Russia had been badly beaten, the people began to complain about inept government, common bribe-taking leading to total system-wide corruption, and how outdated the nation had actually become. Inspired by public outcries for change, Alexander began radical reforms as soon as he became tsar.

In 1861 the tsar signed an imperial *ukase*[7] emancipating several million people. These indentured peasants were known in Russia as *serfs*.[8] These were the people who worked generation after generation in the palaces and houses of wealthy Russians and on untold numbers of Russia's farms, in her mines, in the forestry industry, in the quarries, in the fisheries and on all of the estates of the imperial family and the nobility. For this one act alone Alexander II entered history as the greatest tsar Russia would ever know; earning for himself thereafter the title of "*Tsar-Liberator*."

In Imperial Russia, "everyone was registered in one of five official 'estates'—Noble, Merchant, Burgher, Peasant, Cleric—each of which notionally established the holder's social and legal status, although this often had nothing to do with the occupation or actual position in society."[9] The sovereign and the imperial family were above all the classes, including the nobility and as such they were also outside the laws that confined all classes. The serfs belonged to the peasantry but once liberated by Alexander II some actually rose up out of generational poverty. They legally remained peasants, however, even if they or their descendants could later afford a large town house in the most fashionable part of Moscow or Saint Petersburg. One's wealth or financial position did not change your status in Imperial Russia. You remained in the state you were born into no matter how much wealth you might later accumulate just as some of the nobility who were nearly destitute nevertheless remained nobility with all their exalted privileges.

In 1867 Alexander sold the Russian province of Alaska to the United States for $7.2 million. He feared that in a future war with Great Britain, which he believed was inevitable, Alaska (known as Russian America) would be lost to the British Empire as spoils of war, thus becoming part of the Dominion of Canada. The tsar rightly determined that by selling it early-on as he intended to do he could regain for Russia substantial financial reward for a territory really offering Russia nothing in return.[10]

Generally, Alexander was considered liberal by all the standards of the day, in particular in light of the behavior at that time of other monarchs. Inside Russia he was well aware that he was also considered a radical by many. He reorganized the judicial system setting up elected judges for the first time in every city, town and village and in all the provinces throughout the empire. He established a new penal code based on the *Codex Napoleon* and he greatly simplified the system of procedures for criminal, as well as civil courts. One of his innovations in Russia was the open court system guaranteeing every Orthodox Russian the right to have their case heard both by competent judges and in the full light of day, in view of any spectators who might wish to be present. He also implemented trial by jury as found in Great Britain and the creation of the office of Justice of the Peace who mitigated minor offenses in the smaller towns. He abolished corporal punishment in the military and within the school systems across Russia. He promoted local self-government by his creation of a system known as the *zemstvo*, local assemblies in the districts and provinces across the empire which for the first time were given a voice as to how the tsar's government's regulations and his laws would be implemented locally. He imposed a universal military service for the first time requiring every male to give their country appropriate time in military service and at the same time he abolished the privileges of the nobility to both purchase their way out of military service and to further enslave any of the serfs heretofore owned by them by forcing them to sign on to a prolonged period of military service against their will.

Alexander also promoted university education creating several colleges and universities during the course of his reign. In 1863 he settled a joint uprising which broke out in Poland and Lithuania, but in order to settle down eruptions in Poland (until then a semi-autonomous nation) he responded harshly by stripping the land of its individual constitution and its independent standing within the empire thereafter incorporating the Poles directly into Russia. By so doing, Alexander obliterated one-third of once independent Poland. He was harsh in his treatment of Polish Catholics and Polish Jews as he saw both groups as being hostile to the aims of holy Orthodoxy; his liberal reforms in no way included new freedoms or protection for these two peoples. In fact, in regards to the Jews, Alexander II continued the pogroms inside Russia and where the Jews existed in large numbers in other places, such as in Poland. These pogroms aimed at eradicating the Jews from within pure Orthodox society; they squelched freedom of movement, ownership of property, marriage rights, and even set out to destroy their common language (Yiddish) as well as the practice of their religion. Despite his harsh reprisals against rebellious Poles, in Finland Alexander was far more generous. In that same year he held Finland up as a model state within the empire; he reconvened the Diet (the Finnish parliament), he granted Finland its own currency, its own business regulations so as to foster development and financial interest in the nation, he built railways between Helsinki and Saint Petersburg, eventually these stretched across all of Finland as well, and he encouraged the Finnish language's growth despite having suppressed Polish in Poland and Yiddish for the Jews at the same time. Alexander II, despite all his enlightenment, simply did not see the Jews as whole. His culture and the history of Russia saw these people as far less than chattel and so freedoms granted to Orthodox serfs could never be considered an option for the Jews.[11]

In 1872 Alexander joined the emperors of Austria and Germany in the creation of the *League of The Three Emperors* a military alliance which greatly helped to stabilize Central Europe. In many other ways he sought to bring stability and enlightenment to the continent and to bring peace to it as well. Most of all, except for in his prejudices in which he would never yield, Alexander II steered a generally liberal course for the duration of his tenure as tsar. He certainly was the most liberal monarch Russia would ever see. Despite his liberal leanings and the freedoms that he granted Russia, Alexander was the subject of more assassination attempts than any tsar before him with two each in 1866, 1879, and 1880 respectively, and two more in 1881 the year of his death. The group behind most of these attempts was known as *"The People's Will,"*[12] a nihilist group organized by atheists, (many of these non-adherent secularized Jews whose actions would come to harm Jews throughout the empire as a result). These radical elements were mainly from the burgeoning 'middle class' and most had substantial education credentials. Their aim was to force a reform of the totalitarian, autocratic system by means of violent acts and the absolute overthrow of the imperial government and all its institutions, including the established church.[13]

Despite his liberalism and modernizations in Russia, the "People's Will" were determined to assassinate Alexander II. They were also keen on killing as many Romanov grand dukes as possible, as well as, many senior members of the government wherever possible, both in the capital and further afield. It was said the rail-line between Moscow and Saint Petersburg, a distance of four hundred miles, was lined entirely by Russian soldiers both day and night during the last years of Alexander's life, most definitely whenever a member of the Romanov family was on the move as the railroad network had become the main target of the nihilists.[14] By this time, Russia had fallen into a state under internal siege; so intense had it become that Alexander II remarked to Minnie one evening:

"Am I such a wild beast that they should hound me to death?"[15]

The most daring attempt on the tsar's life, an attempt aimed at also killing numerous members of the imperial family including its female members, took place on a cold winter February night in 1880. The tsar was set to entertain his wife's brother, Prince Alexander of Hesse[16] and the tsarina's favorite nephew, young Prince Alexander, who had been recently installed with the tsar's support as the first sovereign-prince of newly independent Bulgaria. The two Alexanders had traveled to Russia for two reasons: the first was to visit with the tsarina who was now in the end stages of life after a very long pulmonary illness and cancer, and the second was to guarantee the continuance of the tsar's political and financial support for Bulgaria as at this time, as always, the Balkan states were unstable and always at the center of European political concerns. Terror was now found everywhere inside Russia, even inside the tsar's own home.

A palace carpenter by the name of Stepan Khalturin had secretly joined the "People's Will" and was waiting patiently for the most opportune moment to make an attempt to kill the tsar. Over a period of several weeks, Khalturin secretly smuggled hundreds of pounds of dynamite into the palace sellers, each day carrying two or three sticks of dynamite in the bottom of his toolbox, hiding it in a steel case directly beneath the semi-state dining room used most regularly by the imperial family when gathering at the Winter Palace for large dinners. Khalturin saw his opportunity when the household announced the forthcoming visit of the two German princes. The household schedule listed the dinner as a family occasion and as such the grander state rooms would not be used. He knew they would dine in the more intimate surroundings of the family dining room which stood two floors above a secluded basement space where he had been hiding the dynamite, waiting for just such a moment to act. Everything he needed was secretly in place and at the ready. Nothing had yet been discovered so he was confident he would succeed. The forthcoming dinner proved to be the best opportunity and so he put everything into motion. On the evening of the appointed day, 17 February 1880, Khalturin lit the slow fuse which would burn quietly until it made its way to a detonator across the basement floor filled with fulminate-of-mercury foam. He carefully timed the explosion to take place at forty-five minutes passed six o'clock.

Thirty minutes had passed since his fellow workers had left the palace. When Khalturin suddenly appeared outside the staff exit, it was already dark since nightfall came in northern Russian winters by three o'clock in the afternoon. He immediately found himself face to face with a palace gendarme who saw that Khalturin was both out of breath and shivering as he attempted to move quickly away. The gendarme examined his worker's permit under the golden glow of gaslight as heavy snow fell around them. His teeth were chattering, his feet shifted restlessly which the officer attributed to the bitter cold. As his workman's pass was in order and as he had been working in the Winter Palace for three months, and was thus known visually by the guard, he was permitted to pass unmolested. But as his worker's pass was returned to Khalturin the police officer chided him for not exiting the palace with his fellow workers as required as no one was permitted for security reasons to linger after the closing gong.[17]

"I'm late for an appointment with a lady friend; I must hurry!"[18] he proclaimed as he ran off, smiling broadly to the officer. Khalturin picked up speed as he crossed the palace square for the Nevsky Prospekt archway which passed through the Imperial Army Headquarters on the far side of the vast parade ground.[19] Before the blast erupted Khalturin was already out of the view of the gendarme who watched him as he scurried off.[20]

Standing on the floor below the White Dining Room was the State Entrance Hall, one of the main formal entrances of the Winter Palace. This is where important state guests of highest rank came and went. The Winter Palace complex was massive, nearly as large as Versailles and there were many entrances for visitors, each portal set aside for a particular purpose. There were entrances for the imperial family on state occasions and others for them on private visits to the tsar and his empress. There was a ceremonial entrance for visiting royalty near to the famous Jordan Staircase, entrances for ambassadors, entrances for the senior household members when not accompanying members of the imperial family, others for lesser dignitaries both foreign and domestic, and many entrances for business purposes of all sorts. There were also dozens of staircases, both for ceremonial use and for service. The Winter Palace complex covers 1,978,622 square feet excluding the cellars. The inner courtyard alone measures 117,208 square feet.[21] Excluding the storerooms and workrooms in the basements, the Winter Palace contains 1,054 rooms. This grandest of the tsar's palaces "was made up of great corner blocks or wings, each of which forms one of its main facades. These sections are connected by smaller blocks which form enclosed gardens and inner courtyards. The outer walls of all these sections are broken up, diversified and embellished by columns and sculptured motifs, some taking the form of architraves, others of caryatides, masks and the like, all in the elaborate baroque style."[22] During the entire tsarist period, the exterior of the great Winter Palace went unpainted. It was the darkest and most unadorned of all Romanov residences, its brown stone presenting an ominous, almost ugly vision as the stone used had a deep reddish brown hue. Because of its size and it being the seat of the powerful Russian autocracy, however, the Winter Palace was nevertheless one of the most impressive buildings in Europe.[23]

The two visiting German princes (both also called Alexander) were set to arrive by way of a grand interior courtyard. At this entrance, across the hall's sparkling white marble floors, stood a sweeping staircase of granite and marble which rose from the basement level to the attics and from which were found the imperial family's apartments on the first floor.[24] Alexander II was a man who followed an exact regimen each day, something that would come back to haunt him on the last day of his life, and so he fully expected to sit down to dinner with his family and guests at precisely thirty minutes past six o'clock. Unbeknownst to the assassin, however, the dinner had already been postponed by thirty minutes, now set to begin at seven o'clock because of the delayed arrival in the city of the tsar's brother-in-law Alexander of Hesse. Hesse's son, Alexander of Bulgaria, arrived in the capital earlier in the afternoon but had remained behind at the Warsaw Train Station to await his father's arrival so that the two men could travel to the Winter Palace together.[25]

The imperial family was well aware of the delay and the kitchen and household staffs altered their schedules accordingly, but word had never trickled down to the carpenters and other workers who would never have been privy to a change in the tsar's dinner plans at any rate. At forty-five minutes past six o'clock, the carriage containing the two Alexanders entered the main portal of the Winter Palace. Within minutes they crossed into the inner courtyard and up to the diplomatic entrance. Once inside they mounted the steps before them. The two were about to climb to the first floor above. As was the custom, the tsar, the tsarevitch, the tsarevna, and the grand dukes and grand duchesses present had already gathered in the Field Marshal's Hall at the top of the stairs in the northwestern corner of the palace. The room was named for the greatest generals in Russian history, those who had attained the rank of field marshal solely because of their great military accomplishment, and it was here that the tsar and his family always gathered before a formal dinner. Its windows looked down onto the inner courtyard and it was thus easy for them to see when dignitaries began to arrive. The Romanovs were waiting in readiness to welcome their two guests as this was to be a happy family reunion, although Sasha did not like his German uncle or cousin. As the two arrived, the family exited the hall so as to be seen in position at the top of the staircase. It was at this moment when the family should have already been seated in the White Dining Room enjoying the first course of their meal, when Khalturin's holocaust rocked the massive palace complex.

The sound of the explosion was thunderous rumbling across the entire city. For an instant, the imperial family and their guests seemed to pause in time as the massive Winter Palace shook with the accompanying ripple of the concussions. A huge crystal chandelier, weighing more than a ton, and which had been hanging above the entrance hall for more than a century, flew past the imperial party gathered at the top of the stairs at the first explosion, violently swinging backwards and forward before it crashed onto the steps directly in front of Sasha and Minnie. Had they or any of the Romanovs been standing on a lower step the chandelier would have crushed them; killing them instantly. Normally Tsar Alexander would have been at the place where the chandelier fell, but as Alexander of Hesse was his brother-in-law he showed him extra courtesy by moving down the staircase to greet him less stiffly. As it were, many of the Romanovs were cut by flying glass from both the broken crystals of the chandelier and from shards of shattered glass from the many tall windows which crashed to the ground with the blast. Plaster poured down on the tsar's head. He had been thrusted down to the bottom of the staircase and dust and debris covered him as it did all the elegant and costly gowns of the Romanov ladies.[26]

Many of the Romanovs were bleeding profusely from cuts to the face, head and arms and nearly all of those present were dazed and incoherent for several moments. The heavy marble floor of the White Dining Room where they were set to dine imploded down onto the floor below, its marble slabs shattering into many pieces like a large mosaic still to be assembled. Several footmen awaiting the dinner guests perished in the collapse. The walls of the White Dining Room split in two and the ceiling above also risked eminent collapse. In short order, a second explosion again rocked the palace when flames from the burning fires reached the gas lines supplying the hundreds of lanterns which lit the palace. This second explosion roared thunderously but few near the epicenter heard it as their eardrums had been badly damaged by the first blasts of the dynamite. They did feel the might of the force of this impact, however, as the second explosion violently threw them all back to the floor. With it came a wall of heavy black, acrid smoke which streamed up the stairs in continual plumes filling all of the rooms opening off of this stairwell. In the darkness that overwhelmed the interior of the palace, only the glow of the burning fires below enabled those trying desperately to get away to reach safety. For several long moments, the imperial party still lay on their backs choking in the poisonous fumes, groping and clutching at one another in efforts to regain their footing. Amazingly, none had been thrown down the steps during either blast nor were any crushed by the falling chandeliers and stone. The German princes were closer to the source of the impact but as the force immediately moved upward they were blown out of the entrance hall into a side anteroom on the ground level, thus saving their lives.[27] Despite the horrendous nature of the blast, no Romanovs were killed.

The terrifying sounds of the crackling wood, tumbling stonework, fractured marble, onyx, and jasper which had decorated the palace rooms for more than a century and the crisp sounds of splintering glass falling to the floors below seemed to all to go on without end. In the moments immediately following the two explosions an eerie silence prevailed but soon enough blood curdling screams and cries for help echoed throughout the palace. Those cries were not in Russian. They were terror stricken pleas for help in Finnish.[28]

In the total destruction of the basement level forty seven officers and men of the Finnish Guards Regiment on duty that evening lay dead, their bodies torn apart by the explosion, while fifty-eight more were so badly wounded that many lost their limbs, eyes, and some even lost parts of their skulls. More than half this number died within days of the explosion. Many of them were trapped in the basements by falling beams and debris which had then erupted into flames burning palace staff trapped down in the lowest level of the complex where fires continued to burn for hours.[29] Help was long in arriving!

Wild confusion reigned on the first floor, mostly caused by servants rushing to and fro in the darkness. Several people tumbled headlong down the stairs and into open holes where palace salons had long stood. Extra candles and lanterns were stored in rooms on the basement level and thus could not easily be accessed when now needed. Ten or more minutes passed before any light was restored. The staircase, because of the heavy marble with which it was made, with a huge granite base to support it, was unscathed other than being scattered by falling debris. Tsar Alexander and his sons, brothers, and nephews rushed down them offering help to the injured. Their German relations were helped to upstairs rooms to recover from the shock while the tsar and the grand dukes rushed outside into the night to see what they could do by way of rescuing the trapped.[30]

Empress Marie Alexandrovna, too ill with cancer and pulmonary disease to partake in Court life, lay in her bed two floors above where the explosion had occurred, but because of her illness and her near coma-like state, she never knew her home had been attacked. As the second lady of the land and its tsarevna, Minnie had to instantly decide how the ladies of the Court would react. She did not falter nor sink with fear despite having faced death seconds before. She rushed the grand duchesses and other female guests down a service staircase to another part of the palace where she organized the workers to bring as many candles and lights as they could gather, sheets and blankets and all types of linen, pillows and mattresses from various servants' halls and buckets of steaming hot water to a place in the inner courtyard which she determined to be the best place for a temporary field hospital. Minnie also told the staff to gather all the vodka that they could find to use as both anesthetic and pain relief and as an astringent to ward off the onset of infection in the wounds.

Despite the freezing cold, everyone realized they could not remain inside the palace as a second attack could be eminent.

This wintery night, morbidly still as heavy snow fell, eerily quiet despite the crackling of the burning fires caused by the explosions, and despite the screams of those who barely survived it, was the night which changed Russia forever. It was the foundation of the revolution still to come as the imperial family and senior government ministers no longer felt safe in their own homeland. The historic home of the tsar, the powerful symbol of the nation, had been subjected to the ultimate terrorist attack and many of the imperial family were close to being killed. By sheer fate they had not been. The mindset of the ruling powers thereafter moved towards absolutism; even the *Tsar Liberator* no longer felt secure. Life for the Romanovs changed drastically that winter night.

The immediate aftermath of the bombing was a sight to behold—the highest levels of the Court, including the very pampered Romanov grand duchesses led by their future empress, knelt in bloody snow beside badly wounded soldiers and injured palace staff, their gems glittering in the burning fire's soft glow. Large dark brownish-red stains smeared the colorful expensive new Parisian ball gowns which they carefully had chosen for the tsar's dinner. Despite the fear of further attack, this was one of the finest moments of the Imperial Court in the late nineteenth century, but few in Russia would ever learn of the heroic efforts of both the tsar and the grand dukes in rescuing those injured or maimed nor how Minnie and the imperial ladies (and of course the other courtesans and palace staff present as well) reacted so quickly offering selfless care for all those mortally injured regardless of class or rank.

Thereafter the Romanovs lived in a constant state of siege, many leaving the capital for their country estates, some going abroad rather than be subject to another terroristic attack. Life inside the imperial family would never quite be the same again and Minnie and Sasha thereafter looked towards long family visits in Denmark more and more as it was only there that they truly felt free and safe.

Continued........

GLOSSARY OF TITLES

Autocrat: one of the official titles of the Russian monarchs meaning *self-ruling* or more accurately *one in whose hands all power rests.*

Emperor: the highest possible title for a monarch; one who rules an empire which typically comprises several internal kingdoms or autonomous regions. An emperor outranks a king and bears the appellation of *His Imperial Majesty.* The wife of an emperor is an *empress-consort.*

Empress: a female monarch of the highest rank equal to that of an emperor. A female monarch of this rank is known as an *empress-regnant* and carries the appellation of *Her Imperial Majesty.* The wife of an emperor is known properly as an *empress-consort* and the widow of an emperor is known as a *dowager empress.* A morganatic wife or widow of an emperor does not enjoy this rank, title or appellation.

Tsar: The Russian title for emperor deriving from the Latin original for *Caesar.* At a later time the Russians also translated the Latin title of *Imperator* to *Emperor* which was also in use in other nations. In 1721 Tsar Peter the Great issued a decree elevating tsarist Russia to the status of a modern empire and thereafter decreed that the monarch was to be entitled *emperor.* Despite this decree, Russian monarchs were thereafter referred to as both *tsar* and *emperor* interchangeably. When (after this decree) the older Russian title *tsar* was employed, it was equated with the title of *emperor*. Westerners never ceased to refer to the Russian monarchs as *tsar* even though they always accorded them the respect and precedent due to an *emperor*. Tsar Alexander III and his son Nicholas II both preferred the use of the Russian title *tsar* to that of *emperor*.

Tsarina: The Russian title for the wife of a *tsar*. When women ruled Russia, they were generally entitled *empress* rather than *tsarina*. The wife of Tsar Alexander III, Marie Feodorovna, preferred the title of *empress* and later *dowager empress* to that of *tsarina* whereas the wife of Nicholas II, Alexandra Feodorovna, preferred to be known as the *tsarina*.

Dowager Empress: The widow of an emperor; in Russia, after the reign of Paul I, these widows were formally known as *dowager empress* rather than *dowager tsarina*. Marie Feodorovna was the most famous woman to hold this special rank. In Russia, after the time of Paul I, a *dowager empress* always outranked the *empress consort*.

Kaiser: The German language equivalent of the title *tsar* taken in the same way from the Latin imperial accolade for *Caesar*. The German and Austrian kaisers were fully emperors in every way and their families were *imperial* rather than *royal*. The wife of a kaiser was a *kaiserin*.

King: A monarch of the second highest degree; one who rules a kingdom. The appellation of a king is *His Majesty* although for political, religious or territorial reasons other qualifications were sometimes added to this appellation—such as *Her Britannic Majesty* (Great Britain), *His Most Catholic*

Majesty (Spain), *His Most Faithful Majesty* (Portugal), *His Most Sacred Majesty* (Nepal).

King of the Hellenes: The Glucksburgs accepted the Greek throne as *Kings of the Hellenes* rather than as *Kings of Greece* since the previous king, Otto of Bavaria, had not legally abdicated that title and King George I did not wish to cause un-pleasantries as a result. Moreover, by the time of the Glucksburg ascendency, the true Greek nation was far wider than the mere territory to be governed by the new king and so it was also a brilliant political statement on King George I's part by declaring himself *King of the Hellenes*, a title which embraced Greeks everywhere. As such it in no way limited the young king's authority to so small a territory. The direct heir to the king of the Hellenes, or Crown Prince of Greece, was known as the *diadoque* (from *diadochos*) which comes from the Greek for 'successor' or 'one who can claim the inheritance.'

Queen: The title of a woman who rules a kingdom in her own right and who thus under law becomes *queen-regnant*. The title *queen* is also the title of the wife of a reigning king, known as *queen-consort,* or the title of a widow of a king, as well. A widowed queen could be known as *dowager queen,* as the widow of a king, or as *queen-mother* if this *dowager queen* is also the birth-mother of the next monarch. In the case of Queen Alexandra, when Edward VII died, although she legally became *dowager queen* and could also have been styled as *queen mother*, she chose to simply be known as "Queen Alexandra."

Queen-Empress: A title held by Queen Victoria after 1876 at which time India became an empire and Victoria became known as

Queen of the United Kingdom of Great Britain and Ireland, Empress of India. After 1876 she was known commonly as the *Queen-Empress*. As consort of the next king-emperor, Alix was entitled to this title as well, and it was used formally from time to time but she otherwise preferred her British title only. The rank of Queen-Empress also applied to Queen Mary and after her Queen Elizabeth (later the Queen Mother) but like Alexandra, they chose to generally be known as queen only.

Tsarevitch: The title of the crown prince of Russia. This title could be borne by either the heir apparent (one destined to succeed) or an heir presumptive (one who is presumed to succeed 'if' another qualified person is not yet born who would then thus push the presumed heir further down in the direct line of succession). Technically, the Russian *tsarevitch* was entitled *Grand Duke-Tsarevitch* so as to recognize both his birthright and his special position as heir to the reigning *tsar*.

Tsarevna: The title of the wife of the Crown Prince of Russia (entitled *tsarevitch*) although she was also known as a Grand Duchess and by her Russian name and patronym.

Grand Duke *(Russian title):* The title granted to all senior princes of Russia. During the reign of Tsar Alexander III this title, with all of its accompanying privileges, was limited to those males born as sons and grandsons of a reigning tsar through the male line only. All Russian grand dukes bore the equivalent appellation of *Imperial Highness*. To be fully accurate, the translation from the Russian language of this title should have been *grand prince* but as the rank of *sovereign grand duke* was already understood to be a preeminent title in

Western Europe, the translation was altered early-on to that of *grand duke.*

Grand Duke (*Sovereign title*): the title held by sovereigns of those monarchies slightly smaller in size or of lesser importance than empires and kingdoms. Most typically, this class of monarchy was found within the territory of the former Holy Roman Empire which later became known as the German Empire. Examples of such states were: Baden, Hesse-Darmstadt, Oldenburg, and Mecklenburg-Strelitz. One surviving grand duchy exists today—*Luxembourg.* A reigning grand duke was entitled to the appellation of *His Royal Highness* as was his spouse and his direct heir and his spouse. Other members of these grand ducal families were generally styled as *His/Her Grand Ducal Highness* although exceptions to this general rule occurred frequently. The latter was the appellation of Princess Alix of Hesse when she came to Russia to marry (then) Tsarevitch Nicholas Alexandrovitch.

Grand Duchess: The title accorded to all daughters and granddaughters of Russian tsars with the appellation of *Imperial Highness.* This is likewise the title and style of the wives of *Russian grand dukes.* Similarly, the title is accorded to the wives of those men who rule Grand Duchies and to women who inherit a grand duchy in their own right. In regards to Russian grand duchesses, if Romanov by birth, or when a woman became the wife of a grand duke and she had converted at marriage to Russian Orthodoxy, the full title of both would be: *The Truly Believing Grand Duchess* to demonstrate to ordinary Russians that this woman was a member of the Russian Orthodox Church.

Prince of Wales: The title for the heir apparent, or crown prince, of the United Kingdom of Great Britain and Northern Ireland. There may only be one Prince of Wales at a time, his title reverting to the crown when he succeeds to the throne as king. This title must be recreated in each reign. It is not automatically inherited by the heir apparent to the British throne. The *Prince of Wales* is also traditionally the *Duke of Cornwall* and the *Duke of Rothesay.* He holds the appellation of *His Royal Highness.* His wife is known officially as *Her Royal Highness the Princess of Wales,* although the wife of the current Prince of Wales has opted to be known as the Duchess of Cornwall in deference to the previous incumbent in the courtesy title—Diana, Princess of Wales.

Princess Royal: The title of the eldest daughter of the British monarch. It is purely an honorific which designates the first-born daughter as special, but it may not be granted by the monarch until the death of the previous incumbent in the title. When a king has only daughters, and thus his eldest daughter is presumed to be the next monarch, she is not entitled as either the *Princess Royal* or the *Princess of Wales* as the former title is reserved for the eldest daughter of a monarch who has no chance herself of inheriting the throne and the latter is reserved strictly for the wife of the incumbent *Prince of Wales.*

Crown Prince: the title of the heir apparent of a throne in continental Europe such as in Denmark or Sweden. A female heiress apparent is entitled *crown princess* as is the wife of a *crown prince.* All carry the appellation of *Royal Highness.*

Duke: A *reigning duke* is a monarch of a small state, primarily those found in the former Holy Roman Empire, later the

German Empire, whose sovereigns bore the rank of *Duke*. The *reigning dukes*, such as in Saxe-Coburg-Gotha, bore the appellation of *Highness* (although when this small throne passed to Queen Victoria's son and then her grandson these dukes retained the higher dignity of *Royal Highness from Great Britain*).

A *titular duke*, however, has no state to govern and typically has no real connection to the place incorporated into his title, be it a British, Russian or continental European creation. The ducal titles given by Queen Victoria to her sons, such as Alfred, Duke of Edinburgh, were examples of *titular dukedoms*. When a duke governs as a monarch his title is referred to as a *duchy* whereas when a man is raised to an honorary, or titular, ducal title it is referred to as a *dukedom* and when awarded to a royal prince as a *royal dukedom* (never a *royal duchy* other than in the case of Cornwall and Lancaster which are both legal duchies in their own right).

Both the Holy Roman Empire and the subsequent German Empire forbade women from inheriting the thrones in these realms so there were no *reigning duchesses* but a titular duchess title can pass to a woman if the *lettres patent* decree includes this option when initially granted. A wife of a duke, both reigning and titular, is known as the *duchess of...* A widow is known as the *dowager duchess of...*

Prince: A male descendent of a king or one with some other close blood ties to a king. Most royal line princes have the appellation of *Royal Highness*. The title is also accorded to sons and grandsons of grand ducal and reigning ducal families and of all members of princely houses. The appellation granted to each of these depends upon the rank of the family and the terms of their house laws and the laws of that nation. There are also high nobility who enjoy the title of prince. These are not to be confused with members of imperial, royal, or grand ducal houses.

Prince of Russia: When Tsar Alexander III altered earlier imperial house law to limit the persons who could and who could not hold the title of *grand duke*, he created a new class within the Romanov family for those who were thereafter too far removed by blood ties to a reigning tsar to be entitled *grand duke*. For these family members, the new rank of *Prince of Russia* with the appellation of *Highness* was granted. For those that were even more distantly related to a reigning tsar (or to the last reigning tsar), these persons were granted the appellation of *Serene Highness* and these persons were to take the name and title of *Prince Romanovsky* (with the additional designation of one of the imperial estates so as to differentiate the various family lines in the same way the grand ducal lines had always been designated by family branch patronyms).

FORMAL TITLES OF THE TSARS OF RUSSIA

By the Grace of God, His Imperial Majesty Tsar-Autocrat and Emperor of All the Russias, of Moscow, Kiev, Vladimir, Novgorod, King of Kazan, King of Astrakhan, King of Poland, King of Siberia, King of Chersonesus Taurica, King of Georgia, Lord of Pskov, and Grand Duke of Smolensk, Lithuania, Volhynia, Podolia, and Finland, Prince of Estonia, Livonia, Courland and Semigalia, Samogitia, Belostok, Karelia, Tver, Yugra, Perm, Vyatka, Bulgaria and other territories; Lord and Grand Duke of Nizhni Novgorod, Sovereign of Chernigov, Ryazan, Polotsk, Rostov, Yaroslavl, Beloozero, Udoria, Obdoria, Kondia, Vitebsk, Mstislavl, and all northern territories; Sovereign of Iberia, Kartalinia, and the Kabardinian lands and Armenian territories—hereditary Lord and Ruler of the Circassians and Mountain Princes and those others; Lord of Turkestan, Heir of Norway, Duke of Schleswig-Holstein, Stormarn, Dithmarschen, Oldenburg, etc., etc. etc.

APPELLATIONS BY RANK
IN DESCENDING ORDER
OF PRESCEDENCE

(As these apply to persons included in this study)

His / Her Imperial Majesty

His / Her Majesty

His / Her Royal and Imperial Highness

His / Her Imperial Highness

His / Her Royal Highness

His / Her Grand Ducal Highness

His / Her Exalted Highness

His / Her Highness

His / Her Ducal-Serene Highness

His / Her Most Serene Highness

His / Her Serene Highness (known in Russia as *His / Her Serenity*)

His / Her Illustrious Highness

His / Her Ducal Grace

His / Her Princely Grace

PRESIDENCE WITHIN ROYALTY

Emperors outrank kings and queens-regnant. Kings and queens-regnant outrank Sovereign Grand Dukes. Sovereign Grand Dukes outrank Sovereign Dukes, and Sovereign Dukes outrank Sovereign Princes. Those who are not sovereign, such as Russian grand dukes or British princes, find their place of precedence as follows:

I.   Emperors, Tsars, Kaisers
Imperial and Royal Majesty, Imperial Majesty

II.   Kings, Queens-regnant
Majesty, Royal Majesty

III.   Sovereign Grand Dukes; Sovereign Dukes; Sovereign Princes
Royal Highness, Highness, Serene Highness

IV.   Grand Dukes of Russia
Imperial Highness

V.   Princes of the United Kingdom, Denmark, and Greece
Royal Highness

*Second generation British royals at this time bore the lower appellation of "Highness" and those princes of Denmark not in the direct line to the throne also carried the appellation of "Highness" rather than "Royal Highness," which is still the case today.

VI.   Members of several German grand ducal houses providing brides to the Romanovs, such as Mecklenburg and Hesse-Darmstadt etc.
Grand Ducal Highness

VII.   Heads of several German ducal houses such as Saxe-Altenburg, Saxe-Meiningen, etc.
Highness

VIII.   Members of other German ducal houses providing brides to the Romanovs, such as Nassau, Orange-Nassau etc.
Ducal-Serene Highness

IX.   Members of the princely houses such as Waldeck-Pyrmont, Monaco, Liechtenstein, Thurn und Taxis, Waldberg-Zeil etc.
Most Serene Highness (for the head of the house and his consort)
Serene Highness (all other members of the house)

X.   Members of these families stemming from morganatic marriages (if raised to princely rank at marriage)
Princely Grace

*In some instances members of these families were raised to the higher dignity of *Serene Highness*, especially in Russia. The morganatic families of Teck and Battenberg likewise bore the appellation of "Serene Highness."

XI.   Designations clarifying one's worthiness by birth to claim equality with reigning houses; thus the possibility to enter into a royal marriage:

Most Serene and High Born:
*The highest proof of noble status with right of royal kinship.

High and Well Born:
*Later creations which carried the status of royal kinship.

Well Born:
Later creations which did not necessarily carry royal kinship.

NOTA BENE

Directions to Endnotes, Educational Notes, Archival
Information, Bibliography and Photo Library

To all those interested in studying the hundreds of endnotes and educational notations pertaining to the chapters in this three volume set; those wishing to review the archival and bibliographical information; those wishing to study the genealogical charts of the Imperial House of Russia, the British Royal Family and the Danish Royal House at the time of this study; and those interested in reviewing the extensive library of both color and black and white images pertaining to the people and places mentioned throughout this trilogy, may do so by turning your attention to:

www.alixandminnie.com

Made in United States
North Haven, CT
26 January 2022

15313712R00154